Praise for *Imhotep*

"*Imhotep the African* is an archeological dete
make the case that the legendary Egyptian pl
mer Imhotep was not only an historical figu   ... was black. This
remarkable book challenges many assumptions about life along the Nile,
revealing a worldview and technology that was more sophisticated than
anything previously imagined."

—Stanley Krippner, Ph.D., co-author of *Personal Mythology*

"Bauval and Brophy have once again brought their keen intellectual and
scientific skills to bear by examining an aspect of ancient history that contemporary Egyptologists have been either too afraid or too unwilling to
investigate. *Imhotep the African* is the perfect sequel to *Black Genesis,* for it
presents incontrovertible truths that will either be accepted on their merits
or ignored for fear of exposing a house of lies built upon foundations of
historical falsehoods. It is evident to many of their colleagues that Robert
Bauval and Thomas Brophy are the dynamic duo of independent Egyptologists. They are to be commended for their scholarship and their dogged
determination to present an honest assessment of historical events—even
if it flies in the face of conventional dogma."

—Anthony T. Browder, author and independent Egyptologist

Praise for *Black Genesis*

"*Black Genesis* offers astounding new insights as Bauval and Brophy forcefully support, with hard data, the radical idea that Egyptian civilization was
the outgrowth of a sophisticated Black African culture that existed thousands of years prior to the earliest known pharaohs. Their book is a must
read for anyone interested in genuinely understanding the true origins of
ancient Egypt and the dynamics of how civilizations develop."

—Robert M. Schoch, Ph.D., author of
Voyages of the Pyramid Builders and *Pyramid Quest*

"Readers of *Black Genesis* will never think of ancient Egypt in the same way again. Bauval and Brophy make the case that this venerable civilization was originated by Black Africans from the Sahara Desert and that the pyramids, the statues, and the hieroglyphs were the result of their knowledge and ingenuity. The authors trace the series of errors and misjudgments that have obscured the origins of this remarkable civilization. It is time for the record to be set straight, and *Black Genesis* is the book that may well do it. This is an authoritative, excellent, well-written book."

—Stanley Krippner, Ph.D., professor of psychology at Saybrook University and co-author of *Personal Mythology*

"In *Black Genesis*, Bauval and Brophy combined their investigative skills to answer an obvious but often-neglected question, 'who *were* the ancient Egyptians?' With new astroarchaeological evidence they build a strong case for 'the African origin of the pharaohs' and have dramatically altered our understanding of the past."

—Anthony T. Browder, author and independent Egyptologist

"Extremely dense and possibly groundbreaking, Bauval and Brophy make an honest case for a 'very different story of the origins of ancient Egypt.' Their scholarship is meticulous."

—*Publisher's Weekly*, June 2011

". . . packed with revelations!"

—Midwest Book Review, July 2011

"The tales of the authors' 2008 expedition and of explorers in the past century add to the enticing read."

—*Nexus Magazine*, August 2011

"Recommended."

"Both authors are highly accredited researchers who have provided an incredibly detailed book examining the connection between the astronomy of the pharaohs and their Neolithic counterparts."

"*Black Genesis* is a captivating, thought-provoking, utterly intriguing read that traces back the origins of the high civilization of ancient Egypt into deepest prehistory. Buckle your seatbelts for a rollercoaster ride."

Praise for *The Egypt Code*

"In *The Egypt Code* Robert Bauval unveils a sacred landscape, lost for thousands of years, and provides us, literally, with the key that unlocks ancient Egypt."

"Bauval's arguments are very convincing. . . . They are practical, scientific views and they explain a lot that is otherwise difficult to understand. Most of all, this book is imbued with the sense of wonder that is essential for good science, plus the intrigue of a good thriller."

IMHOTEP

THE AFRICAN

IMHOTEP
THE AFRICAN

ARCHITECT OF THE COSMOS

ROBERT BAUVAL & THOMAS BROPHY

Published by Disinformation Books,
An imprint of Red Wheel/Weiser, LLC
With offices at
665 Third Street, Suite 400
San Francisco, CA 94107
www.redwheelweiser.com

ISBN: 978-1-938875-00-7

Library of Congress Cataloging-in-Publication data available upon request

Cover design by Jim Warner
Interior design by Kathryn Sky-Peck
Cover photograph © Omar Buckley

Printed in the United States of America
MAL
10 9 8 7 6 5 4 3 2 1

Dedication

To Michele, my wife, always, for your good nature, love, and support.

ROBERT BAUVAL

*To the memory of my beloved sister, Jayne Brophy, 1956–2012,
and to her two surviving children, Abby and Michael,
whom she loved more than the moon and the stars.*

THOMAS BROPHY

Acknowledgments

As always, our first thanks go to our respective families. Their support, love, and patience are greatly appreciated. We wish to pay special thanks and tribute to the Nile Valley Conference II, Morehouse College president Robert M. Franklin, and conference chair Charles S. Finch III for hosting us to Atlanta (September 2011), where we were honored to present at this unique conference, a twenty-seven-year follow-up to the first conference arising out of the U. S. civil rights movement.

We also thank the many friends and colleagues who, directly and indirectly, have helped us put this book together: Laura Salvucci; Tony Browder; Jean-Paul Bauval; David Rohl; Hesham El Haddad; Hoda Hakim-Taraboulsi; Ahmed Osman; Omar Buckley; Gary Baddeley; Maria Pia Tocco; Richard Fusniak; Joanne Cunningham; Mark Borda; Mayumi Hashiyama; Robert Schoch; Catherine Ulissey; Ambassador Jean-Paul Tarud-Kuborn; Amon Saba Saakana; Terre Brophy-Smith; June and Jim Brophy; Amanda-Jayne and Allison Smith; Hope Umansky; Hideki Baba; and Tamiko Voros. Many others remain unnamed, but they always know our gratitude for their friendship and love.

Contents

Preface

A few kilometers outside the modern city of Cairo, on a large, flat eleva-
tion at the edge of the Sahara overlooking the Nile, is the world's very
first architectural complex. Nearly 5,000 years old, the centerpiece of this
mindboggling complex is a huge stepped pyramid surrounded by strange
temple-like structures, the lot contained inside a giant perimeter wall
whose length is more than 1,500 meters. Aligned conspicuously toward
the four cardinal directions, this strange place evokes a mood, for lack of
better words, of "sacred architecture"—or, perhaps more aptly, "sacred
astronomy." No doubt something extremely potent took place here—
certainly rituals of the highest order that somehow involved the cycles
of the celestial bodies as seen through the eyes of a holy man or shaman.
Amazingly, when one considers the extreme antiquity of this complex,
Egyptologists know for sure who conceived it: Imhotep, the high priest
of Heliopolis and vizier of King Netjerykhet/Djoser of the 3rd Dynasty
in c. 2650 BC. And that, if the truth be told, is just about all they know
with certainty. All else is educated guesses, speculation, and even fanciful
thinking derived from later sources when Imhotep the man had been
mythologized and even deified beyond recognition.

So who was this ancient Egyptian superstar—this pharaonic Da Vinci,
Michelangelo, Galileo, and Newton all rolled into one—whose very name
still commands reverence and awe? From where or from whom did he
acquire his vast knowledge of astronomy and the art of stone masonry?
And perhaps more intriguing still, what was the real purpose of his Step
Pyramid Complex at Saqqara? Is there embedded in it an encoded message? And if so, what? And from whom?

Much has been written and said about Imhotep, from scholarly the-
ses to bizarre novels and movie scripts of pure science fiction. But the
real person—his true origins, his race, the root source of his knowledge
and genius—all seem lost forever in the mist of time. How does one go

about finding the truth about a man who lived 5,000 years ago? Where does one begin the search? There are no written papyri or inscriptions about Imhotep's life that are contemporary or even near contemporary to him, except for his name and his royal titles inscribed on the podium of a broken statue found in the 1920s at Saqqara. So where can one look for more clues? Which stone remains unturned that may reveal the truth of this giant of a man?

There is one aspect of Imhotep's life, perhaps the *main* aspect, that is often overlooked or, at best, trivialized by Egyptologists—his occupation as Chief of the Observers or Chief of the Astronomers, which, in today's terminology, would be Astronomer Royal. This important occupation of sky-watching, when combined with Imhotep's other roles as high priest of Heliopolis and vizier of the pharaoh, provides us with the means to "read" him, as it were, through the complex at Saqqara, which was designed to service the high occult rebirth rituals of pharaohs. Since 1984, I have argued that observational astronomy and a basic knowledge of the precession of the equinoxes should be incorporated into the science of Egyptology or, to be more specific, used to decode the sky religion and associated rituals found in the Pyramid Texts and incorporated into the religious architecture of the pyramid and temple builders of ancient Egypt. I applied this approach to the famous Giza pyramids in the 1990s with great success. I now want to do the same for Imhotep's "Testimony in Stone" at Saqqara.

This was the daunting task I set myself. Knowing myself—and with so many other matters to attend to—I waited for something—a new discovery, new clues—to jumpstart the quest. As is often the case with such things, this came from a totally unexpected quarter.

In early December 2007, I received a phone call from a friend whom I had not heard from in years—Mark Borda, a businessman turned desert explorer. Mark called from his home in Malta to tell me of an amazing discovery he had made a few weeks earlier in Gebel Uwainat—an uninhabited mountain region in the remote southwest of Egypt's Western Desert. Mark informed me excitedly that he had found hieroglyphic inscriptions on a boulder, which, on first analysis, showed that the ancient pyramid builders of Egypt had managed to travel to this distant place and meet with a previously unknown people—something that had so far been deemed impossible by Egyptologists due to the total aridity of the region and the distance involved. Mark's discovery changed all this. To me, however, it also meant that an important "missing link" had been found that could connect the ancient Egyptians to their true black-African origins. For now Mark's crucial discovery could be linked with another all-important discovery made in 1997 by American and Polish anthropologists at Nabta Playa, a prehistoric site of great antiquity located some 100 kilometers due west of the Nile, but still 500 kilometers east of Gebel Uwainat.

At Nabta Playa, a plethora of mysterious man-made megalithic structures—stone alignments, stone circles, strange tumuli, and deep burials—were found to have astronomical alignments and symbolism closely resembling, if not identical to, that of the pyramid builders of Egypt. Was it from these mysterious megalithic stargazers that Imhotep derived his advanced astronomical knowledge and stone-shaping art? The question begged the answer.

No sooner had Mark hung up than I decided, there and then, to investigate this matter further. I had to see these hieroglyphic inscriptions for myself and, hopefully, find more clues in their vicinity that could help resolve this enigma. So I contacted an American colleague and friend from San Diego, author and astrophysicist Dr. Thomas Brophy, who had already carried out extensive research at Nabta Playa, and invited him to join me on an expedition into the Egyptian Sahara. Thomas, too, had a strong hunch that the Egyptian civilization was connected to a prehistoric African people who inhabited the Sahara thousands of years before the pharaohs. In 2003, Thomas had boldly gone on a solo expedition to Nabta Playa to obtain the precise coordinates of the stone alignments and had published his findings in a book, *The Origin Map*, as well as in peer-reviewed articles.

In early April 2008, Thomas and I set off from Cairo with a small convoy of 4-wheel-drive vehicles. We were guided by Mahmoud Marai, a professional desert guide who had been with Mark Borda when the Gebel Uwainat inscriptions were discovered. The story of this expedition and our findings are told in our book *Black Genesis* (Inner Traditions, 2011). In *Black Genesis*, however, we refrained from discussing Imhotep and his true origins because we wanted first to establish a firm foundation for our thesis. Later in the course of 2011, I had the opportunity to visit several times and do research at the Step Pyramid Complex at Saqqara. It was then that Thomas and I reconnected to write the story of Imhotep based on our new research.

In *Black Genesis*, our approach was to apply our knowledge of observational astronomy and precession to "decode" the alignments and other design features of the Step Pyramid Complex. Slowly but surely, we began to enter the mind-set of Imhotep via his *opus magnum* in stone. As if immersed in a whodunit detective story, we followed the clues that took us on an exhilarating magical mystery tour that started at Saqqara and led us beyond its confines to temples in Upper Egypt—and ultimately, as we had suspected, to the stones of Nabta Playa and the black-African stargazers who had placed them there.

Throughout the rest of this book, for simplicity and ease of reading, we always use "we" when describing our travels, researches, and previous publications, even when the actual event involved only one or the other of us. For example, the visit to the Heliopolis area of Cairo (chapter 1) involved only myself and a small group, while the 2003 visit to Nabta Playa (chapter 4) involved only Thomas and a small group. If the actual referent is not obvious from the context, in essentially all cases it can be found in the references we cite.

Thomas and I are proud to have pooled our knowledge and experiences again in this quest for the truth of the origins of Egypt's civilization. It's a rewarding feeling that is not easy to describe. Our ultimate reward, however, will be that you enjoy reading our story as much as we enjoyed writing it.

—ROBERT BAUVAL, JANUARY 8, 2013

⊓ ⊓ ⊓

Why should we attempt to combine the rigors of the science of modern astronomy with the more art-like pursuits of Egyptology and biography? As synchrony would have it, I am drafting this on a very chilly American holiday—Martin Luther King Day—while President Barack Obama delivers his second inaugural address, echoing the words of MLK and offering a poetic route to an answer for that question: "We, the people, declare today that the most evident of truths—that all of us are created equal—is the star that guides us still; . . .[T]o hear a King proclaim that our individual freedom is inextricably bound to the freedom of every soul on Earth." Later in his speech, Obama continued to echo MLK by articulating the many ways in which "our journey is not complete" until we incorporate that "most evident of truths," through our actions, into our worldview. The inextricable linking of the "I" that is "we" and the re-integration of the interior arts with the exterior sciences are the two axes of the integral mission to achieve a sustainable post-postmodern worldview.

I see our attempts in this current book as a small part of that great mission. Attraction to the modern pursuit of archaeoastronomy in general fits into that context as well. Something about the mysterious monuments of deep antiquity that our ancestors have left for us speaks to a time when the inner arts and the outer sciences were more fused—yet somehow more noble, even more aware, in ways that our modern rigid segregation of the inner and the outer blocks us from embracing. And clearly, Imhotep played a key role in bringing those noble truths of awareness into the earliest embodiments of human civilization. The current integral mission to bring together all the disciplines in pursuit of a more powerful, wholistic grasp of reality is a step forward toward completing our journey to reunite with the essence of our own origins. It is in that spirit that I joined Robert Bauval on our journeys to the remotest desert—on a mission toward the reality of our deep past. And in that spirit, I hope we bring to readers of this volume some of the results of those journeys—with both fidelity and enjoyment.

—THOMAS BROPHY, JANUARY 21, 2013

Chapter One

THE CITY
OF THE SUN

*Heliopolis: one of the most important cult-centers of the pharaonic period
and the site of the first sun-temple, dedicated to the god Ra-Horakhty . . .*

IAN SHAW AND PAUL NICHOLSON[1]

*The greatest center of magic in Egypt was probably the holy city of
Heliopolis, the city of the sun, where the most ancient theology developed.
Here were preserved numerous papyri, "magic" in the widest sense of the
word, including medical, botanical, zoological and mathematical texts.
Most Greek philosophers and savants travelled to Heliopolis to study
some of that knowledge.*

CHRISTIAN JACQ[2]

A lonely obelisk stands in the northeast part of the modern city of Cairo.
It represents Heliopolis, the most revered "center of learning" of the
ancient world. Most Egyptologists believe that Heliopolis existed long
before the pyramids. It was known as Innu by the ancient Egyptians; later,
the Hebrews called it On; much later still, the Greeks gave it the current
name of Heliopolis, which means "City of the Sun." Today, local inhabitants call it Ain Shams, "Eye of the Sun."

Egyptologists tell us that Heliopolis was headed by a high priest—the
our mau, or Chief of the Observers—whose main function was to observe
the night sky and the motion of the stars. One such high priest, indeed

the earliest known to us by name and the most revered, was a man called Imhotep, "He Who Comes in Peace." So famous and admired was Imhotep that, during the latter part of the pharaonic civilization, he was venerated as a god. Later, the Greeks regarded him as the Father of Medicine, associating him with Asclepius and thus bestowing on him the unique position of being a historical human, not a king, who was officially deified. Imhotep even gained super-villain stardom status in Hollywood in 1932 in the original movie *The Mummy* starring Boris Karloff, and subsequently in the 1999 loosely remade blockbuster by Stephen Sommers starring Brendan Fraser. The latter grossed 415 million dollars and spawned several sequels—the 2001 *The Mummy Returns* and the 2004 *Revenge of the Mummy*—as well as many spinoffs like the *Scorpion King* and a series of novels, cartoons, and comic books. Second only to Tutenkhamun, or perhaps now even on a par with the boy-king, Imhotep holds a central place in modern pop culture, ranking in the Top 10 list of super villains thanks to Karloff and Fraser.

The truth, however, is that very little is known about Imhotep the man. Although he receives high praise from Egyptologists and historians alike and is often referred to as a genius—or the inventor of architecture, or the father of science—Imhotep's true identity is really largely the subject of guesswork and speculation. In fact, as high priest of Heliopolis during the 3rd Dynasty of Egyptian kings, Imhotep's name appears less than half a dozen times in contemporary texts. The recent academic work on the 3rd Dynasty refers to him in only seven of its 300 pages, with most of the information culled from writings long after Imhotep's time. In short, one could say that Imhotep is a Jesus of deep antiquity—highly mythologized and eventually divinized, but with little or no contemporary archaeological or textual evidence to support the myth. The main reason for this huge lacuna is that Egyptologists have generally ignored one of Imhotep's most important proficiencies: his highly advanced knowledge of astronomy.

Imhotep and Heliopolis

Imhotep's architectural masterpiece, the fabulous Step Pyramid Complex at Saqqara, has for too long been studied as only that—an architectural masterpiece. But we have come to see it as an astronomical "manual" in stone. The Step Pyramid Complex, as we shall see in the coming chapters,

Model of the Step Pyramid Complex of Imhotep now in the auditorium of the Visitors' Center at Saqqara.

View of the Step Pyramid Complex at Saqqara looking northwest.

is a sort of pharaonic "Da Vinci Code," which, if properly understood and decoded, can take us into the mind and even the origin of the architect-astronomer genius who created it.

The first hint of this "Saqqara code" was given to us by Sir I. E. S. Edwards, one of the most eminent Egyptologists of the 20th century and widely acknowledged as the authority on Egyptian pyramids. The first time we met this affable scholar was in the summer of 1985 at his home near Oxford, where we had a long talk about pyramids. It was then, as we talked of the astronomy of the pyramids, that he referred to the new edition of his famous book *The Pyramids of Egypt*, the first edition of which appeared in 1947, the last in 1993. He pointed to this passage, which related specifically to Imhotep:

> On the ground of internal evidence alone it has *been* deduced that the Pyramid Texts [dated c. 2300 BC] which refer to the stars had an independent origin from the solar spells and that eventually they were merged into the Heliopolitan doctrine. Imhotep's title "Chief of the Observers," which became the regular title of the High Priests of Heliopolis, may itself suggest an occupation connected with astral, rather than solar, observation. Here therefore may be the difference between the underlying purpose of the true and step pyramid, the latter being the product of a stellar cult and intended to enable the king to reach the astral heaven.[3]

Later, because of the overwhelming internal evidence of observational astronomy in the Pyramid Texts, Edwards preferred to translate Chief of the Observers as Chief of the Astronomers.[4] He died in September 1996, long before we took up this hint and began to look carefully at the astral aspect of the Step Pyramid Complex.

In 2005, I moved from England to Cairo, and set up a study base near the Giza pyramids. From the balcony of my fourth-floor apartment, I had a view of the Great Pyramid. From the rooftop, I could easily see the majestic Step Pyramid at Saqqara, the principal legacy of Imhotep. The result of my 2005–2006 Egypt study was the book *The Egypt Code*, in which we showed how various aspects of the Step Pyramid Complex were designed according to "sacred astronomy"—i.e., astronomical observations incorporated into the architecture of a sacred complex.[5]

View from the rooftop of our apartment building in Cairo,
with the Step Pyramid at Saqqara in the far distance.

View of the Great Pyramid from our apartment balcony in Cairo.

We will revisit this material in chapters 3 and 4 when we probe the Step Pyramid Complex and the Saqqara code. But first, we need to understand what went on at the cult center of Heliopolis and, more specifically, why it was that Imhotep was both high priest and master architect of the Step Pyramid Complex.

El Massalah

Today, the local Arabs call the spot where the temple of Heliopolis once stood *El Massalah*, the Obelisk. This is because the only visible thing that remains—other than a very small part of a temple's foundation and a few pitiful broken statues—is a lonely free-standing obelisk. When the city of Fustat (medieval Cairo) was built by the Arabs starting in the late 7th

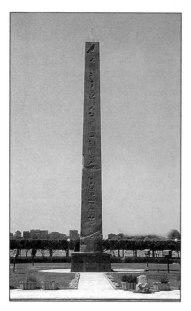

century, the remains of the temples and buildings of Heliopolis were systematically ransacked and used as a quarry for building material. The few remaining artifacts are strewn outside a rickety wooden shed within a large open rectangular space known as *Tel el Hisn*, the Hill of the Horse, which is surrounded ("besieged" is a better word) quite literally by ugly apartment blocks built in the 1960s and 1970s during Nasser's socialist era. Ancient Heliopolis is now an integral part of the Matareya district, swallowed by the ever-growing city of Cairo.

The obelisk of Sesostris (Senurset) I, known locally as *El Massalah*, where the temple of Heliopolis once stood.

We vividly recall our first trip to Matareya, ancient Heliopolis, in March 1993. It was a time of turmoil when anti-government terrorists had set off makeshift bombs in central Cairo, one of which exploded inside a restaurant in Tahrir Square on February 26, killing two students at the nearby American University and injuring many others.

One week later, on March 5, we decided to visit the Egyptian Antiquities Museum in Tahrir Square. We reckoned that, with such low tourism, it would be an ideal opportunity to take photographs unobstructed by the usual throng of tourists. As we happily clicked away in the ground-floor gallery, we became aware of a commotion at the entrance of the museum. A congregation of impressive-looking Coptic bishops had come into the gallery with their bodyguards. Upon seeing us, one of the bodyguards, indicating that he was armed by placing his hand inside his jacket, shouted "no photos!" But one bishop, named Baba Moussa, asked who we were. After we explained that we were taking pictures for a book, he signaled his bodyguards to let us take all the photos we wanted.

Robert Bauval with Ethiopian and Egyptian Coptic bishops
in the Cairo Museum, March 1993.

It was still early when we finished, so we decided to go to Matareya to take some photographs of the obelisk of Sesostris I (a 12th-Dynasty king) and whatever else remained of ancient Innu. The obelisk, 120 tons of solid granite towering some twenty meters, stands like a forlorn sentinel help-lessly watching the ever-encroaching slums of Cairo. A beggar approached me with one palm outstretched and his other hand pointing at the obelisk and cried "*el-massalah! el-massalah! Bakshish, bakshish!*" We wondered if he, or indeed any of the locals today, were aware that this quasi-abandoned archaeological site was once the greatest center of learning of the ancient world, where scholars from as far off as Greece came to be tutored by the Egyptian priest-scientists of Innu. For thousands of years, luminaries like Pythagoras, Eudoxus, Cnidus, and even, it is said, the great Plato came to be taught the sacred sciences of ancient Egypt: geometry, mathematics, medicine, divination, and, above all, astronomy.

The various epithets given to Heliopolis make this more than evident—"the chosen seat of the gods," "the horizon of the sky," and "the sky of Egypt," to cite but a few. Abdel-Aziz Saleh, a professor of Egyptology at Cairo University who spent many years excavating at Heliopolis, noted that "a number of high-priests of *Ounu* [Innu, Heliopolis] were individually entitled 'He who discloses the secret of Heaven [sky]' and the 'Supervisor of the mysteries of Heaven [sky].'" [6]

So important was Heliopolis as a seat of high learning that, even though some of the great scholars from Greece may not actually have made the journey to study there, their biographers nonetheless feigned that they had in order to enhance their scholarly prestige. Even Christ did not escape such a connection, for the district of Matareya was once an enclave of "Followers of Jesus," later to become the Copts, the Egyptian Christians who fervently believe that the Holy Family received sanctuary at Heliopolis. The canonical gospel of Matthew in fact says that the Holy Family sought refuge in Egypt from King Herod's campaign to kill all baby boys in Palestine. Indeed, to this day, just a few hundred meters

Edwin Long's painting of the Holy Family in Egypt, inviting the connection between Isis and the infant Horus, and Mary and the infant Jesus.

IMHOTEP: THE AFRICAN

down the road from *el-Massalah*, the small Church of the Holy Family stands, its interior walls decorated with scenes of the family entering on a donkey into the semi-ruined city of Heliopolis.

Remarkably, there is a superb painting by the 19th-century artist Edwin Long showing Joseph leading the donkey that carries Mary with the infant Jesus in her arms, while passing by a religious procession with an effigy of Isis carrying the infant Horus. Many historians of religion hold that the Isis-Horus myth was absorbed into Christian mythology and converted into the Mary-Jesus myth, complete with the astro-symbology of the Star of the East, a clear indication of the enormous influence that Heliopolis had on world culture.[7]

Church of the Holy Family in Matareya, Cairo.

The guard at the small ticket office outside the Heliopolis archaeological site told us that it was closed. The fact that the guard was alone made it easier to offer the proverbial *bakshish* (bribe/tip) to be let inside. An Egyptian note equivalent to about two U. S. dollars did the trick. The area was littered with garbage, and there were ugly puddles of green sewage water around the ruins. A few broken statues were displayed on the floor outside the small shed. We focused on taking photos of the obelisk, then a few others of the surrounding ruins and broken statuary. Then we drove to the nearby Church of the Holy Family. There, a friendly guard let us into the small but very moving church, and we took some photographs of the murals showing the Holy Family at Heliopolis.

The Bird of Creation and the Marking of Time

The Pyramid Texts comprise the oldest collection of ancient Egyptian religious texts, perhaps the oldest known texts in the world. They were found by French Egyptologist Gaston Maspero in 1881 and 1882, carved on the inside walls of 5th- and 6th-Dynasty pyramids at Saqqara. The oldest version is found in the pyramid of King Unas (last king of the 5th Dynasty, c. 2300 BC), which stands but a few hundred meters to the southwest of the earlier Step Pyramid Complex of Imhotep. The Unas pyramid has been closed since the late 1990s, but we managed to enter it several times between 1992 and 1995. On one occasion in December

The texts in the pyramid of King Unas, a few hundred meters to the southwest of the Step Pyramid Complex of Imhotep.

IMHOTEP: THE AFRICAN

1993, we spent several hours inside it filming a television documentary for the BBC's Everyman series, *The Great Pyramid: Gateway to the Stars*, which aired on February 7, 1994.

There is a passage in the Pyramid Texts (Utterance 600) that speaks of Heliopolis in an intriguing way: "O Atum-Khoprer (the rising sun), you rose high on the heights, you rose up as the benben stone in the Mansion of the Phoenix in Heliopolis." The *benben* stone was a very ancient and very sacred relic that was kept in the main temple at Heliopolis, called the Temple of the Phoenix (see Appendix I). But the most accredited translator of these texts, British philologist Raymond O. Faulkner, imposed the Greek word "phoenix" on the much older ancient Egyptian word *bennu*. The bennu was a magical bird that, according to the Egyptian Creation Myth, had appeared at the "first dawn of creation" to set time in motion by uttering a great cry that initiated life on earth. It is also evident that there is a word-play between *benben* and *bennu*, for both have the same etymological root, *ben*, and both are linked to the same ideas of creation and time. According to archaeoastronomer E. C. Krupp, the ancient priests of Heliopolis had interpreted an actual astronomical observation—not of the rising sun *per se*, but rather of the sun rising along with a very special star, the star Sirius:

> The world began in earnest there (at Heliopolis) when Sirius, the stellar signal for the Nile Flood, in its first return to the predawn sky, alighted as the bennu, the bird of creation, upon the benben and then took wings as the sun followed it into the heavens to bring light, life, and order to the cosmos.[8]

It is well known that the star Sirius, called Spd by the ancient Egyptians, was associated with the birth of Horus, the divine archetype of kings said to be born from the womb of the goddess Isis. It is also known that this star was used as a marker for calendric computations and especially to act as the starting point of the year—as well as to what is loosely termed the "Great Year," but is more accurately referred to by Egyptologists as the *Sothic Cycle* (a name derived from the Greeks, who called Sirius Sothis).

When we speak of time, it is wise to note the words of archaeoastronomer R. W. Stoley. This astute scholar emphasized that "ultimately, our clocks are really timed by the stars. The master-clock is our earth, turning on its axis relative to the fixed stars."[9] Early humans lacked mechanical devices to measure the passing of time. So they, and especially the ancient Egyptians, used the natural "clock" of our world—the earth itself or, to be more precise, the apparent perpetual cycle of the fixed stars as they "sail" from east to west every night. The priests of Heliopolis, as the Chief Observers, were responsible for this important function. And even though they may not have known that it was the earth's own rotation and revolution around the sun that caused the apparent cycles of the stars, they, as we today, could observe the motions, record their duration, and therefore calculate the cycles.

Egyptologists are in agreement that, of all the stars that were observed by the ancients, one special star stood out above all others: Sirius (known as Alpha Canis Majoris by modern astronomers). Egyptologists have recognized how important the first dawn rising of Sirius, technically known as the "heliacal rising," was to the Egyptians:

> The importance of Sirius for the Egyptians lay in the fact that the star's annual appearance on the eastern horizon at dawn heralded the approximate beginning of the Nile's annual inundation which marked the beginning of the agricultural year . . .[10] The Egyptian year was considered to begin on 19 July (according to the Julian calendar) which was the date of the heliacal rising of the dog star Sirius.[11]

The Nile flood near the pyramids, from a pre-1905 photograph.

The Nile River overflows and floods the adjacent valley in Egypt every year at about the time of the Summer Solstice—the last week in June, according to our present Gregorian calendar. By a propitious coincidence, the star Sirius also rises in the east for the first time at dawn after a prolonged period of "invisibility" that lasts some seventy days. It is no wonder, therefore, that the early inhabitants of the Nile Valley saw a connection between the annual heliacal rising of Sirius and the annual inundation of the Nile. And since this event regenerated Egypt's crops with rich detritus and fertilizers brought down from central Africa by the river, it is easy to see how this astronomical event was mythologized into the "birth of Horus" and, by extension, that of his earthly incarnation, the pharaoh.

A powerful and elaborate sky religion centered on the rebirth of kings among the stars gradually developed around, or at least fundamentally intertwined with, this one vital astronomical observation. It would also lead to the design and construction of "resurrection machines" in the form of the great pyramid complexes of the Old Kingdom, whose ultimate function was to bring about the transfiguration of the king's lifeless body into a "living star" in the sky.[12]

The Sothic Cycle

It would have been relatively easy for the ancient Egyptians, or indeed anyone else for that matter, to count the days from one heliacal rising of Sirius to another and come up with the 365-day annual cycle. However, it was eventually noticed that, every fourth year, the heliacal rising was delayed by a day, so that this fourth year of the cycle had 366 days. This was called the *tetraeteris* by the ancient Greeks, and known to the Romans as the *quadrennium*.[13] Today, this "extra day" is taken into account in our Gregorian calendar by having a "leap year" of 366 days once every four years. The leap year was introduced by Julius Caesar in the Julian calendar, which, interestingly, was designed for Caesar by an Egyptian astronomer, Sosigenes of Alexandria.

It seems clear that the ancient Egyptians were quite aware of the extra day in the yearly cycle but, for reasons that we shall soon see, did not adjust for it in their 365-day calendar, known as the civil calendar.

The rising of Sirius, with the constellation Orion high above it.

Today, we know that this extra day occurs because the solar year is not exactly 365 days long, but nearly 365¼ days. At any rate, Egyptologists and astronomers alike agree that the ancient Egyptians did not correct their civil calendar by introducing a leap year, in spite of the fact that they were aware that their calendar "drifted" a lot over time. The question, therefore, is why not? Here, however, is where Egyptologists and astronomers part ways. For the explanation that is self-evident to astronomers is generally rejected by modern Egyptologists—thus the Sothic Cycle debate.

The adoption of a civil calendar of 365 days without a leap year every fourth year meant that the calendar drifted from the true astronomical year at the rate of nearly one full day every four years. A simple calculation shows that this would create a cycle of 365¼ x 4 = 1,461 years (or 1,460 years if the extra ¼ day is left out). This, in a nutshell, is the *calculated* Sothic Cycle for a 365-day civil calendar or a 365¼-day (approximate solar year) calendar. In reality, as we shall see in a later chapter, this value can vary by a few years when and if the cycle is actually observed—that is, its start and end dates are actually recorded. And to be precise, the solar year, also called the tropical year, which is the precise time between one Vernal Equinox and the next is about 365.2422 days, while the sidereal year, which is the time it takes earth to return to the same relationship of the sun to distant fixed stars is about 365.2564 days. In *Black Genesis*, we show how the fact that the solar year is a bit shorter than 365¼ days and the sidereal year is a bit longer than 365¼ days makes the average Sothic year, which is a combination of the two, come out very close to 365¼ days. At any rate, the Sothic Cycle debate among academics is simply this: Many astronomers believe that the Egyptians had to be aware of it and even made use of it in their calendric computations, but contemporary Egyptologists don't.

Much ink has been spilled in this Sothic Cycle debate. It is fair to say, however, that the previous generation of Egyptologists was quite open to the idea of the Sothic Cycle, while today's Egyptologists reject it on the basis that there is no direct evidence to support the notion that the 1,461-year cycle was known, let alone used, by the ancient Egyptians. We shall unequivocally demonstrate in chapter 3 that the ancient Egyptians not only *knew* the Sothic Cycle, but also *used it* from the very earliest times.

Polemics

The first-century Roman historian Cornelius Tacitus, who consulted the works of Egyptian astronomer-priests, reported that the cyclical return of the Egyptian "phoenix"—i.e., the bennu—to Heliopolis was none other than the cyclical return of the heliacal rising of Sirius to its point of origin on the calendar, namely New Year's Day:

> The bird called the phoenix (bennu), after a long succession of ages, appeared in Egypt and furnished the most learned men of that country and of Greece with abundant matter for the discussion of the marvelous phenomenon [of its magical return] . . . it is a creature sacred to the sun. . . . Some maintain that it is seen at intervals of 1,461 years, and that the former birds flew into the city called Heliopolis.[14]

Egypt, with her mysteries, seems to have exercised a special fascination on the imagination of Tacitus; he boasts of knowing her better than others.[15]

British Egyptologist R. T. Rundle Clark also asserts:

> Underlying all Egyptian speculation is the belief that time is composed of recurrent cycles which are divinely appointed: the day, the week of ten days, the month, the year (and) even longer periods . . . 1,460 years . . . in conjunction of . . . stars and inundation. In a sense, when the Phoenix gave out its primeval call it initiated all these cycles, so it is the patron of all divisions of time, and its temple at Heliopolis became the center of calendric regulation. As the herald of each new dispensation, it becomes, optimistically, the harbinger of good tidings.[16]

It seemed obvious to these experts, as it is also obvious to us, that the Sothic Cycle of 1,460 or 1,461 years, namely the calculated return of the heliacal rising of Sirius to its starting point in the calendar, was the same as the return of the mythical phoenix—i.e., the Egyptian bennu—that periodically returned to Heliopolis to begin a "new age." And because the heliacal rising of Sirius symbolized the birth of Horus, the birth/rebirth of the pharaohs, earthly incarnations of Horus, was associated with this astronomical phenomenon.

We suppose, however, that pharaohs who happened to be born when a Sothic Cycle began were regarded as special, perhaps even messianic. In our book *The Egypt Code,* we argue that the birth of the pharaoh Akhenaten in c. 1356 BC coincided in his lifetime with the return of a Sothic Cycle and may have been the impetus for the dramatic religious reform he instigated. It is also possible that the birth of the 3rd-Dynasty pharaoh Djoser, whom Imhotep served as vizier and high priest, also coincided with such a return of a Sothic Cycle and, consequently, may have been the religious, intellectual, and creative impetus that brought about the Step Pyramid Complex.

Censorinus

If a Sothic Cycle ended and a new one began at intervals of 1,461 years, and if we know at least one of these start/end years, it should be relatively easy to work out when other Sothic Cycles begin by simply adding or subtracting increments of 1,461 years. As far as we can make out, however, the ancient Egyptians left us no records of such events.

Censorinus, on the other hand, a Roman writer in the 3rd century AD who was interested in astronomy, philosophy, and antiquarian subjects, wrote about the most recent Sothic Cycle, which began around 100 years before his time:

> The beginnings of these years [the Egyptian year] are always reckoned from the first day of that month which is called by the Egyptians Thoth, which happened this year [239 AD] upon the 7th of the kalends of July [June 25th]. For a hundred years ago from the present year [i.e., 139 AD] the same fell upon the 12th of the kalends of August [July 21st], on which day Canicula [Sirius] regularly rises in Egypt.[17]

Thanks to Censorinus, we know that a Sothic Cycle began on July 21 Julian in the year 139 AD. A check with the astronomical software StarryNight Pro confirms that this statement is correct. Sirius did rise heliacally on July 21 according to the Julian Calendar in the year 139 AD, as witnessed from the city of Alexandria, which is where the observation was most probably made, since it was the capital city of Egypt at that time and the seat of learning and time-keeping. The altitude of Sirius was 1° and that of the sun -9° in the eastern horizon. Sirius would have had an azimuth of 109° 16', a configuration very consistent with its first appearance of the year before sunrise. We thus can easily work out approximate start dates of other Sothic Cycles—1321 BC, 2781 BC, 4241 BC, 5701 BC, 7160 BC, 8621 BC, 10,081 BC, 11,451 BC, and so on. It is thus justified to assume that ancient Egyptian time-keeping probably started with one of these dates.

But which one?

Zep Tepi—The "First Time"

We know from many ancient Egyptian texts that the people who occupied the Nile Valley had a concept of a beginning or starting point—a creation—in their history, very much as Christians take the (assumed) date of Jesus's birth as the beginning of the Christian Era. Indeed, based on the Bible, the 19th-century Irish Archbishop James Ussher calculated that the world began on October 23, 4004 BC!

The ancient Egyptians called their own beginning *zep tepi*, literally the "First Time." Unlike Archbishop Ussher's calculation, however, we believe that the Egyptian First Time is rooted in astronomical reality. Here is what the Egyptologists say about zep tepi:

> The basic principles of life, nature and society were determined by the gods long ago, before the establishment of kingship. This epoch—*zep tepi*—"the First Time"—stretched from the first stirring of the High God in the Primeval Waters to the settling of Horus upon the throne and the redemption of Osiris. All proper myths relate events or manifestations of this epoch. Anything whose existence or authority had to be justified or explained must be referred to the "First Time." This was true for natural phenomena, rituals, royal insignia, the plans of temples, magical or medical formulae, the hieroglyphic system of writing, the calendar—the whole paraphernalia of the civilization ... all that was good or efficacious was established on the principles laid down in the "First Time"—which was, therefore, a golden age of absolute perfection—"before rage or clamour or strife or uproar had come about." No death, disease or disaster occurred in this blissful epoch, known [as] ..."the time of Horus."[18]

In our previous book *The Egypt Code,* we showed how zep tepi could be calculated astronomically to the 12th millennium BC by taking the very first appearance of Sirius at the latitude of Memphis. This date dovetails with the start date of the eighth Sothic Cycle before Censorinus (which, if counted at 1,461 years per cycle, would put it at 11,451 BC).[19] However, such a remote date for the beginning of the Egyptian civilization is violently opposed by Egyptologists and archaeologists, who are adamant that the ancient Egyptian civilization cannot be much older than 3100 BC.

We do not propose to repeat here in detail the reasoning that led us to fix zep tepi in the 12th millennium BC. In brief, however, using astronomy in conjunction with the Pyramid Texts, we showed that the main monuments of the Giza necropolis—namely the three Great Pyramids and the Sphinx—formed an earthly model of the constellations of Orion's belt and Leo as these appeared in the skies of the 12th millennium BC at the time of the Spring Equinox (the day of the year when the sun rises exactly due east). This date corresponds to the first appearance in human history of the star Sirius in the latitude of Giza.

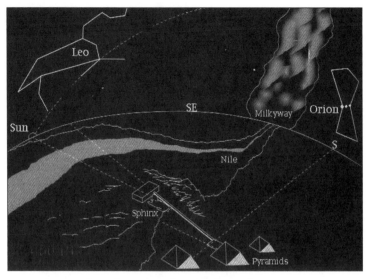

Sky-ground correlation at the latitude of Memphis in 11,450 BC, near the time of zep tepi.

We do not claim, as many have wrongly thought, that the Giza monuments were built in 11,450 BC; what we do claim is that they were built on older alignments or ground plans that date from the time when the location first became a sacred site. Geological evidence, however, suggests that perhaps the Sphinx may be that old, and perhaps other parts of the Giza complex as well—such as possibly a viewing platform on top of which the Great Pyramid was later built, and perhaps the Subterranean Passage.[20] At any rate, when we first published the zep tepi dating in 1993 and then in more detail in 1996,[21] there was a mighty outcry from Egyptologists who were furious at the suggestion that Egyptian civilization could have begun several thousands of years before the Early Dynastic period, which they fixed at c. 3100 BC.

Even some archaeoastronomers—among them E. C. Krupp, director of the Griffith Observatory in Los Angeles, and his colleague in South Africa, Anthony Fairall, professor of Astromony at the University of Cape Town and planetarium director at the South African Museum—joined ranks with Egyptologists in the verbal onslaught. Krupp attacked our

In *Black Genesis*, we revisted the zep tepi discussion and noted that Sirius made its southernmost culmination on its entire 26,000-year journey at that time c. 12,200 BC. And in fact, Sirius's declination at southern culmination precisely equaled the declination of the southern horizon at Giza. What this means is that, during the years around Sirius's southern culmination, the star may have been only glimpsed, just at the horizon, at midnight around the Summer Solstice. The Giza plateau may have been used as a viewing location for that epochal event—perhaps marking the First Time, or zep tepi, when Giza originally became a sacred site. At locations north of Giza, Sirius would have disappeared completely for many years or centuries, whereas locations south of Giza would always have been able to site Sirius sometime during any year. Further, the very bright star Vega (Alpha Lyrae) was the "north pole star" of that time. And Vega achieved its northern culmination, highest declination of about 86.54°, also c. 12,000 BC. And that declination is the same as the declination of the very precisely oriented Subterranean Passage underneath what is now the Great Pyramid.

zep tepi dating in the popular magazine *Sky & Telescope* with the condescending title "Pyramid Marketing Schemes."[22] His objection was that the ancient Egyptians did not know the zodiacal constellation Leo, at least not before it was supposedly introduced by the Greeks in c. 350 BC. Krupp also accused us of allegedly placing the map of Egypt "upside down" to fit our theory.

As for Professor Fairall's criticism, that came in an article published in *The Journal of the Royal Astronomical Society* no less, in which he refuted our zep tepi dating on the grounds that the angle made by the stars of Orion's belt and the pyramids on the ground did not match at the zep tepi date.[23] The dispute finally all came to a huge crescendo in November 1999 when the BBC program *Horizon* presented the attacks of these two scholars, as well as a few others, in one part of a two-episode documentary titled *Atlantis Reborn*. Krupp and another American academic, Kenneth L. Feder, professor of Anthropology at Central Connecticut State University, were particularly vocal in this BBC documentary. We found out later that they were senior members of an organization called CSICOP (Committee for the Scientific Investigation of Claims of the

Paranormal), an ultra-skeptical society of academics and laypeople that claims to defend and protect the public against pseudo-science—in other words, a sort of scientific inquisition that hunts down and debunks whomever they deem unscientific or or anyone who challenges CSI-COP's established status quo. Since 2006, CSICOP has shortened its name to CSI, Committee for Skeptical Inquiry.

Although the producers of the BBC program denied they knew of the CSICOP affiliation of these two scholars, they nonetheless allowed them much leeway to debunk us in the program. Here is a portion of Krupp's conclusion:

> I think, then, it is unlikely the three pyramids of Giza are stand-ins for the stars. For all I know, they may symbolize the Three Blind Mice, the Three Graces, the Three Musketeers, the Three Wise Men, or the Three Stooges. But I don't think they are the three stars of Orion's Belt.

We obviously could not remain silent. The matter was brought to the attention of the British Broadcasting Standards Commission (BBSC) who, upon hearing all the facts, made a rare ruling against the BBC and obliged them to make amends for their unfair tactics. They required the BBC to re-broadcast the program, but with our counterarguments added. They also required them to precede the program with a full reading of the BBSC adjudication and to publish the adjudication in the *Times of London*. The broadcasting corporation also faced the displeasure of senior British astronomers like Professor Mary Brück of Edinburgh University, wife of the celebrated Astronomer Royal for Scotland, Hermann Brück; Professor Emeritus Archibald Roy of Glasgow University; Professor Percy Seymour of Plymouth University; and Professor Chandra Wikramasinghe of Cardiff University, who formally criticized BBC *Horizon* with written statements that supported our views.[24]

Putting these academic quibblings aside, however, there was a far more serious objection by Egyptologists to our claim. They pointed out that there was no direct *archaeological evidence* that supported a human presence in Egypt in the 12th millennium BC, let alone one capable of sculpting the Sphinx or calculating astronomical cycles. The most outspoken Egyptologist on this point was American Mark Lehner, once himself a keen

Robert Bauval at Nabta Playa in 2008.

Thomas Brophy at Nabta Playa in 2003.

believer in a much older date for the Sphinx and Egyptian civilization. Since 1975, however, Lehner has become a zealous opponent to this idea. He summed up the consensus of his fellow Egyptologists with these words:

> I should tell people how this has come down to me personally. Because I actually went over there with my own notions of lost civilizations, older civilizations from Edgar Cayce . . .
>
> Civilizations don't disappear without a trace. If archaeologists can go out and dig up a campsite of hunters and gatherers that was occupied 15,000 years ago, there's no way there could have been a complex civilization at a place like Giza or anywhere in the Nile Valley and they didn't leave a trace, because people eat, people poop, people leave their garbage around, and they leave their traces, they leave the traces of humanity. . . . Well, as I say to New Age critics, show me one pot shard of that earlier civilization. Because the only way they could have existed is if they actually got out with whisk brooms, scoop shovels and little spoons and cleared out every single trace of their daily lives, their utensils, their pottery, their wood, their tools and so on, and that's just totally improbable. Well, it's not impossible, but it has a very, very low level of probability, that there was an older civilization there.[25]

Lehner's claim that civilizations don't disappear without a trace reminded us that, hardly a century ago, scholars used the same argument to discount the existence of ancient Troy, finally to be proved wrong by an amateur, Heinrich Schliemann, in 1876. Recently, the discovery of sophisticated monumental architecture at Gobekli Tepe in Turkey, dating to at least as early as the 9th millennium BC, reveals another previously unknown advanced culture. Indeed, whole civilizations—the Minoans of Crete and the Etruscans of Italy, for example—were totally unknown to archaeologists well into the 19th century. Ironically, Mark Lehner made his comments in 1997, when Egyptologists were well aware that much archaeological, anthropological, and astronomical evidence existed in the Egyptian Sahara at the prehistoric complex at Nabta Playa.

Beginning in 1974, the Combined Prehistoric Expedition (CPE), led by American anthropologist Fred Wendorf and Polish anthropologist

Romuald Schild, and later including astronomer Kim Malville, has brought to light a plethora of archaeological, anthropological, and astronomical evidence that strongly implies, if not proves, that there was a proto-Egyptian civilization in the Western Desert of Egypt, the Sahara, thousands of years before the so-called Early Dynastic period. So it was somewhat ill-informed of Lehner to claim in 1997 that no evidence that supported an older phase for Egyptian civilization existed. At any rate, this issue will be re-examined in chapter 4 and in Appendix IV of this book. Let us now, however, return to Heliopolis, for it is there, we strongly believe, that one should begin the search to understand the intellectual and religious forces that led to the monumental construction of the Step Pyramid Complex.

The Mound of Creation

Although much has been written about Heliopolis in textbooks and novels, the truth is that Egyptologists know very little about its origins and even less about the systems of initiation and teachings that took place there. Scholarly opinions are varied.[26] Let us begin, therefore, with what scholars agree on—that the epicenter of Heliopolis was where the lone obelisk still stands. To be very precise about this, the coordinates of the obelisk are:

30° 07' 45.39" N
31° 18' 37.01" E

Another widely accepted view is that Heliopolis was the main center for astronomical observation and calendric computation, and that records were mostly focused on the cycles of Sirius, especially its heliacal rising. Also, one often reads in Egyptology textbooks that the most sacred location at Heliopolis was a mound or hill called the Mound of Creation; it was on this mound, legend had it, that the bennu bird alighted on the first sunrise of creation. It seems logical, therefore, to consider these three known facts together—the mound, sunrise, and cycles of Sirius—to work out why and how this most holy of ancient centers was established at this location, with its precise latitude and longitude.

Mounds and Hills

There is much textual and archaeological evidence that the ancient Egyptians had a particular interest in and great reverence for certain mounds. A set of these sacred mounds is encompassed by Heliopolis, Letopolis, Abu Ruwash, Giza, and Saqqara. Let us imagine this vast area roughly twenty-five kilometers square with no cities, no villages, no roads or monuments—in other words, a vast region still undisturbed by humans. From a high point like the summit of the Mokattam hills (a long mountain mesa south of modern Cairo on the east side of the Nile), one would be able to see the fanning out of the Nile Valley into the Delta toward the northwest, and the Sahara on the far western horizon. In the inundation season from late June to late September, especially during high floods, the area would be submerged, looking like a lake except for high mounds protruding like icebergs in a sandy sea. One such mound was the Mound of Creation at Heliopolis.

British Egyptologist David Jeffreys, an expert in the topography of this region, gives a good description of how it must have looked in ancient times during inundation season.[27] Let us now imagine the first humans coming into this region and, at some point, witnessing something "falling from the sky" that looked like a fire-bird trailing a long plume and streaming down with a loud screeching noise, finally landing near the Heliopolitan mound. In 1990, we published an article on the origins of the benben stone in which we presented textual and photographic evidence that suggests that the sacred relic of Heliopolis, the stone that is depicted in New Kingdom papyrus as a conical or pyramidal object, could have been a large iron "oriented" meteorite recovered by the inhabitants of the area and placed in the Temple of the Phoenix at Heliopolis (see the substance of the article in Appendix I).

In 1970, Egyptologist John Baines, professor at Oxford University, showed that the root of the word *benben (ben)* has sexual and fertility connotations and, more particularly, often alludes to the semen from a human penis.[28] As for the benben itself, it was associated with the creator god Atum of Heliopolis. According to Egyptologists like Edwards, Henry Frankfort, and James Breasted, a pillar sacred to Atum was worshiped at Heliopolis along with the benben, probably with the benben placed on top of it.[29] From various passages in the Pyramid Texts, it is obvious that

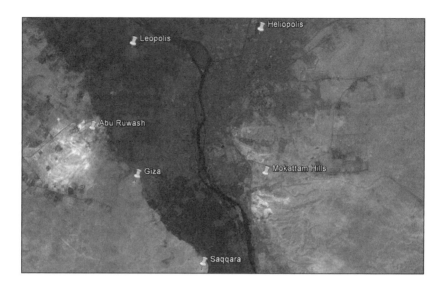

Overhead view of the Memphite/Heliopolitan region and the sacred mounds.

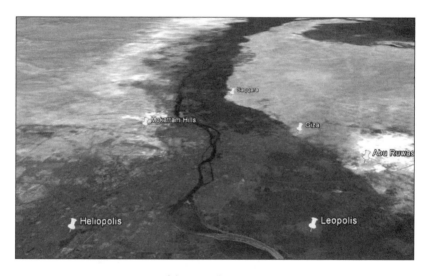

Perspective view of the Memphite/Heliopolitan region and the
sacred mounds looking south.

IMHOTEP: THE AFRICAN

the pillar, a well-known phallic symbol in antiquity, was somehow associated with the phallus of Atum:

> Atum is he who once came into being, who masturbated in (Heliopolis). He took his phallus in his grasp that he might create orgasm by means of it. (pyr. 1248)

> O Atum-khoprer (sunrise), you became high on the heights [pillar/mound?], you rose as the Benben stone in the Mansion of the Phoenix in Heliopolis. (pyr. 1652)

It is thus not hard to imagine, as Frankfort pointed out, that the combination of the pyramid-shaped benben on top of a pillar (later stylized into the obelisk with a pyramid-shaped top) may have represented the phallus and "seed" of Atum.[30]

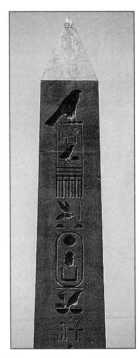

Pyramidion-shaped benben atop a pillar, later stylized into an obelisk.

To all these interconnected ideas we then added the suggestion that this "seed" was probably a fifteen-ton "oriented" iron meteorite, which is commonly conical or pyramidal shaped (see Appendix I). Whatever the object was, everything suggests that the sacred mound, obelisk, or pillar on which the benben was placed served as some sort of main geodetic marker or datum from which astronomical observations and geographical measurements could be made.

Spend time in open deserts where there are hills and mounds, such as Egypt's Western Desert, and it becomes second nature to use the mounds and hills as markers to fix the positions of the rising or setting of the celestial bodies. In other words, the undulated skyline becomes, quite literally, a kind of open-air planetarium from which time-keeping computations can be made and geographical directions established. The easiest and most obvious observation is sunrise or sunset at the solstices, marking the two extreme positions of the solar year. Furthermore, special attention must have been paid to the Summer

Solstice sunrise, because it was at that special time of year that the Nile began to flood the land. Moreover, from 3100 BC and for most of the Dynastic period, it was when the heliacal rising of Sirius occured.

The Living Image of Atum

Standing near the Mound of Creation at Heliopolis and looking toward the west, you can see three distinct mounds across the Nile on the distant horizon. One mound at Letopolis is due west at azimuth 270°; a second mound at Abu Ruwash is southwest at azimuth 243°; a third mound at Giza is more to the southwest at azimuth 225°. Two of these mounds, Letopolis and Abu Ruwash, mark the position of the equinoxes (Letopolis) and the Winter Solstice at sunset, as seen from Heliopolis when looking west.

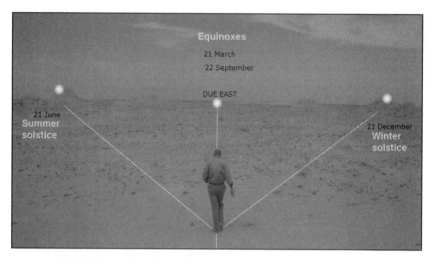

Position of the Summer and Winter Solstices and the two equinoxes, facing due east at sunrise in the desert.

This was pointed out for the first time in 2006 in our book *The Egypt Code*:

> Measuring from a scaled map of the Memphite Necropolis, it is obvious that Djedefre's pyramid is nearer 27° south-of-west of Heliopolis. At this latitude this is the orientation of the setting sun at the winter solstice.[31]

The very same idea was "borrowed" in 2007 by Spanish astronomer Juan Belmonte, who wrote:

> There [at Abu Ruwash], the pyramid of Djedefre was built on top of a rocky outcrop that in antiquity would have been clearly visible from Heliopolis. As a matter of fact, sunset at the winter solstice.[32]

Reversing the position of the observer and looking east from the Letopolis mound toward Heliopolis, the observer would be looking at the equinoxes at sunrise; similarly from the Abu Ruwash mound looking toward Heliopolis, the observer would be looking at the Summer Solstice sunrise. Furthermore, when looking from the Giza mound, Heliopolis would be exactly 45° south-of-west. Unless all this is an amazing set of coincidences, it seems clear that these mounds were chosen because of the special directional interrelationship they have with each other.

At the foot of the Giza mound, as if a sentinel to it, is the universally known statue of the Sphinx. Could the Sphinx have had a connection with Heliopolis? Egyptologists agree that the original god of Heliopolis was Atum, and that Heliopolis was first called *per-atum*, the "city" or "domain" of Atum. This very ancient god was the head of the supreme Egyptian pantheon known as the Great Ennead, or the Nine Gods. The latter was said to have come into existence at the beginning of the world, the zep tepi. It all started with Atum, whose masturbation created Shu, god of air, and Tefnut, goddess of moisture. They, in turn, begat Geb, god of the

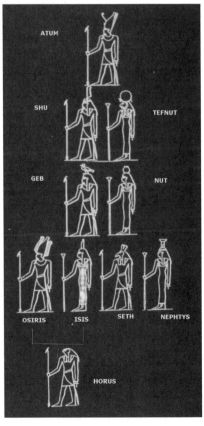

The supreme Egyptian pantheon of the Nine Gods, known as the Great Ennead.

earth, and Nut, goddess of the sky. From Geb and Nut were created Osiris, Isis, Seth, and Nephtys, four anthropomorphic gods who descended from heaven to earth and founded the civilization of Egypt. There was, in fact, a tenth member to this corporation of gods: the man-god Horus, son of Osiris and Isis. Each pharaoh of Egypt unwaveringly believed himself to be the reincarnation of Horus.

However, even though Atum was the supreme god of Heliopolis in pre-pyramid days, sometime around the 4th or 5th Dynasty, the religious focus shifted to another solar deity known as Re-Horakhty, the latter being a merger of the sun god Re and Horus of the Horizon. In our previous books, especially in *Keeper of Genesis* (*Message of the Sphinx* in the United States) and *The Egypt Code*, we show that Horakhty was a stellar deity whose name was given to the Great Sphinx and also the zodiacal constellation we today call Leo, the celestial lion.

The combined name Re-Horakhty was derived from the observable fact that, during the Pyramid Age, the sun was in the constellation of Leo at the Summer Solstice; this "merger" was seen as a cosmic union of Re and Horakhty. Yet the Sphinx does not face the Summer Solstice sunrise (at azimuth 63°, or 27° north-of-east), but instead faces due east, the place of sunrise at the equinoxes. How can this anomaly be explained? Egyptologists have often pointed out that one of the identities attributed to the Great Sphinx, probably the oldest, was none other than Atum, the original god of Heliopolis. As such, and for reasons that Egyptologists cannot explain adequately, the Sphinx was called Seshep-ankh Atum, the Living Image of Atum. According to Lehner, an expert on the Sphinx: "The ancient Egyptian general term for sphinx, *shesep ankh Atum*, means 'living image of Atum,' Atum being both the creator god and the setting sun."[33]

This Sphinx = Atum = lion imagery was, in any case, confirmed by the eminent Swiss Egyptologist Edouard Naville, who wrote: "There can be no doubt that the lion or the sphinx is a form of Atum."[34] Furthermore, the highly respected Egyptologist Rosalie David also confirmed the antecedence of Atum at Heliopolis at the opening of the Pyramid Age, pointing out that "... the god Re [sun god] had taken over the cult of an earlier god Atum."[35]

Egyptologists concur that, according to ancient Egyptian beliefs, the world came forth from Atum as he appeared on the Primeval Mound

The Great Sphinx, the "Living Image of Atum," depicted as a lion with a human head.

or Mound of Creation. In the Pyramid Texts, the Coffin Texts, and the Book of the Dead, a lion is said to emerge from this primeval mound before all other creatures, including humankind. Polish Egyptologist Karol Mysliwiec of Warsaw University, who did an extensive study of the god Atum, showed that there is a direct association between the birth of Atum and this primeval lion. In other words, Atum first appeared on earth as a lion.[36] Around the Pyramid Age, however, the Egyptians saw the Sphinx as Horakhty, Horus of the Horizon, which we have identified as a lion, even though it was also still referred to as the living image of Atum.[37] So, if the Sphinx was originally seen as the living image of Atum and depicted as a lion with a human head and later called Horakhty, then might it not make more sense to consider an earlier date for the astronomical alignment of the Sphinx?

Heliopolis was sacred to these two gods, who are alter egos of each other at different epochs: Re-Horakhty during the Pyramid Age (c. 2650–2300 BC) and Atum at an earlier date. But which earlier date? Since Heliopolis was the site of the Temple of the Phoenix or bennu, who regulated time and initiated the Sothic Cycles, then would it not be logical to wonder if a Sothic Cycle did begin when the sky figure of Leo, the cosmic lion, was in direct alignment with the Sphinx—i.e., due east?

Leo and the Equinox

The sun rises due east (azimuth 90°) at two dates in the year: the Spring Equinox (March 21–22) and the Autumn Equinox (September 22–23). The question, therefore, is better formulated as follows: Was there a time when the constellation Leo marked one of the equinoxes? The answer is a resounding "Yes." Leo marked the Spring Equinox between the 12th and 9th millennia BC.

Using powerful astronomical computer software that reconstructs the sky for any epoch in the past or future—StarryNight Pro, for example—it can easily be verified that the first time that the constellation Leo was seen in its entirety due east on the horizon on the day of the Spring Equinox was about 11,500 BC. This date dovetails neatly with the beginning of the very first Sothic Cycle, which we have identified as zep tepi—the First Time—when sky and ground mirror each other at the Giza necropolis, with the three main pyramids "reflected" as the three stars in Orion's belt in the lower southern sky and the leonine Sphinx "reflected" as the constellation Leo in the lower eastern sky.

That the Giza complex was believed to have been initiated at zep tepi is confirmed by the pharaoh Thotmoses IV, who left a written testimony—a sort of pharaonic "message in a bottle"—inscribed on the stele he had placed between the paws of the Sphinx with these words: "The Holy Place of zep tepi," the place of the First Time. The whole passage reads:

> Then the hour came to give rest to his followers, at the limbs of Horemakhet [the name of the Sphinx in the New Kingdom], beside Sokar in Ra-Setjaw [Giza], Renutet in Northern Djeme, Mut the mistress of the Northern Wall and the mistress of the Southern Wall, Sekhmet who presides over her Kha, Set, the son of Heka, the Holy Place of the zep tepi (First Time), near the Lords or Kheraha, the divine road of the gods toward the West of Iunu (Heliopolis).

And although we have stressed this point in our books *Keeper of Genesis, The Origin Map,* and *Black Genesis* with archaeological, geological, anthropological, and astronomical evidence, most of modern Egyptology remains intractable. After nearly two decades of time-wasting debate, rebuttals, and counter-rebuttals, there was only one way forward: We had to leave modern Egyptologists arguing among themselves and move on. As far as we are concerned, the question is no longer whether there was a deliberate interrelationship in the positioning of the various pyramids and temples, but *why*? What could have been the real motive—or function—of such a scheme?

Sacred Astronomy and Geometry

In 1990, French Egyptologist George Goyon, after serving as personal Egyptologist to King Farouk I of Egypt from 1936 to 1952 and studying the geography of the pyramid fields in the vast Memphite necropolis, could not help but wonder if "the Egyptians of the Pyramid Age had much more astronomical and geographical knowledge than hitherto assumed by us."[38] Goyon, however, was not the first person to suspect this, although he was the first modern-era Egyptologist to do so as far as we can determine. Before him, however, there had been non-Egyptologists like the Italian classicist Livio Catullo Stecchini (1913–1979), professor of Ancient History at William Paterson University in New Jersey, who published a thesis in 1971 about the highly advanced geographical and astronomical knowledge of the ancient Egyptians. Egyptologists largely ignored Stecchini's thesis, branding him a pseudoscientist,[39] although the idea of a deliberate interrelation between the Giza plateau and Heliopolis had, in fact, been proposed as early as 1852 by an Armenian-Egyptian engineer, Joseph Hekekyan, a fact pointed out in an article published in 1998 by British Egyptologist David Jeffreys.[40]

Hekekyan (1807–1875) served as director of the School of Engineering in Egypt. In 1852, he conducted a detailed survey of the Giza-Memphis region that was published under the title *Topographical Sketch of Heliopolis and Surrounding Lands*, which is now kept in the manuscript archives of the British Library in London. In this paper, Hekekyan showed that the southwest-to-northeast diagonal passing through the apex of the Great Pyramid, if extended toward the northeast, will also pass through the apex of the Sesotris I obelisk at Matareya-Heliopolis some twenty-four kilometers away.[41] Predictably, virtually all Egyptologists ignored him.

Joseph Hekekyan, who first proposed a link between the apex of the Great Pyramid at Giza and the apex of the Sesotris I obelisk at Matareya-Heliopolis in 1852.

In 1970, however, Goyon also conducted an investigation of the astronomical orientation of the Great Pyramid at Giza and arrived at the same conclusions. He further noticed that a third mound some eighteen kilometers due north of the Giza plateau marked the location of ancient Letopolis, which, furthermore, was precisely eighteen kilometers due west of Heliopolis. These three locations formed a huge right triangle. But that was not all. Goyon also suggested that the ancient astronomers who aligned the Great Pyramid were sighting the Big Dipper constellation, called Mesekhtiu (the Bull's Thigh) at its upper culmination when it hovered over Letopolis, since Letopolis was the capital of the ancient nome (district) whose symbol was a bull's thigh.[42]

Goyon, too, was all but ignored by his fellow Egyptologists. Then, more than a decade later, in November 1983, a journalist at the *Washington Post* surprised everyone by proudly announcing that an American Egyptologist, Hans Goedicke of John Hopkins University, had discovered a connection between the Giza pyramids and Heliopolis![43] Goedicke, who was clearly inspired by Hekekyan's earlier discovery (1852) and Goyon's publication (1970), claimed to have identified the "Giza diagonal"—with a minor variation: apparently a line could be drawn from the southeastern corners of the three pyramids and extended straight to Heliopolis "and the sanctuary of the Benben Stone."

This new Giza diagonal proved to be erroneous, however, due to Goedicke's unfamiliarity with the precise layout and measurement of the Giza pyramids. Working from a small-scale drawing or photograph of the Giza complex, he made an error typical of amateurs who draw lines, even with very fine pencils, which actually represent several meters of width in the actual Giza complex. Putting the Giza complex on a

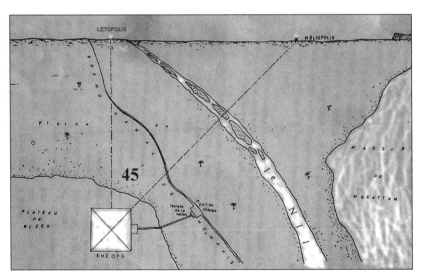

George Goyon's 1970 map of the interrelationship between
Giza, Heliopolis, and Letopolis.

standard A4 sheet (8.27 × 11.69 inches), the scale would have to be about 1:5000, with every centimeter representing fifty meters. In such a drawing, even the thickness of a pencil line would represent several meters! Further compounding this error, it seems that Goedicke used an even smaller image that fit on an A5 sheet (5.83 × 8.27 inches). On a map of this size, it may appear as if the southeast corners of the three pyramids can be joined in a straight line, but the reality is that the line would, in fact, miss the southeast corner of the third pyramid by several meters. In fact, British engineer Chris Tedder, who has spent many years studying the layout and measurements of the Giza pyramid complex, confirmed this:

> The three SE corners are *not in a straight line*. . . a line between the SE corners of G1 and G3 misses the SE corner of G2 by 12m (39ft), and a line between the SE corners of G1 and G2, extended to G3, misses the SE corner of G3 by 23m (76ft)—either G2 is set back from the line about 12m (39ft), or G3 is offset to the east by 23m (76ft).[44]

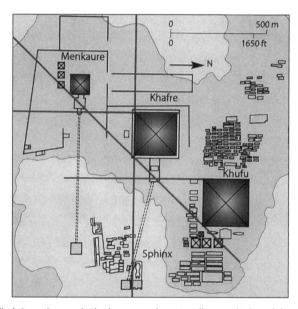

The so-called Giza diagonal. The lines are about 1 millimeter thick and thus represent about 10 meters actual distance on the ground.[45]

Scholars who at first supported the Giza diagonal were thus forced to acknowledge this large deviation of either twelve meters (at G2) or twenty-three meters (at G3). Yet, amazingly, some still obstinately retain as gospel this defunct Giza diagonal theory, claiming it as the only motive of the ancient builders for the layout of the Giza pyramids.[46] Moreover, they keep flaunting it ad nauseam in articles and textbooks.[47] (See Appendix II for a full discussion on this issue.)

In 1989, a few years after Goedicke's Giza-diagonal declaration, we published our own thesis in the academic journal *Discussions in Egyptology*, showing for the first time the correlation between the layout of the three Giza pyramids and the pattern of the three stars in Orion's belt, based on the religious ideologies found in the Pyramid Texts and the symbolic astronomy incorporated into the design of the Giza complex.[48] Again, most Egyptologists ignored it, with the solitary exception of Edwards.

In private correspondence dated October 16, 1984, Edwards said the following:

> Let me say that I found your astronomical observations very interesting. . . . I am very much in agreement with your contention that the stars of Orion's belt were an important element in the orientation of the Great Pyramid. . . . I think you have made a very convincing case that the two other pyramids were influenced by it.

Dr. Richard Parker—eminent Egyptologist, renowned expert on ancient Egyptian astronomy and calendars, and a colleague of Edwards—concurred in another letter in 1985.

When *The Orion Mystery* was published (Bauval, 1994), the Orion Correlation Theory (OCT), as it was now being called, received widespread notoriety, since the book was accompanied by the major BBC documentary *The Great Pyramid: Gateway to the Stars*, which forced Egyptologists out of their comfort zone. They simply could not ignore it and attacked the thesis in the international media and popular science magazines. A handful, however, were open to the idea—notably Edwards and Jaromir Malek of the Griffith Institute in Oxford. The latter did the honor of reviewing the book, and cautiously commented:

> The idea that the distribution of the pyramids is governed by definable ideological (religious, astronomical, or similar)

considerations is attractive. After all, if there were such reasons for the design of the pyramid and for the relationship of monuments at one site, why should we shut our eyes to the possibility that similar thinking was behind the apparently almost perverse scatter of the pyramids over the Memphite area? The argument that the Egyptians would not have been able to achieve this had they set their mind to it cannot be seriously entertained.[49]

Robert Bauval's proposed correlation theory—on the left, the position of the Giza pyramids; on the right, the stars in Orion's belt.

To be clear, Professor Malek did not sanction the thesis, but seemed particularly open to to idea of a deliberate interrelationship between the various pyramids based on religious ideologies. In a similar vein, Miroslav Verner, an eminent Czech Egyptologist who is also an expert on Egyptian pyramids, puzzled over this issue of their distribution:

> The reasons why the ancient Egyptians buried their dead on the edge of the desert on the western bank of the Nile are evident enough. The same, however, cannot be said of the reasons for their particular choice of sites for pyramid-building. Why, for example, did the founder of the 4th Dynasty, Sneferu, build his first pyramid at Meydum then abandon the place, building another two of his pyramids approximately 50 kilometres farther north of Dashur?

Why did his son Khufu build his tomb, the celebrated Great Pyramid, still farther to the north in Giza? ... the question are numerous, and, as a rule, answers to them remain on the level of conjecture.[50]

While most Egyptologists equivocated over these issues, Jeffreys, a director at the Egypt Exploration Society (EES) in London, became convinced that a planned (as opposed to haphazard) interrelationship did exist between certain pyramids and the city of Heliopolis:

> The archaeology and topography of Heliopolis and Memphis have often been the subject of comment, but these two important sites have usually been discussed in isolation from one another; only rarely have they been considered as elements in the wider landscape of this crucial area of the Nile Valley. Work on the EES Survey of Memphis has convinced me that any regional study of this area must take into account the local (and no doubt conflicting) territorial claims of both urban centers, and indeed that of Letopolis-Ausim to the west as well.... It is difficult today to appreciate just how prominent and visible these sites and monuments actually were ... in the last century the Giza pyramids could also be seen from Heliopolis.... It is therefore appropriate to ask, in a landscape as prospect-dominated as the Nile Valley, which site and monuments were mutually visible and whether their respective locations, horizons and vistas are owed to something more than mere coincidence?[51]

Jeffreys did not discuss possible astronomical motives for a deliberate interrelationship between the various sites, but he did at least suggest, albeit with the exaggerated caution that plagues modern scholarship, that it seemed to be "something more than mere coincidence."[52] In brief, Jeffreys, who had headed the Topographical Survey of the Memphite region in the late 1990s for the EES, noted that there were clear "lines of sight" to Heliopolis from the pyramid fields starting at Abu Ruwash in the north to the so-called Sun Temples of Abu Ghorab in the south, but that beyond this point the "line of sight" was cut off, as it were, by the high hills of the Mokattam range.[53]

Jeffreys, however, gave no explanation for why the pyramids farther south of Abu Ghorab, especially those at Abusir, Saqqara, and Dashur,

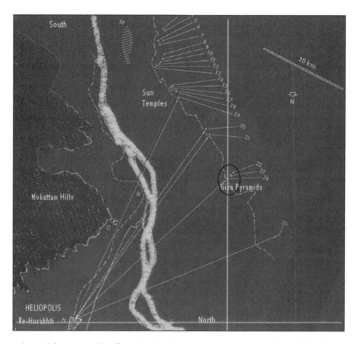

Map adapted from David Jeffreys's sketch showing the relationship of the Giza pyramids and the Sun Temples to Heliopolis in the northeast.

did *not* have lines of sight to Heliopolis. Jeffreys's insight was nonetheless intriguing and definitely worth a closer look. We, too, were convinced that the locations of pyramids were chosen for reasons related to Heliopolis, but we did not think that simply having lines of sight was the primary motive. If this were the case, we would expect Imhotep, of all people, to have positioned the Step Pyramid Complex with clear visibility to Heliopolis as well, especially since all the choice sites north of Abu Ghorab were as yet unexploited and thus available to him.

The same argument goes for Djoser's immediate successors—the pharaohs Sekhemkhet (3rd Dynasty), Huni (3rd Dynasty), and Snefru (founder of the 4th Dynasty)—who chose sites even farther away without lines of sight to Heliopolis. Something clearly was amiss in Jeffreys's theory, even though there was definitely something to it. There surely was an explanation for this apparent anomaly that had to do with the sacred astronomy of the Heliopolitan priest-scientists. Starting with Imhotep himself, they,

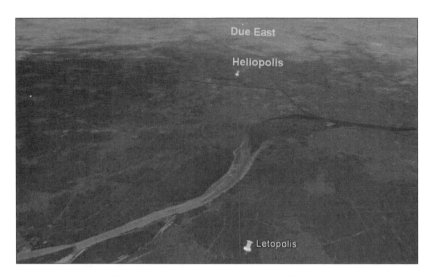

View from Letopolis due east toward Heliopolis,
azimuth 90° at equinox sunrise.

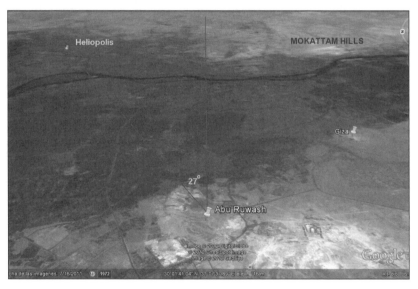

View from Abu Ruwash northeast toward Heliopolis,
azimuth 63° at Summer Solstice sunrise.

after all, were largely responsible for the design, the choice of location, and the alignments of the various pyramid complexes.

When one looks at the overall positions of the various pyramid fields, the ancient cult centers of Heliopolis and Letopolis, and the Sun Temples of Abu Gohrab, there are at least two alignments emanating from (or extending toward) Heliopolis that clearly have important solar meaning: the Letopolis–Heliopolis line at azimuth 90° implicit of the equinoxes, and the Abu Ruwash–Heliopolis line at azimuth 63° implicit of the Summer Solstice.

The Giza Mound

According to Egyptologists, the city of Letopolis, today called Aussim by the local Arabs, was known as Khem in ancient times. George Goyon says it was sacred to Horus of Khem and was the cult center of a priesthood that served the rebirth cult of the pharaohs during the Pyramid Age. It is located precisely due west of ancient Heliopolis and due north of the Giza plateau. At this precise location, it defines a latitude and longitude that are directly related to the Heliopolis sacred mound and the Great Pyramid.

It is well known that under the Great Pyramid there is an ancient mound that was originally about twelve meters high with a rough circumference of 200 meters. This mound was terraced into "steps" and the Great Pyramid was built on top of this stepped terrace/pyramid, sitting on the latter like a giant cap. On the north face of this mound is a rectangular opening, about a meter square, that forms the entrance of a descending shaft some seventy-two meters long (the Subterranean Passage). This passage leads to a large space, a sort of man-made cave, that Egyptologists call the Subterranean Chamber. This chamber does look very ancient indeed. In direct contrast to the perfect symmetry of the rest of the internal features of the Great Pyramid, however, it is extremely roughly cut. In it, there are strange features that have yet to be explained—a pit or "well" going down some ten meters below the floor, a rectangular horizontal tunnel in the east side that reaches a dead end after a few meters, and, in the western part of the chamber, a strange elevated platform reminiscent of a throne or seat.

It has long been assumed that the Subterranean Chamber was cut out by the same people who built the Great Pyramid. However, although

The "throne" in the Subterranean Chamber of the Great Pyramid at Giza.

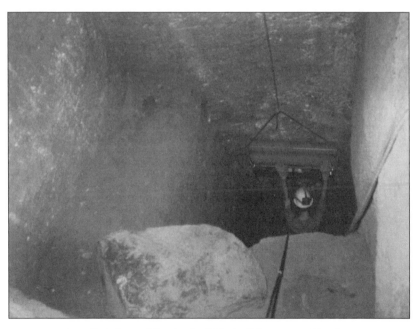

Jean Kerisel examining the "well" in the Subterranean Chamber
of the Great Pyramid at Giza.

every Egyptology textbook about the pyramids states this as fact, there is nothing that proves or, to be fair, disproves the claim.

In January 1993, we discussed this matter with Edwards in an exchange of letters, suggesting that this so-called Subterranean Chamber might be far older than the Great Pyramid itself:

Dear Dr. Edwards,

[H]as anyone thought that the Subterranean Chamber may have existed before the Cheops [Khufu] Pyramid was built? It may explain many things. It is not impossible that it was an ancient ancestral tomb. Thus found "as is" by the Egyptians of the Pyramid Age. . . . It may also explain why the rock mound was left within the core of the Great Pyramid. The consensus that the rock mound was left to "save work" is, from a construction viewpoint, not really tenable. . . . The ideal building site is a leveled site where ground bearing capacity is good enough to take the load of the proposed structure, but not so hard as to make excavation too difficult. The last site you would select is one with a rock mound on it. Normally, if such a site was unavoidable, an experienced engineer would have the mound leveled. Such groundwork is necessary not only to ensure proper load distribution in the case of, say, a pyramid edifice, but also so that you can set out the corners of the structure, before construction, to ensure proper leveling as the building goes up. It is also awkward to lay large stone blocks level and true when you work around and over a rough, uneven mound. In short, leaving the mound is more of a nuisance than to remove it. Also the risk of uncertain load distribution . . . is too much of a risk to consider, especially when one is responsible for the greatest structure ever built. . . . [An] engineer or architect today would insist on having the mound removed, or persuade the owner of the new edifice to select another site. . . . [My] conclusion . . . is that the builders of the Great Pyramid did not "abandon" the Subterranean Chamber [as Egyptologists say] but, quite the contrary, meant to *preserve* it in its original state . . . the same way we, today, would insist on leaving an old monument untouched even though it was in a poor state and badly finished [as is the Subterranean Chamber].

View of the Third Pyramid (G3) with the Mortuary Temple in the foreground.

The Sphinx Temple directly in front of the Great Sphinx.

In recent years, the same conclusion was arrived at independently by American geologist Robert Schoch:

> [A] suggestion [was] made by Robert Bauval, one I had independently been thinking about too. Perhaps the Subterranean Chamber, and the natural rock mound in which it is found—a rock mound that is now covered over by and enclosed in the Great Pyramid—is much older than the Great Pyramid itself? Was it considered sacred for thousands of years before the Great Pyramid was actually built?[54]

Schoch, who is best known for having teamed up with John A. West to investigate the age of the Sphinx in 1991–1993, is a great advocate of an older origin for Egyptian civilization. Between 2009 and 2012, he expanded his research to the site of Gobelki Tepi in Turkey, which is estimated to date to c. 8000 BC or perhaps even earlier. He has used his exceptional knowledge of geology to argue the case for an older Sphinx at Giza. It was natural, therefore, that we would team up on several occasions—on television documentaries and at conferences—to present both the geological and astronomical evidence for an older Sphinx.

Schoch is convinced that there was a previous, older phase at Giza, which we both term the "megalithic phase." This possibly includes not only the Subterranean Chamber of the Great Pyramid and the Sphinx, but also the so-called Valley Temples, Sphinx Temple, and Mortuary Temples located east of the pyramids.

But if the mound at Giza absolutely had to be retained no matter the huge construction risks and difficulties it would have caused, then clearly the reason could not have been a practical one. The risks could easily have been avoided by placing the pyramid 100 meters or so farther west. The only other motive, then, would have been *religious*. In other words, the mound and the prehistoric chamber underneath it had to be retained at all cost for a cultic reason.

So what was so important about this mound? We return to this issue in a later chapter. Suffice it here to say that its resolution further brings together the amazing story of the sacred astro-ceremonialism of these interrelated sites.

Meanwhile, let us recall that Imhotep was not only the high priest of Heliopolis, but also, and more signficantly, the personal architect of King

Djoser of the 3rd Dynasty and, as such, the designer of the celebrated Step Pyramid Complex at Saqqara. Before Imhotep, there was no construction done in Egypt using quarried and hewn stone blocks; everything built before him used mud bricks. Before Imhotep, there were no pyramids, and it would be another century before Khufu erected the Great Pyramid at Giza. So it is appropriate to ask: If the mound of Giza was so important and so sacred, then why did Imhotep not choose this site for his project? Why did he instead choose a site some eight kilometers farther south? As we shall see, Imhotep indeed had good reason to do so.

In the next chapter, we examine the mysterious complex of Saqqara in order to discover the true motive behind Imhotep's choice of location. As we do so, we will come closer to understanding who this genius really was.

Chapter Two

ARCHITECT
OF THE COSMOS

Imhotep was initiated into the mysteries revealed at Heliopolis, the oldest religious city of the country, and was raised to the position of high priest. . . . There existed at Saqqara a school of magicians under the aegis of this ancient sage who was both astronomer and astrologer. He was "Architect of the Cosmos" . . . and taught the motion of the stars and constellations.

CHRISTIAN JACQ[55]

It is significant that the high priest of the center of the sun-cult at Heliopolis bore the title "Chief of the Astronomers" and was represented wearing a mantle adorned with stars.

SIR I. E. S. EDWARDS[56]

For his discovery of the solar year and the use of astronomy to design pyramids and predict the Nile Flood, we honor Imhotep representing the Egyptian astronomer-priest as first amazing astronomer of antiquity.

THE AMAZING ASTRONOMERS OF ANTIQUITY,
HOUSTON MUSEUM OF NATURAL SCIENCE[57]

On clear days in Cairo, we often went to the rooftop of our apartment building to get a bird's-eye view of the Memphite necropolis. We had an almost unobstructed view that stretched far to the north, where we could easily see the "unfinished pyramid," Abu Ruwash, and to the distant south, the profile of the Step Pyramid at Saqqara. Between these two extremes,

Aerial View of Giza necropolis looking southeast.

we also could see the giant pyramids of Giza straight ahead, and farther to the south, the cluster of small pyramids at Abusir.

It is a remarkable feeling to see these pyramids scattered like strange yellowish icebergs in a sea of sand that disappears into the horizon. You cannot help imagining soaring high above this "land of the pyramids." Past, present, and future momentarily merge in a warp in which time has no meaning, and the notions of life and death no longer apply. There is only a sense of a static eternity or, better, of a Golden Age frozen forever, with the pyramids the stunning physical proof of its existence. And even when noisy Cairo life inevitably breaks the spell, one powerful image lingers: the hazy, almost ghostlike sight of the great Step Pyramid Complex in the far distance.

It was here that it all started, and it is here that we must begin our search for Imhotep.

Notions of the Cosmos

According to Egyptologists, the site for the Step Pyramid Complex was chosen because it afforded a clear view across the Nile toward the nearby city of Memphis, the first capital of pharaonic Egypt. As Edwards tells us:

The site which Imhotep selected was a stretch of high ground at Saqqara overlooking the city of Memphis. It covered an area measuring approximately 597 yards from north to south and 304 yards from east to west. A short distance to the north lay the large cemetery of 1st and 2nd Dynasty mastabas.[58]

His view is shared by other Egyptologists. Mark Lehner even permitted himself a little unbridled license when he speculated about the Step Pyramid Complex:

> [This] city of the dead in stone and sand is the otherworldly counterpart of the living city of Memphis. . . . [The city of] Memphis migrated southward to stay ahead of the sands drifting in from the desert as the climate became increasingly drier throughout the Old Kingdom, and to follow the Nile as it retreated eastward. As the city moved, so did the necropolis up in the high desert.[59]

The idea that Imhotep chose the site of Saqqara because it had a clear view toward Memphis seems, a priori, reasonable. Yet the nagging question remains: If the center of religious and cultic activities was Heliopolis, then why did Imhotep not choose to be nearer to it—perhaps at the much more imposing promontory of Giza? Was there something special about Saqqara—something so vitally important that Imhotep, or the king he served, just had to select that site? Since Imhotep, as Chief Astronomer, was responsible for studying the motion of the stars, could not the choice have been dictated by astronomical factors? French Egyptologist and author Christian Jacq, always so perceptive about such matters, hinted at something like that:

> [The Step Pyramid complex of] Saqqara was the "book in stone" of Imhotep, destined to translate in a physical manner the thoughts of the god-king [the pharaoh], Djoser. "The sky lives at this site," affirms a text.[60]

In a similar vein, German Egyptologist Dietrich Wildung, director of the Berlin Museum, aptly refers to Imhotep as the Architect of the Cosmos,[61] and American Egyptologist Florence Dunn Friedman, former curator of Ancient Art at the Rhode Island School of Design, saw Imhotep's Step Pyramid Complex as having "notions of cosmos" that reflected an idea of the "sky above, the sky below."[62] However, it was astronomers at the Houston Museum of Natural Science who were more specific about this issue:

> Imhotep designed the Step Pyramid [Complex] to allow the deceased to mingle with the circumpolar stars that arc across the northern sky each night—to link heaven and earth. . . . As scientist and priest, Imhotep would have predicted and monitored the flooding of the Nile. . . . Along its banks, ancient astronomers observed the turning star-field from dusk to dawn. They were looking for signs to predict the yearly Nile flood. Night after night, they studied the constellation of the Egyptian god Osiris, called Orion . . . they followed its three stars in a row [Orion's belt] downward toward the eastern horizon, lit by the glow of dawn. Orion would be a bit higher before dawn, allowing astronomer-priests to see more stars below it in the predawn sky. Finally one morning, they saw the bright star Sirius for the first time. They realized that Sirius would be visible for the first time on the same day each year, just after the Summer Solstice. This day marked the New Year in the world's first solar calendar. The first sighting of Sirius also promised that the nourishing Nile flood would soon begin.[63]

Thus, the "architect's brief" for the Step Pyramid Complex surely involved concerns with the astral rebirth rituals for the king. Such high rituals had to be performed in the correct setting to ensure the safe passage of the soul of the king into the starry heaven to be reunited with his divine ancestors.

So what was Imhotep's architect's brief? And who was this king for whom he would create such a magnificent ritualistic setting at Saqqara?

Memphis—The White Wall

Before we answer these questions, let us try to imagine the region of Memphis and Saqqara before Imhotep laid the first stone for his famous project. Egyptologists have deduced from Early Dynastic palettes, seals, and fragments of pottery that some time around 3100 BC, a chieftain or king called Narmer or Menes came from the south and united his own southern kingdom with the north, thus creating the double kingdom of

Upper (southern) and Lower (northern) Egypt. Then, in an area east of Saqqara, he founded Egypt's first national capital called Ineb Hedj, the White Wall—which much later, in classical times, was called Memphis by the Greeks. Today, the ancient city of Memphis has virtually disappeared, partly due to its having been used as a quarry by medieval Arabs, and partly because much of the ruins that remained were covered up under layers of silt deposited by thousands of years of Nile floods.

The Nile today flows west of Memphis, but Egyptologists think that the course of the river may have been different in ancient times. Indeed, it is possible that, during the early part of the Egyptian civilization, it flowed immediately west of Memphis. According to Egyptologists, there may have been an "archaic Memphis" located in the existing Abusir wadi, today a dry riverbed immediately below the escarpment where the archaic *mastabas* stand. So far, however, no archaeological evidence has confirmed this.[64] Originally, Memphis was a fortified settlement perhaps built of mud bricks and with habitations made of straw or palm branches.[65] Four centuries after Narmer founded Memphis, however—when Imhotep began his project at Saqqara—it must have been an imposing urbanized region.

Of course, another important city in the region—perhaps *the* most important and one that existed *before* Imnhotep—was Heliopolis. A third was Akhem, the Letopolis of the Greeks (today called Aussim). Letopolis, as we have seen, is located due west of Heliopolis and due north of the Giza complex. In geographer's jargon, Letopolis is on the same latitude as Heliopolis and the same longitude as the Giza complex, suggesting a deliberate connection between the three locations that would have required precise astronomical sightings to establish.

Letopolis was the home of the priesthood responsible for the Opening of the Mouth ceremony that was performed on the king's mummy. It was also the home of the four sons of Horus who, in the Pyramid Texts, are said to assist the dead king's ascent to the stars. The Opening of the Mouth ritual may have once entailed the actual forcing open of the mouth of the deceased king in order to give him the "breath of life," but it was also probably performed symbolically on the mummy. A set of sharp instruments were used, the principal one being a sort of carpenter's adze called *nw3*. All these tools were said to be made of a material called *bja,* probably meteoritic iron—i.e., iron that "fell from the sky" or material from a falling star.[66] American Egyptologist Ann Macy Roth undertook an extensive study of these ritualistic instruments, also collectively known as *ntrwj*, and arrived at these startling conclusions:

> [A]ll the tools used in the "opening of the mouth" ritual are associated with iron, meteoritic material, or stars. Iron bladds chisels found in the tomb of Tutankhamun resemble closely chisels shown in representations of "opening of the mouth" tools. The adze itself theoretically had a blade of meteoritic iron and was originally and most frequently called *dw3-wr*, a name that is written with a star and is clearly related to the *dw3t*, the place where stars are. The constellation we see as a Great Bear or Big Dipper was called *mskhjw (mesekhtiu)* by the Egyptians, and was compared to both the adze and the *hps*, the foreleg of an ox. Both the foreleg and the adze were added to the offering ritual at the same time in the Pyramid Texts of Merenere, and their association there was probably due to their common association with this constellation. The stellar element was presumably connected principally to the realm of the dead, which in some conceptions of the afterlife was clearly located in the region of the circumpolar stars. The orientation of the stellar adze/foreleg toward the circumpolar stars is similar to the orientation of the mouth-opening implements toward the mummy/statue in depiction of the ritual. Even before the adze and foreleg were introduced into the offering ritual of the Pyramid Texts, its text was placed on the north wall of the burial chamber of Unas, hinting at the same relationship with the northern circumpolar stars.[67]

As if this connection were not intriguing enough, Roth pointed out that Letopolis, where the Opening of the Mouth priesthood resided and where the ritualistic sacred instruments were kept, was the capital of the second nome (a sort of archaic governorate) of Lower Egypt whose emblem, as mentioned earlier, was a bull's thigh (or foreleg) and which, according to George Goyon, "means the constellation of Ursa Major"—i.e., the Big Dipper.[68]

The high priest of Letopolis assumed the role of Horus of Letopolis, and it is presumably he who personally conducted the Opening of the

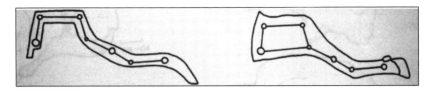

The Big Dipper seen as the Opening of the Mouth adze (left) and the foreleg of an ox (right). Drawing by A. M. Roth.

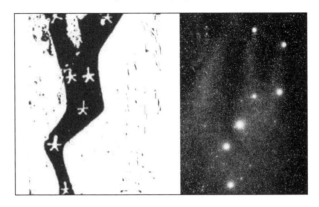

The Big Dipper seen as Mesekhtiu—a bull's thigh or foreleg (left); the Big Dipper constellation as it appears in the sky (right).

Mouth ritual with the sacred adze on the king's mummy, perhaps even inside the pyramid itself. As Roth further explained:

> The connection of Letopolis with *bja* [meteoritic iron] and the "opening of the mouth" ritual is further reinforced by several circumstances: the high priest of Letopolis was called *wn-r*, "the opening of the mouth"; the standard of the Letopolite nome is the foreleg of a bull, which is used in the ritual and is associated with the mouth-opening adze through the constellation *mskhtjw (mesekhtiu)*.[69]

Letopolis is due north of the Giza complex and due west of Heliopolis; moreover, it is equidistant from Giza and Heliopolis, so that the three locations form a huge right triangle with sides of about seventeen kilometers and a hypotenuse of about twenty-four kilometers. This "sacred triangle," as we noted earlier, contained three very sacred mounds at its angles and the whole had formed a vast religious landscape since Early

Dynastic times. George Goyon also postulated that there was once a high observation tower at Letopolis, from which stellar observations were made in ancient times.[70]

So, bearing in mind all these interconnections and tantalizing clues, we may now ask what it was that drove Imhotep to choose the site of Saqqara.

The answer to this question can be encapsulated in two simple words: "stones" and "stars."

Let's start with the stones.

The Mokattam Quarries

The Mokattam Hills are located just south of modern Cairo and some fifteen kilometers southeast of the Giza plateau. Here we find some of the limestone quarries that have been used since ancient times. A little farther south along that range, almost opposite Abusir, are the famous Tura and Ma'sara quarries, the source of the very fine-grained limestone that was used extensively for casing pyramids. It was first used in that way by Imhotep for much of the architectural revetment and decorative work at the Step Pyramid Complex. This type of fine limestone can still be seen today on the eastern base of the Great Pyramid.

Looking down into a quarry pit in the Mokattam Hills, south of modern Cairo.

The Tura quarry is mentioned in texts as early as the 4th Dynasty (c. 2500 BC), and its high-quality limestone was employed extensively at Saqqara in the 3rd Dynasty by Imhotep. The earliest inscriptions that survive on the quarry walls, however, date from the 12th and 13th Dynasties (c. 1800 BC).[71] Egyptologists Somers Clarke and Reginald Englebach, two specialists in the study of ancient Egyptian stone constructions, give us a vivid image of these very ancient quarries of the pharaohs:

> Few things are more impressive than the large covered quarries. At Tura and Ma'sara, for example, they appear from the river as almost rectangular openings—some like great doorways, others wider than they are high. The entrances appear as dense black spots against the intense brightness of the sunlit cliffs.[72]

Today, coming from Cairo airport on the busy Saleh Salem Street, you get a dramatic view of the Mokattam Hills and some of the open quarries on the northern edge of the range as you drive past the Mohammad Ali Citadel Mosque.

Looking left—i.e., toward the south—the huge man-made horizontal and vertical gashes into the limestone hills are clearly visible, some from modern quarrying and others dating from the time of the pharaohs. In 2007, we decided to visit these parts of the quarries with our friend Sandro Mainardi, an Italian photographer from Florence. Our first impression was that giants had been at work here, as we felt ourselves totally dwarfed by the sheer size of the quarries. Scrambling up a rugged path, we reached a high point from where we had a bird's-eye view. All around us were huge rectangular pits, on the walls of which could be seen the markings of cutting tools. According to Clarke and Englebach, one could easily get lost in quarries at Tura:

> On approaching one of the openings, one begins to see that within there are massive pillars, more or less square in plan, but very irregularly placed. They support the overlying strata, in which the rock is not of sufficiently good quality for building. The opening, which appears of insignificant size from a distance, is often in reality more than twenty feet high, and the gallery sometimes goes hundreds of yards into the mountain, pillar following pillar until they are lost in pitch blackness.[73]

It is only when you visit these ancient quarries that you become fully aware of how incredibly difficult it must have been for ancient people to quarry out massive stones—some of the pieces weighing more than ten tons—then somehow drag them to the banks of the Nile, take them across the river, tow them up the promontories, and raise them into perfect position on the growing pyramid. The magnitude of the enterprise is truly amazing. Our visit to the ancient quarries also drove home how important they were to the ancient builders and, especially, to Imhotep, who "invented" the construction techniques using hewn stone.

We can imagine how this genius may have come to these quarries, touched the fine white limestone with his hands, feeling its texture, and then, in a flash of inspiration, visualized the stone in beautiful geometric shapes that mimicked those in nature and rendered them eternal—papyrus plants, palm trunks, and bundles of reeds. Was this when architecture as we know it was born? Perhaps. But certainly there was some creative spark that started a frenzy of construction in stone that lasted three thousand years.

If you draw a straight line between Heliopolis and the Step Pyramid Complex, it passes through the northern edge of the Mokattam Hills. The azimuth bearing of this imaginary line is 16.5°, a value that is, remarkably, the same as the slope of the steps of the Step Pyramid, which have an inclination of 16.5 °. Our experience in investigating the sacred

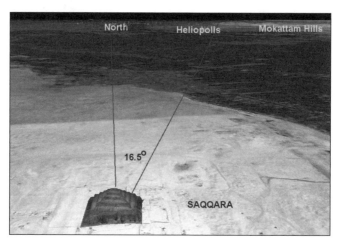

Azimuth of Heliopolis (16.5°), looking northeast from
the Step Pyramid Complex at Saqqara.

astronomy of the monuments of ancient Egypt convinces us that such parallels are rarely coincidental. But what can this orientation toward Heliopolis mean?

We will return to this intriguing line of investigation when we examine the sacred astronomy of the Step Pyramid Complex. But we first need to consider the explorers and archaeologists who visited or worked at the Step Pyramid Complex and see whether their findings can provide more clues to the identity and origins of Imhotep.

Prussian Barons and Eccentric Englishmen

Heineich von Minutoli (1772–1846), a high-ranking Prussian military man turned amateur archaeologist, was probably the first modern explorer to investigate the Step Pyramid Complex. Minutoli taught himself languages—including Greek, Latin, Italian, and English—and eventually became the private tutor of young Prince Carl, son of King Friedrich Wilhelm III of Prussia. In 1821, under the aegis of the king, Minutoli, by that time a baron, headed an expedition to Egypt, taking along a small group of eminent German scientists and scholars. They were probably the first Europeans to enter the subterranean system of the Step Pyramid Complex. To their immense delight, they discovered the beautiful blue faience-tiled walls of the pharaoh's apartments, today displayed in the newly opened Imhotep Museum at Saqqara. Minutoli's own private collection of Egyptian antiquities was sold for a small fortune to the King of Prussia, and was the basis for the Egyptian Museum in Berlin.

Shortly after Minutoli came British Egyptologist James Burton, who had been invited to Egypt in 1822 by its ruler, Mohammad Ali Pasha, to join the recently formed Geological Survey. In 1824, Burton began private explorations at several ancient sites, including Abu Simbel, Medinet Habu, Karnak, and some tombs in the Valley of the Kings. He also entered the subterranean system of the Step Pyramid Complex. The eccentric aristocrat left Egypt in 1835, taking with him a substantial collection of Egyptian antiquities that he ultimately had to auction off at Sotheby's to pay his private debts.

Next came John S. Perring, a British engineer employed by a retired British colonel, Sir Richard William Howard Vyse. Together, they traveled to Egypt to conduct explorations at the Giza pyramids. In those days,

Mohammad Ali Pasha was completely disinterested in the ancient legacy of his country and had no qualms about letting the blocks of ancient temples be used to build dams and factories, or even having the old stones pulverized to extract saltpeter in order to make gunpowder. Mohammad Ali was thus more than happy to grant Vyse a *firman* (permit) to do more or less as he pleased at Giza—presumably including permission to use gunpowder to blast into the pyramids in search of secret chambers and treasure. It was Vyse who, along with his team of engineers, discovered the four so-called "relieving" chambers in the Great Pyramid.

Vyse quite literally attacked the Third Pyramid (of Menkaure) with charges of gunpowder in order to clear the blocked entrance and internal passageways. Inside the burial chamber, he found the beautiful, but empty, granite sarcophagus of the king. He also found the broken lid of a wooden coffin and fragments of human bones, now at the British Museum. The coffin lid, which bore the name of Menkaure, was at first thought to belong to the builder of the pyramid. Recent carbon 14 tests by the British Museum, however, date it to the Saite period c. 500 BC, and the bones to the 1st century AD. As was quite common in those heydays of archaeology, Vyse claimed the precious artifacts as his own, promptly offering the sarcophagus to the British Museum for a large sum of money. He had it packed in a large wooden crate and placed aboard a small "snow" schooner bound for England out of the port of Alexandria. On its journey home, the top-heavy ship hit a violent storm, capsized, and sank with all its crew, taking down with it the sarcophagus along with two hundred other boxes also thought to contain ancient artifacts. This precious cargo still lies at the bottom of the Mediterranean Sea.[74]

Vyse left Egypt in late August 1838, leaving behind Perring to carry on with the exploration, but now at Saqqara. It must be said that John Perring was a professional and very meticulous engineer, and the excellent and very precise account of his exploration at Saqqara, which is reported in volume 3 of Howard Vyse's voluminous *Operations Carried on at the Pyramids of Gizeh in 1837*, is a delight to read.

Perring proceeded to Saqqara July 24, 1839, and, notwithstanding the great heat, began his operation, reporting:

> [T]he pyramids of Saccara are eleven in number . . . they are much decayed, excepting the large one built in degrees [the Step

Pyramid], which, together with another toward the northeast (No. 2 in the map) are the only two at present open.

Perring first attacked the smaller of the two (his "No. 2 in the map"), a 5th-Dynasty pyramid (of Userkaf) that the Arabs called Al Haram el Mekurbash ("the broken pyramid"), which had previously been opened in 1831–1832 by a certain Signor Maruchi. Since then, however, its entrance had been blocked by falling masonry. After this initial exploration, Perring gave his full attention to the Step Pyramid, which he called the Great Pyramid of Saccara (his No. 3 on the map), and which the Arabs called Al Haram el Modargheh, meaning "The Step Pyramid."

Perring carefully measured the pyramid's base and height, as well as its orientation to north and the inclination of its steps. He remarked that this monument "is the only pyramid in Egypt, the sides of which do not exactly face the cardinal points, the northern front being 4° 35' east of true north"—a deliberate "error" by Imhotep that we will examine in chapter 3.[76] Perring also noted that "the face of each story or degree has an angle of 73° 30' with the horizon."[77] A quick calculation shows that 73° 30' with the horizon gives an inclination of 16° 30'—which is, significantly, the same angle of azimuth that the monument has with Heliopolis. We are confident that this similarity is not a coincidence, and

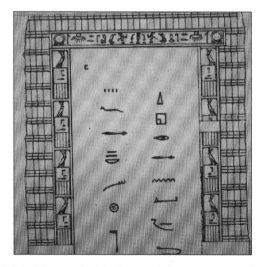

A 1839 drawing by John Perring of the inscriptions on the decorated door frames inside the Step Pyramid at Saqqara.

in chapter 3 we will show how and why these seemingly random angles are part of an elaborate and deliberate plan by Imhotep to incorporate sacred astronomy into his design.

Perring also managed to investigate part of the elaborate subterranean system of the pyramid, and made accurate sketches of the beautifully decorated stone door frames of the small rooms beyond the so-called large apartments.

> The doorway in one of them [a small room] is bordered with hieroglyphics in relief, and in another has a similar inscription traced in black. The characters had been much defaced since M. Burton copied them: they contain the title, but not the name, of a very early king . . . the headings of these doorways are covered with small stars, sculpted in relief.[78]

Copies of these inscriptions were sent by Perring to the eminent British philologist Samuel Birch. The doorway with the inscriptions was taken to the Berlin Museum in 1843 by German Egyptologist Richard Lepsius. The quest for the identity of the mysterious and elusive owner of Imhotep's fabulous architectural masterpiece was about to begin.

Netjerykhet and Djoser

When Samuel Birch examined the inscriptions sent to him by Perring, he was surprised to find that, although there were several rounded cartouches (enclosures) that usually contain the name of the king, these were left empty, implying perhaps a deliberate attempt by the ancient sculptors or scribes to keep the given name of the king a mystery. What the ancient scribes clearly wanted to highlight, however, was the so-called "Horus name" of this mysterious king—Netjerykhet, which is commonly translated as "Divine of Body."

The Horus name is the first of a series of titles (usually five) given to the king. It was commonly placed inside a rectangular space called a *serekh,* which, apparently, represents the façade of a palace with the crowned falcon (Horus) perched on top. Clearly this king, whoever he was, had a preference to be known by his Horus name. Or, to see it perhaps in the correct way, the king was regarded unequivocally as the physical reincarnation of the god Horus. Wilkinson sees Netjerykhet as meaning "(most) Divine of the Corporation"—the corporation being the pantheon of gods. It is usually understood, however, as "Divine of Body," indicating that the corporal king, as the reincarnation of Horus, is divine. The inscription itself was written with three hieroglyphs surmounted by a crowned falcon—i.e., Horus.

Horus, the Divine Falcon, was the quintessential sky god of Egypt, and perhaps the most ancient deity of this civilization. Although generally said to be the posthumous son of Osiris and Isis, this can apply, strictly speaking, only from the 5th Dynasty onward—that is, from 2300 BC, some three centuries after Imhotep. No mention of Osiris prior to the 5th Dynasty has yet been found, forcing Egyptologists into a sort of scholarly quandary. Common sense requires them to assume that the cult of Osiris existed before the 5th Dynasty, but the textual or archaeological evidence to support that assumption has, so far, not been discovered. The first mention of Osiris (Ausar in ancient Egyptian) is from the Pyramid Texts, the earliest

Serekh containing the Horus name Netjerykhet.

version of which was found in the 5th-Dynasty pyramid of King Unas at Saqqara that was built just behind the Step Pyramid Complex. Some Egyptologists have suggested, however, that prior to the 5th Dynasty, Osiris was referred to by his well-known epithet Foremost of the Westerners (*khenti-amenti*), which is found in inscriptions dating as far back as the 1st Dynasty. This is not universally accepted, however, since two other deities, Anubis and Wepwawet, were given this epiphet as well.[79]

So who was Horus before he became the son of Osiris?

In hieroglyphic language, the name Horus, as expected, is shown as a falcon and transliterated as *hr.w* or *heru*. Thus this word is generally assumed to mean "falcon," but other meanings may be "the distant one" or "one who is above." All these meanings are implicit of a sky god or, as we believe, a constellation or a special star.

As we know, as of the 5th Dynasty, Horus is said to be the son of Osiris, born from the womb of the goddess Isis. It is generally agreed that Osiris and Isis were, in their celestial form, constellations in the night sky—Osiris being Orion (Sah) and Isis being Canis Major (Spdt). Although Egyptologists still identify Isis/Spdt with the star Sirius, French Egyptologist Nathalie Beaux has convincingly shown that, at least in the Pyramid Age and before, Spdt was the constellation Canis Major, which contains the star Sirius. Beaux's argument is based on the fact that, in the Pyramid Texts, there is a feminine form, without the suffix "t," that is written simply as Spd. Beaux examined a vital passage of the Pyramid Texts translated by the British philologist R. O. Faulkner:

> O Osiris the king, arise, lift yourself up . . . Your sister Isis comes to you rejoicing for love of you. You have placed her on your phallus and your seed issues into her, she being ready as Spdt, and *Horus-Spd* has come forth from you as "Horus who is in Spdt."[80]

Although Faulkner did recognize that Horus-Spd represents a star, he could not explain why this male star, Spd, was said to "come forth" from another female star that had the same name—Spd-t. Clearly, the translation makes no sense unless we consider that Spdt is the constellation (womb?) that *contains* the star Spd.

In Beaux's own words:

> It is evident that there originally existed a masculine form, *Spd*, and also a feminine form, *Spd-t*, and it would be logical that they refer to two different stellar entities. Dr. V. L. Davis [a well-known Egyptologist specialised in ancient Egyptian astronomy] has proposed that the second form (i.e. *Spd-t*) is the name of the constellation to which belongs Sirius, in view that most constellations carry feminine names. This proposal has the advantage to make comprehensible texts which, without this distinction, do not make sense as in line 458a (Unas) "*Spd is alive, because Unas is alive, the son of Spd-t,*" where it is clearly demonstrated that the filial relationship Spd/Spd-t represents the belonging of the star to the constellation.[81]

Beaux also correctly points out the following:

> . . . in the decans table, we can see an evolution, with the name of Spd alternating with that of Spd-t and finally disappear to the

advantage of the latter, often accompanied by the name of Isis as from the 18th Dynasty. These changes reflect the increased importance, from the mythical viewpoint, of the mother-constellation (Canis Major) identified to Isis in the Pyramid Texts (lines 632a-d; 1635b; 1636 a-b), and explains the redefinition of the star in relation to the constellation under the *nisbe* form Spd-ty 'He of Spd-t,' and the previous unique use of the feminine of Spd-t, for the constellation as well as, by metonymy, for the star. The *nisbe* (adjective) form of Spd-t, Spd-t(y), is attested as from the texts of Teti in the name Hr-Spd-t(y) (line 331a), confirmed reading, as was shown by R. Anthes ('*Horus als Sirius in den Pyramidtexten*' in ZAS 102, 1975, p.1 sq.) with the graphic Hr-Spd-ty cf. Pyr. Line 330a (Pepi II)."[82]

According to Beaux, the passage given above from the Pyramid Texts translated by Faulkner should read:

> O Osiris the king, arise, lift yourself up . . . Your sister [wife] Isis comes to you rejoicing for love of you. You have placed her on your phallus and your seed issues into her, she being ready as Spd-t [Canis Major], and Horus-*Spd* [Sirius] has come forth from you as "Horus who is in Spd-t" [Sirius which is in Canis Major].

The passage clearly now makes perfect sense, and is also a correct metaphor for what the ancient priests of Heliopolis actually saw in the sky—the constellations Orion and Canis Major (i.e., Osiris and Isis) appearing in the east in the dawn sky at the time of the Summer Solstice, followed by the heliacal (first annual) rising of Sirius (i.e., the birth of Horus). The following passage from the Pyramid Texts supports this interpretation:

> Orion is enveloped by the dawn-light, while the "Living One" [the king] washes himself in the Horizon. Canis Major (Spd-t) is enveloped by the dawn-light, while the "Living One" washes himself in the Horizon. This king Unas is enveloped by the dawn-light, while the "Living One" washes himself in the Horizon. (pyr. 151)

> Let the sky brighten, let Sirius (Spd) live, for this king Unas is the "Living One," the son of Canis Major (Spd-t). (pyr. 458)

The "Living One" is obviously the Horus king (the pharaoh Unas, in this case) who is reborn as the star Sirius—i.e., Spd, which is within Canis Major; i.e., Spd-t. The original hieroglyphs read: *nh spd n wnjs js nh s3 spd.t* (Spd is alive because Unas is the Living One, the son of Spd-t).

Returning to the Horus name of the owner of the Step Pyramid Complex—Netjerykhet, meaning Divine of Body—we must assume a stellar association with the star Spd—i.e., Sirius. This stellar identification is made the more obvious by the name given to the Step Pyramid itself—"Horus Is the Star at the Head of the Sky"—as confirmed by the recent work of British Egyptologist Stephen Quirke in a list he has drawn of the original names of pyramids.

> The following list of Old Kingdom Pyramid names follows the interpretation of Wolfgang Helck: even if in some instances the name denotes a different part of the pyramid complex, it remains important to examine the general tendency in associations.
>
> 3rd Dynasty:
>
> Netjerykhet, Step Pyramid, Saqqara, "Horus is the star at the head of the sky"
>
> In this list, the Step Pyramid . . . [is] *explicitly* stellar . . .

From various inscriptions related to the so-called domains and estates of 1st- and 2nd-Dynasty kings, it is obvious that Horus was not, as many Egyptologists insist even now, a solar god in early times, but rather a stellar god, likely representing the bright star Sirius. In the reign of the 1st-Dynasty King Aha, for example, there was a festival called the Festival of the Horus Star of the Gods.[85] Another 1st-Dynasty monarch, Anedjib, called his domain Horus, Star of the Corporation (of the Gods); Khasekhemy, father of Netjerykhet, also called his domain Horus Risen as a Star.[86] The evidence is overwhelming that, originally, Horus was equated with a star that, as Natalie Beaux has argued, was the bright star Sirius. German Egyptologist Rudolf Anthes arrived at the same conclusion.[87]

It thus seems very likely that the owner of the Step Pyramid Complex wanted his afterlife abode to be connected somehow with the star Sirius via the rituals associated with its "rebirth"—i.e., its heliacal rising. The complex had to be a sort of "resurrection machine" intended to metamorphose the physical Horus king into a star—a very special star. This very idea is seriously entertained by at least two eminent Egyptologists, Wolfgang Helck and Michel Baud:

> [T]he title of the local high priest was "priest of the Lord of Heliopolis" (*hem-netjer neb Iounou*)—a designation of Atum. He [the high priest] is also given the title "Chief of the Observers" (*our manou*), meaning the superior of a college of priests to whom was given the important task of scrutinizing the sky, carefully observing the motion of the stars and planets, and ensuring the proper functioning of the Universe. This distinction, which could have been a title for non-royalty, was held by Imhotep, the architect of the [Step Pyramid] complex, as well as other chief architects after him. According to Wolfgang Helck, it is therefore probable that there is a very close connection between the art of building and this priesthood; indeed the foundation of sacred buildings involved precise operation of stellar alignments which could have been made by the "observers" of Heliopolis.[88]

Hence, we conclude that there is more than just a symbolic connection between the Step Pyramid Complex and the holy city of Heliopolis—a connection that has to do with the various cycles of Sirius and the alignments and location of the complex itself. But before we unpack this idea, we need to consider who the pharaoh was who commissioned this grandiose project. A clue to this king's identity is found in the serekh, the Horus name, of his two immediate predecessors.

The typical serekh is surmounted by a falcon, sometimes shown wearing the double crown of Upper and Lower Egypt. All the kings of Egypt, from earliest times to the end of Dynastic times, have the falcon (Horus) symbol perched over their serekhs, except for the last two kings of the 2nd Dynasty, who reigned immediately before Netjerykhet. One of these kings, Peribsen, had the Seth symbol (a doglike creature with long flat ears and a protruding snout) on his serekh. No other king before or after him had Seth on his serekh. In choosing Seth, he was putting himself in total opposition to those who followed Horus, for Seth was the traditional

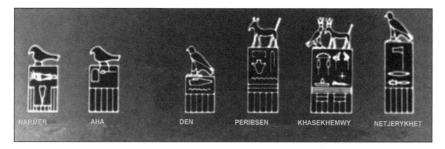

Serekhs of Early Dynastic kings from Narmer to Netjerykhet. Note the Seth symbol on Peribsen's serekh and the combined Seth and Horus symbols on Khasekhemwy's serekh.

mortal enemy of the falcon-headed god. Peribsen was then followed by Khasekhemwy (probably the father of Netjerykhet) who kept the Seth/dog symbol, but also added the Horus symbol next to it. This was also unique, because no other king before or after used this combined symbolism on his serekh.

Khasekhemwy's successor (perhaps son), Netjerykhet, dropped the Seth symbol and again took up the single Horus/falcon symbol. All kings who followed Netjerykhet then used the Horus symbol in an unbroken chain that lasted more than 3,000 years.

So what could have driven Peribsen to deviate so dramatically from the tradition of kingship by adopting the Seth symbol; and, even more intriguing, why did his successor, Khasekhemwy, combine both the Horus and Seth symbols on his serekh? The explanation of this mystery may be found in the so-called Memphite Theology, a text carved on a black slab known as the shabaka stone.

The shabaka stone, found near Memphis
and now in the British Museum.

IMHOTEP: THE AFRICAN

The Battle between Horus and Seth

The shabaka stone was found in 1800 at a farm near Memphis by a soldier of Napoleon's army. When the French surrendered to the British in Egypt in 1801, the latter claimed the stone as a spoil of war and took it to England. It was given to the Earl of Spencer, who donated it in 1805 to the British Museum, where it is still displayed in the main Egyptian gallery.

The shabaka stone measures 92 x 137 centimeters and has sixty-four lines of hieroglyphic text carved on it. Many of the original inscriptions have been worn away—apparently it was used as a millstone by Arab farmers!—but enough remains to provide Egyptologists with a narrative of how the ancient Egyptians viewed the divine origins of their kings.

The stone itself dates from about 710 BC from the reign of King Shabaka; however, Egyptologists believe that the inscriptions were copied from a much older source, which is confirmed by the ancient scribe who carved the text on the stone:

> This writing was copied out anew by his majesty (King Shabaka) in the house of his father Ptah-South-of-his-Wall (Memphis), for his majesty found it to be a work of the ancestors which was worm-eaten so that it could be understood from beginning to end. His majesty copied it anew so that it became better than it had been before.[89]

American Egyptologist Miriam Lichtheim, an expert on ancient Egyptian texts, regarded the text as "a work of the Old Kingdom," but admits "its precise date is not known. The language is archaic and resembles that of the Pyramid Texts."[90] Likewise, Henry Frankfort, an authority on pharaonic kingship, asserted that certain doctrines in the Memphite Theology came from "traditions of the greatest antiquity."[91]

The first part of the inscription recounts how the creation of Egypt had taken place when the primeval waters receded and the Mound of Creation first appeared at Heliopolis. It then tells of an epic conflict between Horus and Seth over who was the legitimate ruler of Egypt. The conflict is temporarily resolved by the earth god Geb on behalf of the Great Ennead, or Nine Gods:

> Geb, Lord of the Gods, commanded that the Nine Gods gather to him. He judged between Horus and Seth; he ended their

quarrel. He made Seth king of Upper Egypt . . . up to the place where he was born which is Su [a place near Herakleopolis]. And Geb made Horus king of Lower Egypt . . . up to the place in which his father [Osiris] was drowned which is "Division of the Two Lands." Thus Horus stood over one region and Seth stood over one region. They made peace over the Two Lands at Ayan [near Memphis]. That was the division of the Two Lands. Geb's word to Seth: "Go to the place in which you were born." Seth: "Upper Egypt." Geb's words to Horus: "Go to the place in which your father was drowned." Horus: "Lower Egypt." Geb's words to Horus and Seth: "I have separated you" into Lower and Upper Egypt.

But then Geb has a change of heart:

Then it seemed wrong to Geb that the portion of Horus was like the portion of Seth. So Geb gave to Horus Seth's inheritance, for he is the son of his firstborn [Osiris]. Geb to the Nine gods: "I have appointed Horus, the firstborn." Geb's words to the Nine Gods: "Him alone, Horus, the inheritance." Geb's words to the Nine Gods: "To this heir, my inheritance." Geb's words to the Nine Gods: "To the son of my son, Horus . . . " Then Horus stood over the land. He is the uniter of this land, proclaimed in the great name: Ta-tenen, South of his Wall, Lord of Eternity. Then sprouted the two great magicians [crowns] upon his head. He is Horus, who arose as king of Upper and Lower Egypt, who united the Two Lands in the nome of the Wall [Memphis], the place in which the Two Lands were united. Reed and Papyrus were placed on the double door of the House of Ptah [a creator god]. This means Horus and Seth, pacified and United. They fraternised so as to cease quarreling in whatever place they might be, being united in the House of Ptah, the "Balance of the Two Lands" in which Upper and Lower Egypt had been weighed.[92]

From the above inscription, we can deduce that, at some point, ancient Egyptians regarded the land of Egypt as shared between Horus and Seth. Then, for reasons that are not so clear, Horus was given total control of the whole of Egypt. Could it be that the Memphite Theology reflects historical events that occurred in the late 2nd and early 3rd Dynasties? Could the Memphite Theology explain the placing of Seth on the serekh of King Peribsen, and then the placing of both Seth and Horus on the serekh of King Khasekhemwy, only to revert back to just Horus on Netjerykhet's serekh? This idea has indeed occurred to some Egyptologists.[93]

The god Seth's peculiar animal head requires special consideration. Belgian Pierre de Maret has recently argued that this bizarre doglike head, far from representing a dog or a mythological creature as many Egyptologists believe, in fact depicts an African animal called the *orycteropus,* commonly known as an aardvark—a sort of large anteater that today is native to sub-Saharan Africa where there are savannahs and grasslands.

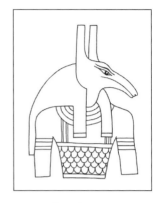

Line drawing of the head of Seth.

According to de Maret:

> Although many attempts have been made to identify the Seth-animal, it is usually regarded as an imaginary creature. However, there are striking similarities between the shape of its ears, forehead and snout with those of the aardvark. In many parts of sub-Saharan Africa this animal plays an important symbolic role, as the appearance and the behavior of this very peculiar mammal make good "food for thought." It is often associated, like Seth, with the night, the underworld and the dead. Furthermore, such an identification may also explain most of Seth's characteristics, such as why it is linked to the origin of kingship, disorder, confusion, sexuality, strength, drunkenness, voracity, etc.[94]

To be fair, the features of the aardvark that de Maret attributes to Seth mainly involve the head and face, whereas the body, at least the one seen on the serekhs, is canine—probably a type of wild desert dog. We should bear in mind, however, that the usual depiction of Seth is as a man with the alleged aardvark head, so de Maret's thesis is likely correct.

Thus, these questions arise: First, why would Netjerykhet's immediate predecessors, King Peribsen and King Khasekhemwy, select a Central

African creature for their symbol of kingship? And second, could the aardvark have existed in Egypt in the Early Dynastic period (c. 3000 to 2650 BC)? Aardvarks do not now live in Egypt.

Drawing of a prehistoric aardvark found near Arkenu in rock art discovered by Mark Borda.

De Maret did point out that the aardvark must have existed in the Sahara when the climate was much more humid, because prehistoric rock art depicting this creature has been found in the desert of Libya. Hardly five years after de Maret published his thesis, in November 2010, Mark Borda discovered prehistoric rock art depicting an aardvark near the mysterious Arkenu Mountain located near the modern Egyptian-Libyan border. Was the adoption of the Seth animal by the immediate predecessors of Nejerykhet indicative of some sub-Saharan African connection?

In many ancient Egyptian texts, including the Pyramid Texts, Seth is often identified with the constellation of the Big Dipper, Mesekhtiu, the Bull's Thigh. According to British Egyptologist E. A. Wallis Budge:

> The Kingdom of Seth was supposed to be placed in the northern sky, and his abode was one of the stars which formed the constellation Meseskhtiu or the "Thigh," which has been identified as the Great Bear [Big Dipper], and it was from this region that he made use of his baleful influence to thwart the beneficent designs

of Osiris, whose abode was Sah or Orion, and of Isis, whose home was Sept, or Sothis. A little consideration will show that the northern sky was the natural domain of Seth, for viewed from the standpoint of an Egyptian in Upper Egypt, the north was rightly considered to be a place of darkness, cold, mist and rain, each of which was an attribute of Seth. . . . From a passage in the Book of the Dead (xvii.89) we learn that Seth was accompanied by the Four Sons of Horus . . . who were said to be "behind the Thigh in the northern sky" . . . in the texts from which these details are quoted it is said definitely that the "Mesekhtiu [Big Dipper] is the Thigh of Seth."[95]

In the "offering spells" of the Pyramid Texts, the Bull's Thigh, Mesekhtiu, which was shaped like the ceremonial iron adze used for opening the mouth of the deceased king, is clearly said to belong to Seth, while the act is performed by Horus:

> To repeat four times: Osiris-King [the king's mummy], I open for you your mouth with the Thigh. . . . How good is the condition of your mouth after. I have adjusted for you your mouth to your [jaw] bones. I open for you your mouth. . . . I open for you your mouth with the *nw3*, the *mesekhtiu*-adze of *bja* [iron], which opens the mouth of the gods. Horus opens the mouth of this king . . . with the *bja* (iron) which comes forth from Seth, the *meskhtiu-adze* of *bja* (iron), which opens the mouth of the gods.

The Jumilhac papyrus in the Louvre Museum, although dated to the Ptolemaic period, was copied from much older sources dated from the Old Kingdom, as attested by the ancient scribe himself. In it, we read (in section VII, 11–12) about the epic combat between Seth and Horus:

> And after he [Horus] had cut out his [Seth's] fore-leg he threw it into the sky. Spirits guard it there: The Great Bear of the northern sky. The great Hippopotamus goddess keeps hold of it, so that it can no longer sail in the midst of the gods.

In his excellent study on Seth, Dutch Egyptologist H. Te Velde also confirmed that, "In the stars of the Great Bear [Big Dipper] the Egyptians saw an adze or a foreleg."[96]

In New Kingdom and Late Period depictions of the northern sky found on the ceilings of tombs, there is often shown a falcon-headed man brandishing a spear at the Bull's Thigh, the latter clearly being the constellation of the Big Dipper. The scene is clearly a representation of the well-known act of Horus slaying Seth, especially from the Late Period:[97]

> These [are] ... representations of the Late Period when Seth was considered to be Mesekhtiu and the ancient *dwn-nwy* (a name of the falcon-headed man with the spear) as the god Horus attacking his enemy Seth with a spear. The falcon-headed man with the spear, oddly enough, is called either *dwn-nwy* (He who stretches out the arms, or wings, or claws) or *Nemty*, spelled previously as *Anti* or *An-u*, (the Wanderer). Wallis Budge calls this figure "Horus the Warrior *An*, who holds in his hand a weapon with which he is attacking the Great Bear (Big Dipper)."[98]

Regarding the spear-brandishing falcon-headed man called *Dwn-nwy*, Wilkinson asserts:

> In the Pyramid Texts *Dunanwi* (*Dwn-nwy*) appears in several contexts, including that of the purification ritual in which the god represents the east in accompanying Thoth, Horus and Seth who together personify the four cardinal points (PT 27, etc.). From the end of the Old Kingdom, however, *Duwanwi* seems to have been assimilated with the falconiform god Nemty and is known only in that form thereafter ... like most other local falcon gods, Dunanwi was assimilated to Horus.[99]

Dwn-nwy (Anu) has often been wrongly assumed to be the constellation Cygnus. Zbynek Zaba also wrongly thought that the spear represented the celestial meridian.

In chapter 4, we look more closely at the black-African connections of the pharaoh and, more specifically, of Imhotep. But for now, let us find out who this mysterious King Netjerykhet was and what evidence— archaeological or textual—connects him to Imhotep.

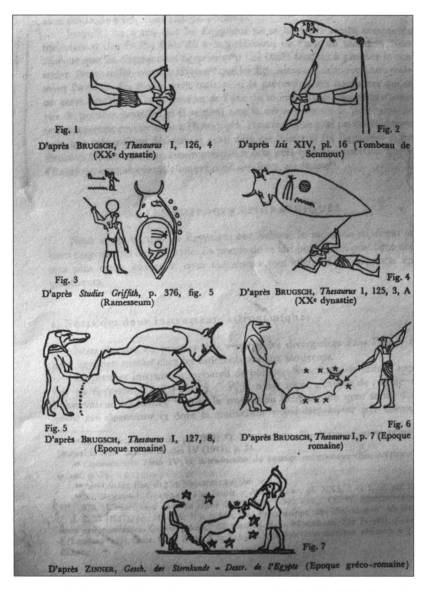

Fig. 1
D'après BRUGSCH, *Thesaurus* I, 126, 4
(XXᵉ dynastie)

Fig. 2
D'après *Isis* XIV, pl. 16 (Tombeau de
Senmout)

Fig. 3
D'après *Studies Griffith*, p. 376, fig. 5
(Ramesseum)

Fig. 4
D'après BRUGSCH, *Thesaurus* I, 125, 3, A
(XXᵉ dynastie)

Fig. 5
D'après BRUGSCH, *Thesaurus* I, 127, 8,
(Epoque romaine)

Fig. 6
D'après BRUGSCH, *Thesaurus* I, p. 7 (Epoque
romaine)

Fig. 7
D'après ZINNER, *Gesch. der Sternkunde – Descr. de l'Egypte* (Epoque gréco-romaine)

Drawings of a falcon-headed man, Dwn-nwy, spearing the "Thigh of Seth" (the Meseskhtiu constellation), from tombs of the New Kingdom and the Ptolemaic period.

King Djoser

In all Egyptology textbooks, guidebooks, and professional articles, you will assuredly be informed, with little or no reservation, that the Step Pyramid Complex belonged to a king called Djoser, apparently the founder of the 3rd Dynasty, who reigned some thirty years—according to the latest estimates, from c. 2690 BC on. Recent radiocarbon tests confirm the start of his reign to be between 2691 and 2625 BC, earlier than some previous historical estimates.[100] That Netjerykhet is also the same person as Djoser is perhaps true; yet it is well known in Egyptology that this conclusion is not supported by contemporary archaeological or textual evidence. So what makes Egyptologists so sure that Netjerykhet is Djoser?

Let us begin with a quote from the latest research by Mark Lehner:

> Djoser is the name given to this king by New Kingdom visitors to this site a thousand years later. But the only royal name found on the walls of the complex is the Horus name, *Netjerykhet*.[101]

Egyptologists Ian Shaw and Paul Nicholson of the British Museum concur:

> Only the Horus name *Netjerikhet* was found in 3rd-Dynasty inscriptions associated with the pyramid, and it is only through New Kingdom graffiti that an association has been made between this name and Djoser.[102]

As far as we can make out, nowhere on the Step Pyramid Complex or near it—or indeed anywhere else in the whole of Egypt—has the name Djoser been found on monuments contemporary or even near-contemporary with Imhotep, let alone next to the name Netjerykhet.

According to Michel Baud, the earliest known appearance of the name Djoser is on the base of a statue of Sesostris II c. 1880 BC, thus nearly 900 years after the reign of Netjerykhet.[103] Indeed, the only time that both names, Netjerykhet and Djoser, are associated is more than 2,000 years after Netjerykhet's reign. They are carved on a boulder, the so-called Famine Stele, on the small island of Sehel located about three kilometers south of Aswan. The Famine Stele speaks of a king called Djoser-Netjerykhet, who is concerned about a protracted drought due to poor Nile floods that has caused famine throughout Egypt. It tells how this king sent his high priest Imhotep to investigate the matter at the legendary source of the Nile flood—the First Cataract near Aswan.

So why are Egyptologists so confident that Djoser and Netjerykhet are one and the same person? Well, some say, there are the graffiti from visitors of the New Kingdom that claim that Djoser was the owner of the Step Pyramid Complex. But frankly, when it comes to graffiti—especially those that allude to events that happened 1,000 years earlier—we feel justified in questioning the soundness of such a conclusion.

The Kings Lists

So let's look at this alleged Djoser = Netjerykhet equation more closely and see if the evidence available can prove or disprove the association. For this, we need to refer to the so-called "kings lists" that have been the basis of Egyptian chronology. These, in order of their antiquity, are:

1. The Palermo stone, dating from the 5th Dynasty c. 2350 BC
2. The South Saqqara stone, inscriptions on the sarcophagus of Queen Ankhesenpepi of the 6th Dynasty c. 2100 BC
3. The Karnak tablets, dated from the reign of Thutmoses III c. 1450 BC
4. The Abydos king list, carved on a wall of the Seti I temple c. 1290 BC
5. *The Turin Royal Cannon*, a text on papyrus of the 19th Dynasty c. 1250 BC
6. The Saqqara tablets, dated to the 19th Dynasty c. 1250 BC
7. Manetho's *Aegyptiaca*, a chronology compiled for King Ptolemy I Soter by an Egyptian scribe called Manetho in c. 250 BC

None of these lists or sources, however, associates the names Djoser and Netjerykhet. In fact, they only name Djoser; none mention Netjerykhet. So what conclusion can we draw? Well, it is beyond doubt that a king called Netjerykhet is connected with the Step Pyramid Complex at Saqqara (and was almost certainly its owner); but we cannot be absolutely certain that he and the Djoser mentioned in the various lists are one and the same person. They may well be, but it is by no means a proven fact. It is, at best, a good deduction based on circumstantial evidence.

According to E. R. Bevan, an expert on the Ptolemies of Egypt, an Egyptian of the priestly caste, Manetho, wrote a history of Egypt in Greek, with the encouragement apparently of the first Ptolemy. Manetho really had some knowledge of the ancient records, and what he wrote was largely based on them, though he brought in a certain amount of Egyptian popular legend. It is, however, to his credit that we find him—in one connection, at any rate—specially pointing out that what he is giving is legend, and not something taken from the documents. The chronology by Manetho was the fullest, most authentic history of ancient Egypt that the Greeks and Romans ever possessed. The work has now perished, but considerable fragments, preserved by Josephus and other writers, gave Europe almost all the substantial information it had about ancient Egypt until the 19th century, when scholars discovered the key to the old Egyptian writing. "If we estimate aright the spirit of the Alexandria of that day," Bevan observed, "we shall not hesitate to say that Manetho's dry enumeration of early dynasties of gods and kings stood no chance in popularity against Hecataeus' agreeable romancing." He went on to say, however: "In Manetho's day his work was a failure, though centuries later Jews and Christians in their controversies raked it out of oblivion."

But what of Imhotep himself? Can he be linked to Netjerykhet and also to the Step Pyramid Complex with certainty? Until 1926, even though Egyptologists had long suspected that Imhotep was indeed the architect of the Step Pyramid Complex, there was absolutely no contemporary evidence to support the fact.

The Lepsius Expedition

Following the explorations of Perring, the next serious activity at Saqqara came from "the first true Egyptology expedition of history." This began in 1842, when the Prussian scholar Karl Richard Lepsius was sponsored by Prussian King Frederick Wilhelm IV for a scientific expedition to Egypt and the Sudan.

Karl Lepsius followed in the steps of the great Champollion and diligently studied the *Grammaire égyptienne*, gaining a reputation as an expert in Egyptian hieroglyphs and ancient texts. The passion he felt for his work led him to visit many of the museums of Europe. By 1841, his reputation got him recommendations from the brilliant geographer and naturalist Alexander von Humboldt and the famous diplomat and scholar Baron Christian Bunsen (at the time, Prussian Ambassador at the Court of St. James's) to King Frederick Wilhelm, who was also deeply fascinated by this ancient exotic culture.

Highly impressed by Lepsius's scholarship, the Prussian king promptly commissioned him to undertake a full-scale expedition to Egypt and the Sudan with the unpublicized proviso, of course, that he collect and bring back artifacts for the national museum in Berlin. No expense was spared. Like Napoleon four decades earlier, Frederick Wilhelm empowered Lepsius to gather a group of scholars, geographers, and scientists to accompany him, and the Lepsius Expedition, as it is now called, reached Giza in November 1842. Not surprisingly, one of the first things Lepsius did was to carve in hieroglyphs a commemoration for the King of Prussia on the entrance of the Great Pyramid (on the second level of pitched lintel, on the block on the right/west side). To our chagrin, it can still be seen today.

The expedition spent several months making detailed scientific studies of the pyramids of Giza, Abusir, Dashur, and Saqqara. Let us note in passing that, while working at Saqqara, Lepsius dismantled an entire ancient chapel, packed the blocks in wooden boxes, and shipped the lot to Germany along with other antiquities taken from the Step Pyramid Complex. According to Egyptologist Michel Baud:

> In two months of excavations at Saqqara, fraught with all sorts of problems, he [Lepsius] discovered and recorded a number of important tombs from the Old Kingdom. And he sometimes removed them, because Lepsius is also, like many personalities who preceded him, a hunter of monuments. After Paris, London and Turin, which bought big collections [of antiquities] amassed by adventurers and consuls in Egypt, Lepsius wants Berlin to also become a capital of Egyptology. It is thus that the decorated chapel of *Metjen*, discovered north of the Step Pyramid, is dismantled block by block, packed in boxes and shipped to the metropolis [Berlin]. . . . The door frame of Netjerykhet is also a choice piece. Dislodged [from the wall], it was shipped to Berlin where it is given inventory number 1185.[105]

The staggering inventory number 1185 for Lepsius's shipment to Germany implies that a huge number of ancient artifacts were taken out of Egypt to fill the Berlin Museum's Egyptian section—all, presumably, with the full approval of Mohammad Ali Pasha. At any rate, Lepsius later became the director of the Berlin Museum and wrote extensively on Egyptology. For these works, he is generally honored by his peers as the father of Scientific Egyptology.

Lepsius identified the king of the Step Pyramid Complex as being Netjerykhet, although in these early days of Egyptology, the name was misspelled as "Nouterot" and "Neterirkhet." Noting also the New Kingdom graffiti at Saqqara that mentioned Djoser, Lepsius began the trend that led many Egyptologists to identify Netjerykhet with Djoser—assuming them to be the same king and owner of the Step Pyramid Complex. As Michel Baud recently pointed out:

> Thanks to the royal lists that places Djoser in the long lineage of Kings of Egypt, and thanks to the comment of the historian Manetho who associates Tosorthros, a deformation in Greek of the name Djoser, to the invention of architectural works in stone which is attributed to Imhotep, the main pieces of the puzzle could at last be fitted together: Horus Netjerykhet is the same as the "king of Upper and Lower Egypt Djoser," and can be placed under the 3rd Dynasty. For now, he is in fact the first monarch to be truly identified in the ancient sources, because his eternal home, the Step Pyramid, has been identified.[106]

With the departure of Lepsius from Saqqara in 1845, a strange silence befell the ancient burial site, and it was again left to the mercy of adventurers, dabblers, and treasure hunters. Then, in 1856, French archaeologist Auguste Mariette founded the Services des Antiquitées and gradually put a stop to all that.[107] No further important work, however, was undertaken at the Step Pyramid Complex until 1924, when a gifted British Egyptologist named Cecil Firth was commissioned by the Egyptian Antiquities Services to take over where Lepsius had left off.

Things were now about to move quickly toward a full restoration of Imhotep's architectural masterpiece.

The "Black Box" of Imhotep

Cecil Mallaby Firth (1878–1931) was well placed in British scientific circles, including astronomy and especially Egyptology, since his wife's family was closely connected to the larger-than-life father of British Egyptology, Sir William Flinders Petrie. In 1924, after having served as an inspector for the Services des Antiquitées in Cairo since 1913, Firth was entrusted with one of the most important archaeological sites in Egypt—Saqqara. He paved the way for the extensive restoration of the Step Pyramid Complex. Little did Firth know, however, that one of his first discoveries would prove to be the key to our understanding of the true motives of the ancient pyramid builders.

While removing fallen debris on the north face of the Step Pyramid, Firth and his assistant, James E. Quibell, uncovered a most unusual structure—a small box-like stone cubicle that we have recently come to regard as the pharaonic equivalent of the "black box" on a jetliner. Firth and Quibell were intrigued by its most peculiar design. First, it was not level, but tilted against the lower step of the pyramid. The tilt was clearly not due to settling or subsidence, because the structure was solidly built into the Step Pyramid itself. Even more intriguing, there were two small round holes drilled in the north face of the box at about eye level. When Firth peered in through one of them, he was astounded to find staring back at him the lifeless eyes of a pharaoh! It was a life-size seated statue of King Netjerykhet, as the inscription on the pedestal confirmed.

Head of the statue of King Netjerykhet found
inside the serdab at Saqqara.

French Egyptologist Jean-Phillipe Lauer, who joined Firth's team at Saqqara at about this time, described the moment of discovery and the curious impression he had of this strange artifact:

> One day Firth was called to Cairo. It was nearly midday when he had to leave, and gave instructions to his workers to clear away a sand mount where he felt nothing would be found, and which still blocked the slope of the pyramid and the funerary temple on the north side. He then made his way to Cairo where he had lunch and spent the early hours of the afternoon. It was a day like any other and, without worries, he took his time, but a huge surprise awaited him on his return: the workers had cleared, up to the foot of the pyramid, leaning against the facing blocks [of the pyramid] which still existed at the base, a curious edifice of cubic shape inside of which, *like a cosmonaut inside his space capsule*, was the statue of Djoser.[108]

Statue of Netjerykhet found inside the serdab at Saqqara. It is now in the Cairo Museum; a replica is in the serdab.

The *serdab*, as this stone cubicle is now called, was made from good-quality Tura limestone blocks, and designed like a cube with sides of 2.6 meters. It is inclined against the first step of the pyramid and thus has the same inclination of about 16.5° to the horizon, as well as the same orientation of the pyramid, namely 4.5° east-of-north (azimuth 4.5°). The two round holes on the north face are at the eye level of the statue, and thus clearly intended to direct the king's gaze toward the circumpolar region of the northern sky. Looking through the holes from *inside* the serdab, your gaze would be directed to a specific spot in the circumpolar northern sky at azimuth—a sort of pharaonic "X marks the spot" in the sky, if you will.

Many Egyptologists who have recently commented on this unique serdab have arrived at more or less the same conclusion: The peepholes were intended for the statue of the king—which represents his *ka*, his spirit—to gaze eternally toward the circumpolar sky and the so-called "imperishable" or "indestructible" (fixed) stars. According to French Egyptologist Christiane Ziegler, ". . . through the two peep-holes the king would gaze towards the 'imperishable' stars near the North Pole."[109]

The inclined serdab on the north face of the Step Pyramid at Saqqara, directed toward the circumpolar region of the northern sky.

In the same vein, Mark Lehner wrote:

On the northern side of his Saqqara Step Pyramid Djoser emerges from his tomb in statue form, into a statue-box, or *Serdab*, which has just such a pair of peepholes to allow him to see out[110] . . .

with eyes once inlaid with rock crystal, Djoser's statue gazes out through peepholes in the serdab box, tilted upwards 13° to the northern sky where the king joined the circumpolar stars.[111]

Lehner quoted a passage from the *Book of the Dead* that, according to him, explains the function of the two holes or peepholes:

> Open for me are the double doors of the sky, open for me are the double doors of the earth. Open for me are the bolts of Geb, exposed for me are the roof . . . and the Twin Peepholes.

Russian astronomer Alexander Gurshtein gives a more scientific viewpoint when he writes:

> On the north side of Imhotep's Step Pyramid there is a small stone cubicle canted towards the north, with a pair of tiny holes in its façade likely for astronomical observations by the dead pharaoh.[112]

We totally agree with these scholars that a stellar function of the serdab is overwhelmingly supported by textual, astronomical, and architectural evidence. So upon what circumpolar star or constellation was the king's statue intended to gaze? And why?

To examine the serdab, you have to walk past the northeast corner of the Step Pyramid and then turn sharply left along the north face of the monument. As you approach the serdab, the head of the *ka*-statue can be seen through a small window on the east side. When standing in front of serdab—i.e., facing the north side—you see the twin peepholes. Leaning against the north face of the serdab, your body is inclined 16.5°, and your gaze is directed toward the circumpolar region of the sky. The reason for directing the gaze of the king's spirit (the statue) toward the circumpolar stars is given in the Pyramid Texts, where numerous passages instruct the soul of the departed monarch to travel to the "stars that never die," which they called the *ikhemu-set*.

It is easy to verify with astronomy software that, during the time of Imhotep (c. 2690 BC), the stars that occupied the circumpolar region were those in the constellations Draco, the Big Dipper, and the Small Dipper. All three constellations are attested in the ancient Egyptian religious texts, but the one that held special importance to them was the Big Dipper. Strictly speaking, however, the Big Dipper, in modern astronomy, is considered to be an *asterism,* because its seven bright stars are part of the larger constellation of the Great Bear, or Ursa Major. This often causes people to use the name Great Bear when they, in fact, really mean the Big Dipper.

To the ancient Egyptians, it was for the very distinct shape of the seven stars that form the Big Dipper that they had special reverence. They perceived these seven stars, not as a dipper (or plow or chariot, as others do), but rather as a bull's thigh or foreleg—*khepesh* (*hpš*), which was called Meskhetiu. As early as 1912, Breasted recognized the importance of these special circumpolar stars when he wrote:

> [I]t is especially those (stars) which are called "the Imperishable Ones" in which the Egyptians saw the host of the dead. These are said to be in the north of the sky, and the suggestion that the circumpolar stars, which never set or disappear, are the ones which are meant is a very probable one.[113]

Speaking of the circumpolar stars, Clark commented:

> [N]o other ancient people were so deeply affected by the eternal circuit of the stars around a point in the northern sky. Here must be the node of the universe, the centre of regulation.[114]

In the same vein, Krupp, an accredited specialist in this field, also pointed out that the Egyptians associated the Big Dipper "with eternal life because its stars are circumpolar. They were the undying, imperishable stars. In death the king ascended to their circumpolar realm, and there he preserved the cosmic order."[115]

According to Lehner:

> The "Imperishable Ones" are the circumpolar stars....Since these stars revolve around the celestial North Pole and neither rise or set, the long, narrow passages sloping up from the burial chamber in the northern sides of many pyramids were aimed like telescopes in their direction.[116]

The belief that the king was responsible for preserving the cosmic order or harmony of the universe via the circumpolar stars as the center of regulation may thus explain the function of the serdab. We look at this more closely in the next chapter.

There was something else, however, that made the circumpolar stars vitally important to the astronomical alignment of the Step Pyramid Complex. It involved one of the most ancient, intriguing, and beautiful goddesses of the ancient world—Seshat.

Seshat—Our Lady of the Stars

From earliest times, well before the epoch of Imhotep, the mysterious astronomer-priests of Egypt had performed a dramatic ceremony known as the Stretching of the Cord in order to align the sacred monuments to the stars. This ceremony, which involved the pharaoh himself, was performed, not by a priest, but by a very fetching priestess who took the role of a goddess called Seshat. This intriguing goddess was the most learned among all others—so much so that, among her many epithets, she was known as Lady of Builders and as the patron of the sacred books and libraries. Always depicted as tall and slender, Seshat was especially admired and venerated by the scribes in the Houses of Life (temple libraries) as the patron of hieroglyphs and the keeper of the royal annals, especially the records of the coronations and jubilees of kings.[117] Above all these important functions, however, Seshat had what may be termed a scientific role—or, to be more precise, an astronomical task—that required assisting the pharaoh in defining the corners of a temple or pyramid, and aligning the axis toward the stars in the northern sky. This was the essence of the Stretching of the Cord ceremony.

In many ancient reliefs, the goddess Seshat is shown with a tight leopard-skin dress cut low to expose her breasts. Sometimes, the spots on the leopard skin are replaced with stars or rosettes. The leopard skin, which is traditionally worn by priests, may also symbolize Seshat's ability to see in the dark.[118] Another feature of the goddess's attire is a golden tiara with a stem surmounted by a seven-pointed star.

Seshat is the wife-companion of none other than the great god of wisdom, Thoth, inventor of the sacred hieroglyphs and the sciences, especially astronomy. With such an illustrious partner, as well as her own important responsibilities, Seshat was given many impressive titles—Foremost in the Library, Mistress of Writing in the House of Life, Keeper of the Royal Annals, and, more important, Lady of the Stars.[119] In the reliefs, she is seen either alone or with Thoth recording important dates of royal events like births, coronations, and jubilees by cutting notches on a palm branch. Seshat was thus the divine time-keeper—or, to use a modern term, the Astronomer Royal *par excellence*—who recorded calendric events by observing the cycle of the stars. The French expert on the Egyptian calendar Anne-Sophie Bomhard makes this appropriate comment about Seshat:

> The recognition of the annual cycle and its definition, the linking of celestial phenomena to terrestrial happenings, are essential preliminaries to establishing any kind of calendar. This enterprise requires long prior observations of the sky and the stars, as well as the recording, in writing, of these observations, in order to verify them over long periods of time. It is quite natural, therefore, that the divine tutors of Time and Calendar should be Thoth, God of Science, and Seshat, Goddess of Writings and Annals.[120]

Lady Seshat was thus not only a very smart and important official of the royal court, but also, as we shall see, the one who held the king's life, quite literally, in her able hands.

Tutor of Time and Controller of Jubilees

As the "tutor of time" and keeper of the king's annals, Seshat was directly responsible for computing and supervising the royal jubilees. Wallis Budge describes a relief from the New Kingdom:

> [Seshat is seen] standing before a column of hieroglyphics meaning "life" and "power" and "thirty-year festivals" which rest upon a seated figure who holds in each hand "life" and who typifies "millions of years." In connection with this must be noted a passage in a text in which she declares to a king that she has inscribed on her register on his behalf a period of life which shall be "hundreds of thousands of Thirty-Year periods" and has ordained that his years shall be upon the earth like the years of *Ra* (the sun god) i.e. that he shall live forever.[121]

Egyptology consensus is that the first royal jubilee—or *heb-sed* festival, as it is known—was generally celebrated on the king's thirtieth year of reign. Indeed, the term "thirty-year festivals" was simply another designation for royal jubilees. Moreover, the linking of the thirty years with the "years of Ra" implies some sort of astronomical cycle and, therefore, a calendric computation. Indeed, it is highly probable that the Seshat priestess was learned in astronomy, the workings of the calendar, the keeping of records, and, more specifically, the circular motions of the stars of the Big Dipper about the north celestial pole.

It is well known that the Stretching of the Cord ceremony involved the observation of the circumpolar stars. As British Egyptologist George Hart affirmed:

> As early as Dynasty II she [Seshat] assisted the monarch . . . in hammering boundary poles into the ground for the ceremony of "stretching the cord." This is a crucial part of a temple foundation ritual.[122]

Details of this mysterious astronomical ceremony are culled mostly from inscriptions and reliefs from the temples at Karnak, Edfu, Dendera, and Kom Ombo; but it is fairly certain that the ritual can be projected back in time to the beginning of the Egyptian civilization and, in our opinion, very likely beyond it. As Edwards explained:

> In spite of the relative late date of the inscriptions referring to the episodes of the foundation ceremonies [Stretching the Cord], there is no reason to doubt that they preserved an ancient tradition. Some indication that similar ceremonies were already current in the Pyramid Age is provided by a fragmentary relief found in the Vth Dynasty sun-temple of Niuserre, which shows the king and a priestess impersonating Seshat, each holding a mallet and a stake to which a measuring cord is attached. The scene is in complete agreement with the text in the temple at Edfu which represents the king saying: "I take the stake and I hold the handle of the mallet. I hold the cord with Seshat."[123]

In the various scenes that depict the Stretching of the Cord, the Seshat-priestess faces the king; each of them carries a peg in one hand and holds a mallet in the other. A cord or rope is looped between the two pegs. From the accompanying text, it is clear that the king and the Seshat-priestess carefully align the cord to the Big Dipper. When the

Seshat and the pharaoh performing the Stretching of the Cord ceremony, from the temple at Dendera.

Reenactment of the Stretching of the Cord ceremony for a television documentary. (Courtesy Raoul Oostra)

desired direction is reached, they hammer the pegs into the ground with the mallet. The axis of the future monument is thus established. In the beautiful temple of Dendera, the following inscriptions accompany a relief showing Seshat and the pharaoh performing the Stretching of the Cord ceremony:

> (The king says): "I hold the peg. I grasp the handle of the mallet and grip the measuring-cord with Seshat. I turn my eyes to the movements of the stars. I direct my gaze towards the bull's thigh [Meskhetiu; Big Dipper]. . . . I make firm the corners of the temple."

> (A priest says): "The king stretches joyously the cord, having turned his head towards the bull's thigh and establishes the temple in the manner of ancient times."

> (The king says): "I grasp the peg and the mallet; I stretch the cord with Seshat; I observed the trajectory of the stars with my eye which is fixed on the bull's thigh; I have been the god who indicates Time with the Merkhet instrument. I have established the four corners of the temple."

(A priest says): "The king . . . while observing the sky and the stars, turns his sight towards the bull's thigh."[124]

It has always been thought by Egyptologists and astronomers alike that the pyramid builders wanted to align their monuments to true north—i.e., at the north meridian—as accurately as they could. (The meridian is an imaginary line in the sky connecting due south to due north.) But was it really so? Or were they aiming at a specific star in the Big Dipper at a specific time and not, as assumed, necessarily at true north? As far as we know, none of the ancient texts of the pyramid builders or those accompanying the Stretching of the Cord ceremony stated or even implied that it was true north that was the objective. On the other hand, it is clear from the Pyramid Texts that the circumpolar stars were considered a highly favored destination for the soul of the king, and the Stretching of the Cord inscriptions make it obvious that the Big Dipper is the celestial target in the alignment ritual.

Jean-Philippe Lauer, who is regarded as the supreme authority on the Step Pyramid Complex, acknowledged that the main axis of the monument was almost certainly aligned according to the Stretching of the Cord ritual. Moreover, he even considered that Imhotep was the inventor of this ritual: "In the Old Kingdom there existed a ritual for the foundation of temples, [of] which Imhotep presumably was the author."[125] And historian Michael Rice, another expert on the Saqqara monuments, comments:

[The Step Pyramid was] a veritable stairway to the region of the Imperishable Stars [the circumpolars], beyond which the King would reign for all eternity. A stellar orientation for buildings, rather than a solar one, is a characteristic of the Third Dynasty and represents the culmination of what may have been one of the most important aspects of aboriginal Egyptian cults.[126]

There can be little doubt that the ritual of the Opening of the Mouth and the ritual of the Stretching of the Cord are to be considered together as part of the stellar rebirth rituals for the deceased king. This is made obvious by the direct association both rituals have with the Mesekhtiu/Big Dipper constellation—i.e., the "celestial adze." Moreover, there is another important instrument in the toolbox of the Opening of the

Mouth called *peshemkef* (*pss-kf*), which is shaped like a fishtail hook, of which Zaba commented:

> The Egyptian . . . instrument which much resembled a *b'y n imy unwt* [a sighting instrument made of wood] and which, when fixed on a wooden slab, could be adapted better to astronomical observation as described [in the Stretching the Cord ritual]: this instrument was the *pss-kf*, used for the "opening of the mouth."[127]

In 1872, British engineer Waynman Dixon discovered the so-called star-shafts in the Queen's Chamber of the Great Pyramid. Inside the northern shaft that was directed toward the circumpolar stars, he found a small instrument made of bronze, which, in 1993, Edwards identified as a *pss-kf*. On the handle of the instrument, there can be seen small bolts that were perhaps used to fix a wooden arm, thus making the instrument perfect for accurately sighting distant objects or stars.

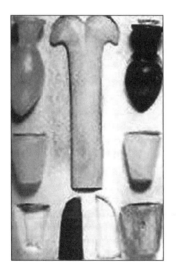

A *pss-kf* in the toolbox of the Opening of the Mouth ceremony (left); the bronze *pss-kf* found by Waynman Dixon in 1872 in the northern star shafts of the Queen's Chamber of the Great Pyramid (right).

Circle in the Sky

The circumpolar stars, as seen from the Saqqara region, occupy a large circular portion of the northern sky, having a radius of nearly 30° with the focal point being the celestial North Pole. The stars within this circle transit true north—i.e., the north meridian—only twice each day for just a minute or so. Otherwise, they are found either east or west of true north during the rest of the day. Thus, the apparent "misalignment" of 4.5° toward the east of the Step Pyramid Complex does not seem a misalignment at all, but a deliberate alignment toward a star in the Big Dipper that was 4.5° east-of-north at the time of the Stretching of the Cord. But why choose this specific star at that specific time? We return to this intriguing question in chapter 3. Meanwhile, let's flash back to 1926, when Cecil Firth was about to make another stunning discovery—one that would resolve once and for all whether Imhotep was really the architect of the Step Pyramid Complex.

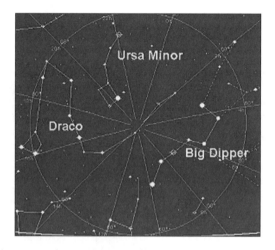

The circumpolar region as seen from Saqqara in c. 3000 BC.

A Pedestal with No Statue

Hardly two years after his sensational discovery of the serdab, Cecil Firth was clearing the southeast corner of the entrance of the Step Pyramid Complex when he unearthed a small pedestal of a statue of which only parts of the feet could be discerned. As Firth cleared the dust, he was delighted and astounded to read the inscriptions that decorated the front of the pedestal. There, finally, was the name of Imhotep next to the name of King Netjerykhet! Smoking-gun proof—as good as it gets in archaeology—that Imhotep was, indeed, a contemporary of this king. But there was more. The inscriptions also attested that Imhotep was *our maou*—Greatest of Seers or Chief of the Observers or, as Edwards preferred to translate this title, Chief of the Astronomers—the title held by high priests of Heliopolis. There were other titles on the inscription as well: Chancellor of the King (*khetemou bity*), Delegate of the King's Command (*khery-tep nesout*), Chief of the Great Domain (*heka hout aat*), and Master of Sculptors and Masons (*medjeh genoutyou*).

Firth's discovery sent a wave of excitement through archaeologists. It was now certain that Imhotep had indeed been the great astronomer-priest-architect who, as texts of much later periods had persistently affirmed, was also the inventor of stone masonry and the designer and builder of the Step Pyramid Complex. Furthermore, the fact that no

Statue base found by Cecil Firth in 1926, showing the name of
Imhotep next to that of Netjerykhet.

contemporary evidence other than the pedestal bearing his name had been found suggested that his own tomb might still be undiscovered and, more thrillingly, unviolated. It became the dream of many excavators to find the tomb of Imhotep, especially since, over the last few decades, his name had become universally known through popular novels and movies.

Grand Master of the Pyramids

When Cecil Firth died in 1931, the management of the Saqqara site passed to his assistant, James Quibell. In 1926, however, a young French architect had joined the team. Straight out of architectural school and only twenty-four years old, Jean-Philippe Lauer (whom we cited earlier) was eventually to exceed all expectations and enter the annals of Egyptology among greats like Champollion, Mariette, Maspero, Edwards, and Flinders Petrie. Ultimately, he was dubbed by his peers the Grand Master of the Pyramids, an epithet given to him in 1985 by German Egyptologist Dr. Rainer Stadelmann.[128]

Lauer entered Egyptology, as it were, through the back door. In early 1926, he was informed by a cousin working in Egypt that the director of the Antiquities Services, Pierre Lacau, was looking for an architect to join Cecil Firth's team at Saqqara. Lauer jumped at the opportunity and, in December, was received at Saqqara by Firth and Swiss Egyptologist Gustave Jéquier.[129] A warm friendship developed between Lauer and Firth. It was with Firth, in early 1927, that Lauer discovered the so-called South Tomb, a sort of dummy tomb or *cenotaph* of the pharaoh Netjerykhet (his actual tomb was under the pyramid itself), with its fine reliefs depicting the pharaoh performing rituals. The walls of the cenotaph had been decorated with beautiful small blue ceramic tiles, all of which had fallen off. Lauer's wife, Marguerite, the daughter of the director of the Institut Français d'Archaeologie du Caire, restored the tiles to the walls with the help of Mrs. Firth, after carefully washing them "at Mrs. Firth's home in a bath of water" to remove the dust and grime.

Their friendship, alas, was to be short-lived. Firth died suddenly in 1931 while on leave in England. His untimely death was a huge blow to Lauer, who became the only archaeologist at Saqqara. He was soon to be joined, however, by James Quibell, a no-nonsense Shropshire man educated at Oxford and a pupil of the great Flinders Petrie. Quibell was the epitome of the British Egyptologist. He had worked with Flinders Petrie at various important excavations in Egypt—including Coptos, Nagada, and Hierakonpolis—and had been employed in the Egyptian Antiquities Service as Chief Inspector for the Delta region from 1899 to 1904. It was while working at Hierakonpolis in 1899 that Quibell and his team discovered the famous Narmer palette of the 1st Dynasty, now one of the most important items on display in the Cairo Museum. Also in 1905, while working at the Valley of the Kings in Upper Egypt, Quibell discovered the tomb of Yuya, a vizier of the 18th Dynasty whose daughter, Tiye, and her husband, Amenhotep III, were the parents of the celebrated pharaoh Akhenaten.

Quibell also served as keeper at the Cairo Museum until 1923. He was then appointed director of excavations at Saqqara shortly after Firth took charge of the site, while Lauer remained responsible for excavations and restoration work. Quibell, who was already retired and well into his sixties, primarily concerned himself with publishing Firth's research papers and notes, although much still remained unexplored in the subterranean parts of the Step Pyramid Complex. In 1932, Quibell and Lauer decided to re-enter the subterranean galleries and together discovered a deposit of thousands of beautifully fashioned stone vases

Stone vases discovered by Quibell and Lauer in 1932 in the galleries under the Step Pyramid at Saqqara.

or jars, many of which had royal inscriptions—although, oddly, not of King Netjerykhet/Djoser or any of his 3rd-Dynasty contemporaries, but rather of kings of the 1st and 2nd Dynasties.

The consensus now among Egyptologists is that these vessels were handed down from generation to generation and then put into the complex during the reign of Netjerykhet/Djoser. But what if the subterranean system, or parts of it, were already there long before the time of this king? In the north of Saqqara, not far from the Step Pyramid Complex, are the mastaba tombs of 1st- and 2nd-Dynasty kings, proving that the Saqqara site was in use long before Djoser. But there is much more evidence to consider, to which we will return in chapter 4. For now, it is time to take a tour inside the Step Pyramid Complex, where there are very mysterious structures that do not appear to be of practical use, but may rather have been for the use of the spiritual or unseen.

A Complex on the Scale of a City

"Nothing," wrote the enthralled Egyptologist Wendy Wood, "in the architecture of archaic tombs, would constitute an adequate preparation to the technical mastering which suddenly appears in the Step Pyramid Complex."[130] Indeed, nothing of this type of construction and scale had occurred before. It is as if, totally out of the blue, the principles of architectural design and hewn-stone construction were born in the mind of one man: Imhotep. The surface area of the complex alone is mind-boggling: 545 x 277 meters, vast enough to accommodate more than 560 tennis courts! The whole complex is surrounded, as noted in chapter 1, by a gigantic rectangular boundary wall some ten meters high made of high-quality Tura limestone.

Lauer claims that the north-south length of the boundary was originally shorter, but later extended by 160 meters toward the north. This may be so, but the proportions and details of the design are too perfect for the wall not to have been designed in its entirety from the outset. At any rate, we discuss this matter in greater depth in chapter 3 when we investigate the astronomical character of the complex. For now, suffice it to point out that this giant boundary wall has 211 "bastions" (rectangular projections) about three meters wide, each having fifteen long vertical "panels" (six inserts and nine flats). Fourteen of these bastions are much larger than the rest and are, in fact, false doors. The largest of the bastions is near the south end of the east side of the wall, and has a real, open door leading into the complex. The whole wall is decorated with long vertical indents that create a panel effect. The precision of these indents and the effect they create is breathtaking, and would alone—there are 1,722 of them—be considered a supreme example of the mason's art.

As you pass through the high open doorway, you find yourself at the east end of a long narrow corridor flanked with wonderful fluted columns. This colonnade, as it is now called, had two rows of twenty columns. At the other end of the colonnade, there are two sets of four columns built back to back, giving each row a total of twenty-four columns. Past the colonnade and immediately to the left is the so-called South Tomb in which Lauer discovered the king's apartments with the blue ceramic tile walls and the ceremonial stele. To the north of the colonnade is the jubilee court. The latter has two rows of small "dummy buildings" or "pavilions," the western row containing three *zeh-nejer* (divine) pavilions and ten *per-our* (Great House) pavilions. The eastern row contains twelve *per-nou* (associated to the city of Bouto) pavilions.

The Step Pyramid is more or less at the center of the enclosure. On its north and south are vast open-air rectangular courts. The south court apparently was used for a ceremonial "race" in which the king had to run around the perimeter to mark the four cardinal sides of his domain (Egypt) symbolically. Other buildings in the complex are the North House and the South House, which are located along the east part of the complex. There is also a temple on the south part of the complex, a northern temple on the north side of the Step Pyramid, and, of course, the mysterious serdab attached to the north face of the pyramid. There are store rooms along the west and north walls as well.

The base of the Step Pyramid is not quite a square and, oddly, not at the exact center of the enclosure. Rather, it is offset a few dozen meters toward the east. The base of the pyramid occupies an area of some 12,000 square meters, enough to hold forty-five tennis courts. The pyramid is about sixty meters high and the base measures 118 x 105 meters, according to the latest published data by Michel Baud. There is some disagreement on the size of the base, however. Lehner, for example, says it's 121 x 109 meters; Malek says 140 x 118 meters.

Lauer has claimed that the Step Pyramid was built in five successive stages: the project started as a small square mastaba and, after four other extensions, it finally ended up looking like the Step Pyramid we see today. Rainer Stadelmann, however, rejects this "progressive *ad hoc* construction" thesis, and insists that the Step Pyramid was planned and built as it is seen today—i.e., as one project.

As noted earlier, John Perring carefully measured the angle of the steps in 1838 and concluded that "the face of each story or degree has an angle of 73° 30' with the horizon,"[131] which means that the steps are inclined 16° 30' to the vertical. Lauer, Edwards, Vandier, and Baud agreed with this measurement, give or take 0.5°. Thus the serdab, which is integrated into the first step of the pyramid, should also have the same inclination of 16° 30' to the vertical.

Very often in matters to do with the orientation of ancient monuments, an error quoted by one highly respected colleague is taken at face value and perpetuated in other works, so that it becomes accepted as true. This, unfortunately, has been the case for the orientation of the Step Pyramid Complex. Granted, Egyptologists are not astronomers; nor are they particularly concerned if a monument's axis is measured approximately, give or take 1 or 2° here or there. After all, what could such minor deviations matter to an archaeologist engrossed in the meticulous study of artifacts and shards and ensuring that these are properly recorded and stored for posterity? Although Perring had ascertained that the orientation of the Step Pyramid was 4° 35' east-of-north (azimuth 4° 35'), unfortunately Lauer, who later came to be regarded as the prime authority for this site, stated that the orientation was "about 3° east-of-north."

Then in 1953, Zaba claimed that the orientation of the Step Pyramid is "approximately 3° towards the east" in his landmark article on the astronomical orientation of Egyptian pyramids. Zaba asserted that this measurement was provided by Polish astronomer B. Polak, who measured it off the drawings in Edwards's book *The Pyramids of Egypt*. Edwards, in turn, had obtained it from Lauer in the first place.[132] Then in 2000, in another landmark article on the astronomical orientation of Egyptian pyramids, Kate Spence used the value given by Zaba.[133] Amazingly, Spence confirmed that she had consulted the recent thesis of German Egyptologist Josef Dorner on the astronomi-

Confusion about the inclination of the serdab was perpetuated by Lehner who, in his book *The Complete Pyramids* (1997), wrongly claimed that it was "tilted upwards by 13° towards the northern sky."[134] This error was quoted in a major television documentary produced for the Discovery Channel by the BBC. The value of 13° quoted by Lehner was, in fact, taken from one of Lauer's publications, and refers to the almost vertical walls of the alleged original mastaba. However, in the same publication, Lauer stated that "two round holes drilled in the north face of the serdab, whose sides are inclined parallel to that of the Pyramid, allowed the statue to communicate with the outside world. . . . The slope of its faces is *near 16° to the vertical*."[135] This value of "nearly 16°" is also given by Edwards;[136] Vandier gave a value of 17° to the vertical.[137] It is obvious that the "near 16°" (Lauer and Edwards) and the 17° (Vandier) were taken from Perring's value of 16.5°.

Given the importance of this value to our work, we took several readings from all three faces of the serdab, as well as other readings of the slope of the lower step onto which the serdab abuts. Our conclusion was that the inclination of the serdab, as well as the step of the pyramid, was close to 16° 30', as Perring had stated when he measured it in 1838.

cal orientation of Egyptian pyramids, who stated that the sides of the Step Pyramid "do not exactly face the cardinal points, the northern front being 4° 35' east of true north"![138] Stadelmann also gives about 4° east-of-north, probably using an approximation of Perring's value.[139]

So we were back to square one. Today, thank goodness, a very good value can be obtained by anyone using Google Earth satellite GPS. So we checked the measurement on a high-resolution screen, and the value obtained tallies with the one Perring obtained in 1838, give or take 0.20°—which also confirms the high quality of workmanship of this 19th-century engineer.

Egyptologists attribute this rather large deviation of 4° 35' from true north to carelessness or inefficiency by the ancient astronomers and surveyors. We do not agree. In our professional opinion as engineers and astronomers, the 4° 35' east-of-north alignment was deliberate, and we need to find out why.

As we have seen, the alignment of monuments was established in the Stretching of the Cord ceremony, during which the astronomers/surveyors aimed at a star in the circumpolar constellation of the Big Dipper. In the famous Palermo stone, dating from the 5th Dynasty, we are told that, in the fourth year of the reign of King Netjerykhet, this ceremony was performed for a rectangular complex called Qebeh-netjerou (Qbh Ntrw), the Refreshing Water of the Gods, perhaps an allusion to the flood season. The actual text reads: "Year IV-Appearance of the King of Upper Egypt; appearance of the King of Lower Egypt; Stretching the cord for the *Qbh Ntrw.* "

According to Baud:

> The (4th year) sees the foundation (ceremony) *pedj shes* "Stretching the Cord," which was to define a line and an orientation of a building which had a rectangular plan, and called *Qebeh-netjerou* . . . it is tempting to see in this name of *Qebeh-netjerou* the funerary complex of Saqqara.[140]

It is tempting, to put it mildly, to imagine that the ceremony for the Qebeh-Netjerou complex took place at the religious moment when the star Sirius rose heliacally to mark the start of the annual Nile flood.

The Whole Sky Is Within It

One's first impression of the Step Pyramid Complex can be strangely deceiving and awe-inspiring at the same time. Deceiving, because on approaching the entrance and the huge boundary wall, a newcomer may think that it is too modern a structure so well preserved (and restored) are the architectural features. Awe-inspiring, because it is very hard to believe that what you are seeing is the world's first-ever architectural project in stone. You cannot help getting an other-worldly feeling about the place—a sort of connection with the wider cosmos. Perhaps this is what an ancient scribe who undertook a pilgrimage there in 1300 BC meant when he remarked that the ancient complex appeared "as if the whole of the sky was within it."[141]

Today, you approach the Saqqara site along a small tarmac road that runs through a lush palm grove from the canal right to the edge of the Western Desert. The ticket office has recently been renovated and now includes a small auditorium where visitors can see a short film on the history of Saqqara. In the middle of this auditorium is a wonderful scale model of the Step Pyramid Complex that provides a great view of how this amazing and vast compound must have looked in its original state. Not far from the auditorium is the new Imhotep Museum, which contains many of the artifacts that were found by Firth, Lauer, and Quibell—items like the stone vases and the plinth of the statue on which were inscribed the titles of Imhotep. After visiting the museum, you drive up the escarpment onto the Saqqara plateau, passing on the way the small and very dilapidated pyramids of the 5th and 6th Dynasties and coming finally to a large unpaved parking area.

The small, dilapidated 5th-Dynasty pyramid of Userkaf on the Saqqara plateau, with the Step Pyramid in the background.

You then walk toward the original entrance of the Step Pyramid Complex. Standing outside and looking at the ten-meter-high stone wall, you feel dwarfed and humbled, as well as thrilled by the sheer scale of the construction. Although largely reconstructed and restored by Lauer and his team beginning in the late 1920s, many of the blocks, especially those that were decorated and rounded, are original. It is, again, hard to believe that they are more than 4,500 years old. This is especially true for the two rows of beautifully fluted columns that you pass as you walk along the colonnade that leads to the open courtyard. No matter how many times we have seen and touched these columns, we are always dumbstruck by their sheer perfection and smooth texture.

At the end of the roofed colonnade, you emerge into a vast open-air courtyard and, as you gaze to the left, you see the Step Pyramid with its six graduated tiers looking like a giant wedding cake that is melting under the heat of the sun. To the left are the rows of dummy ceremonial pavilions.

The imposing entrance colonnade of the Step Pyramid Complex, with its two rows of fluted columns.

When we conduct tours for visitors, we approach the pyramid from there so that they can not only marvel at the elaborate architectural details, but also get a dramatic perspective on the Step Pyramid from an ideal vantage point.

You then walk along the eastern side of the pyramid to reach the serdab on the north face of the monument so that, when you reach it, you can peep into the round holes and see the stony face of King Netjerykhet, eternally frozen in a gaze toward the circumpolar region of the northern sky. At that point, you are tempted to lean against the serdab so that your own gaze also locks on the hazy blue sky 16° 30' above the horizon and 4° 35' east-of-north.

All you see in the daytime is the infinite expanse of the sky. But were you here at night, in the crystal-clear darkness of the open desert, you'd see the northern stars, the brightest being the seven stars of the Big Dipper, majestically moving around the pole. Casting your thoughts to a distant time when this place was new, you wonder what the effigy of the pharaoh in the serdab was looking at so intently. How did he imagine that, by being in this peculiar stone box, his soul could communicate with the heavenly ancestors in the golden age of zep tepi? And how could Maat, the order of the cosmos, be controlled from this spot?

When the constellations were thought of as gods and kings were deemed responsible for the proper functioning of the cosmos, what role was the serdab supposed to play? We had to imagine ourselves as the figure inside it, seated and gazing through the two holes toward that spot in the northern sky that we now could confidently mark with an imaginary X: azimuth 4° 35', altitude 16° 30'.

A marvelous journey into a far-off time and into the mind of Imhotep is about to begin.

The *heb-sed* jubilee courtyard at the end of the roofed colonnade, with the "dummy" ceremonial pavilions in the foreground and the Step Pyramid in the background to the right.

Chapter Three

A TIME MACHINE IN STONE

[The pyramid builders]clearly associate their owner with an astral after-life.

I. E. S. EDWARDS[142]

The (names of the) Step Pyramid of Netjerykhet (Djoser) [are] . . . explicitly stellar.

STEPHEN QUIRKE[143]

The last time we were at Saqqara was in February 2012, a year after the Tahrir Revolution and the ousting of the Mubarak regime. We had especially come to see, yet again, the mysterious little serdab. The site was practically abandoned, although some renovation work was going on on the northern side of the Step Pyramid Complex. A group of unsupervised laborers were lethargically standing on a rickety wooden scaffold raised against the north face of the pyramid. Annoyingly, an armed guard was blocking access to the serdab. In the pre-Revolution days, a little *bakshish* would have had him roll out the red carpet for us; but now, in the new Egypt, we opted not to perpetuate this corruptive custom.

Suddenly, there was a loud noise like the sound of thunder from above. We all looked up to see where it came from. Seemingly totally indifferent or oblivious to the sacredness of this place, a worker had emptied a wheelbarrow from the top of the scaffolding. We watched in horror as some of the contents splattered on the serdab, a puff of dust engulfing the small monument. The guard next to us simply smiled, then mumbled to us Egypt's universally used magic word: *maalesh* (never mind). We handed him a pack of cigarettes. He looked at the label, saw they were British, and, with a broad grin, excitedly pulled one out and lit it. We signaled that he could keep the pack. To show his appreciation, he indicated that it would, after all, be alright for us to go see the serdab. He then uttered Egypt's second magic word: *etfadal* (welcome). The Egyptian-born French superstar, Dalida, coined the phrase *ahssan nass* to describe the gentle and jovial Egyptians. It means "the best people." There is indeed a lot of truth in this.

We looked around and, for the umpteenth time, wondered how old this site really was. When you have been exposed to these ancient and powerful places as much as we have over the past twenty-five years or so, you tend to develop a sort of sixth sense about the ancient stones. You can almost tell which are much older than others. There was something about the Step Pyramid Complex that had always goaded this sixth sense, but we could never quite put a finger on it. We glanced again at the workers on the scaffolding and saw that they were replacing the crumbling, weatherworn ancient limestone blocks with bright new ones. In some months from now, when this facelift is complete, the pyramid will surely

appear much younger than it really is.

It was only then, in one of those endearing chaotic moments you find only in Egypt, with the dust settling around the serdab, that we realized what had been taunting our sixth sense all along: the *contrast* between the high state of preservation of the site and the quality, advanced design and workmanship of the boundary wall—and the entrance colonnade, the stone pavilions, the chapels, and so

Scaffolding on the north face of the Step Pyramid.

on—with the pathetic state of preservation and almost shoddy workman-ship of the Step Pyramid itself. Although we had seen these monuments dozens and dozens of times, we were looking at them with the blinders of preconception on. We were told or had read so many times that the Step Pyramid Complex belonged to one man, King Djoser, that we always had perceived it as such. But in the famous axiom of Groucho Marx, which may as well be attributed to the proverbial Egyptologist: "Are you going to believe me, or what you see with your own eyes?"

The remarkable knowledge of architecture characteristic of the complex as a whole is not, in fact, exhibited in the building of the Step Pyramid. There's nothing simpler than drawing a pyramid. And although we are impressed, of course, with the sheer effort and determination it took to build the Step Pyramid, it cannot, in all honesty, be considered an architectural masterpiece. In contrast, the sheer perfection of design of the complex as a whole—the beautifully proportioned fluted columns,

Details of the boundary wall of the Step Pyramid Complex (left); the fluted columns of the colonnade seen from the north court (top right); the cobra frieze on the chapel wall with the Step Pyramid in the background (below right).

the delicate architraves and friezes on the pavilions and chapels, and the amazing features of the boundary wall—displays an advanced knowledge of architecture and highly skilled workmanship. It was as if a veil had been lifted, as we began to see two totally different projects in the so-called Step Pyramid Complex. Had everyone been looking at this place in the wrong way? Could it be that the Step Pyramid was much older than the auxiliary buildings and the boundary wall around it?

Hallowed Ground

It so happened that, a few days earlier, we had come across an article by French Egyptologist Maurice Alliot, who rightly reminded his colleagues that "inscriptions carved on the walls of Egyptian temples often affirm that their sanctuary goes back to very ancient times."[144] Indeed, our previous book *The Egypt Code* investigated several temples that are built over older structures or even use the layouts of older ground plans. Our idea was that, if older ground plans had been used—or, better still, the outline of older foundations—then the astronomical alignment of the new temple would provide the date of the older one, because of the precession shifting of the stars over time. This was ABC for astronomers, but not at all obvious to Egyptologists.

An example of the value of looking with an astronomer's eye is seen at the great sun temple complex of Amun-Ra at Karnak. This temple has a 500-meter axis directed at 27.5° south-of-east. For anyone remotely familiar with basic astronomy, this alignment shouts Winter Solstice sunrise. But even with such a blatantly obvious clue, it took an astronomer and not an Egyptologist to point this out. Upon visiting the Karnak temple in 1894, Norman Lockyer immediately realized that the temple had a solstice sunrise alignment. The Amun-Ra temple dates from the New Kingdom, c. 1450–1200 BC, and the buildings that we see today are principally the collective work of 18th- and 19th-Dynasty monarchs. But there is textual and archaeological evidence showing that it rests on the foundation of a much older temple that goes back to the Middle Kingdom, probably begun by Mentuhotep II of the 11th Dynasty c. 2028 BC.[145]

In fact, it was common practice in ancient times—not just in Egypt, but also elsewhere, to make use of an older sacred site to raise a new temple. We have striking examples of this at Elephantine Island with the temple of Satet, at Edfu with the temple of Horus, at Dendera with the temple of Hathor, and on Thoth Hill with a small temple of Horus, to name but a few.[146] The temple of Satet was fully restored by a German team in the 1980s as a sort of hybrid reconstruction using the ruins of the 18th-Dynasty temple of Thotmoses III (c. 1400 BC) and, to a lesser degree, the ruins of the last Ptolemaic temple. Indeed, the recently restored temple of Satet on Elephantine Island at Aswan, which dates from the Ptolemaic period, rests on six successive temples built one on top of the other like the tiers of an inverted wedding cake over a period of 2,000 years. Thus, it makes compelling sense to re-examine the Step Pyramid to see if it was also built on an older sacred site.

Before examining the astronomical alignments of these successive temples, however, let us briefly explore who the goddess Satet was and why she was given such special attention over nearly three millennia on this same spot.

The temple of Satet on Elephantine Island.

The Source of the Nile Flood

Hardly six kilometers south of Elephantine Island is the last natural change in level of the Nile River in northern Lower Nubia. It is known as the First Cataract of the Nile. From this point on, the river gently flows all the way to the Mediterranean, some 830 kilometers to the north. In ancient times, the whole region of the First Cataract, and especially Elephantine Island, was sacred to the god Khnum, who fashioned humans with his divine potter's wheel. But it was his beautiful daughter (some say young concubine), Satet, who was the real star of this magical place. Satet (Satis in Greek) is depicted as a slender young woman wearing the White Crown of Upper Egypt with horns of the desert antelope.

Satet is generally shown carrying a bow and four arrows that symbolize her vigilance and protection of Egypt's southern border and the Nile cataract. The ancient Egyptians believed that the waters of the annual inundation of the Nile emerged from a cavern near the First Cataract. As the goddess of the Nile flood, Satet was associated with Sirius—or, more specifically, the heliacal rising of this star that occurred at the start of the seasonal flood.

The goddess Satet, from a relief on her temple on
Elephantine Island.

There is much archaeological evidence of human occupation on Elephantine Island since prehistoric times and the Early Dynastic period. Indeed, the oldest shrine—that is, the lowest point under the Satet temple—is dated to the Early Dynastic period, c. 3100 BC. And according to American astronomer Ron Wells, the axis of this Early Dynastic temple has an azimuth of 120.6° (30.6° south-of-east).[147] Wells had a hunch that this might be the same azimuth as the rising of Sirius over the eastern hills. Using old photographs to see what the horizon looked like before modern buildings blocked the view, he established that Sirius was visible in archaic times when it was 11° altitude, which gave it an azimuth of 120.6°, the very same as that of the archaic temple.

Checking Wells's conclusions with StarryNight Pro, we confirmed that the best "fit" between the axis of the archaic temple and the rising of Sirius was around 3100 BC. Spanish astronomer Juan Belmonte (Instituto Astrofísico de Canarias) conducted studies at the Satet temple with Egyptian astronomer Mosalam Shaltout (Minufiya University), and allocated a date of about 3200 BC to the archaic temple underneath.[148] Bearing all this in mind, we felt compelled to look more closely at the Famine Stele, which we briefly mentioned in chapter 2. For it may well be that it reports an actual historical event that occurred during the epoch of Netjerykhet/Djoser and, furthermore, that the archaic temple of Satet on Elephantine Island may also have been a part of these events.

The Famine Stele

The Famine Stele is inscribed on a natural granite boulder on the river bank off Sehel Island. As the name implies, it records a protracted famine caused by the nonappearance of the Nile flood for seven years during the reign of King Netjerykhet/Djoser.

However, most Egyptologists have deduced from the style of writing that the inscription dates from the Ptolemaic period, thus nearly 2,500 years after the reign of Netjerykhet/Djoser. Their conclusion is that the story it tells is apocryphal, probably an invention by the Ptolemaic clergy to give their region the illustrious pedigree of a link with the golden age of Djoser and Imhotep. Others, including us, are not so sure. In fact, when all the clues are considered together, it appears

The Famine Stele, a natural granite boulder on the riverbank off
Sehel Island near Aswan.

that the events are historical, albeit couched in the mythical semantics
of the Ptolemaic era.

At any rate, the gist of the story told in the Famine Stele is that the
annual inundation failed to come for seven years, causing untold calami-
ties in the land of Egypt. It relates how the distraught King Netjerykhet/
Djoser asked Imhotep to investigate the matter and report to him forth-
with. Here are some selected passages from the Famine Stele as translated
by American philologist Miriam Lichtheim:

> I [King Netjerykhet/Djoser] was in mourning on my throne.
> Those of the palace were in grief . . . because Hapy [the Nile]
> had failed to come in time in a period of seven years. Grain was
> scant, Kernels were dried up. . . . Every man robbed his twin.
> . . . Children cried. . . . The hearts of the old were needy. . . .

Temples were shut, Shrines covered with dust, Everyone was in distress. . . . I consulted one of the staff of the Ibis [Thoth], the Chief lector-priest of Imhotep, son of Ptah South-of-the-Wall [Memphis]. . . . He departed, [then] he returned to me quickly, He let me know the flow of Hapy [The Nile].[149]

After Imhotep completed his investigation, he reported thus to the king:

[T]here is a town in the midst of the deep surrounded by Hapy [Nile], Abu [Elephantine] by name. . . . "Twin Caverns" is the water's name; they are the breasts [fountains] that nourish all. It is the house of sleep of Hapy [Nile], he grows young in it in [his time], [it is the place whence] he brings the flood. . . . He holds the door bolt in his hand, Opens the gate as he wishes. . . . His temple opens *southeastward*.

Re rises in its face every day. . . . Learn the names of the gods and goddesses of the temple of Khnum: *Satet*.[150]

Could the mysterious "temple of Hapy (Nile God)" that "opens to the southeast" be one and the same as the archaic temple that also opens to the southeast toward Sirius?

Alignments and Coffin Lids

It is interesting in this context to note that the azimuth of sunrise on the Winter Solstice, six months exactly after the heliacal rising of Sirius, was the same as that of that star in 3100 BC. Is this what Imhotep meant by "his temple opens southeastward, Re (the sun) rises in its face every day"? That is, on the sun's annual journey, moving north and south of due east, it never rises farther south than the axis of this southeast-facing temple, and so rises "in its face every day."

While investigating the Satet temple in 1985, Ron Wells noted that there was another alignment toward the northeast and, more specifically, toward the circumpolar constellation the Big Dipper:

[T]he upright position (of the Big Dipper) would have been depicted by the ancient Egyptians as an oxleg with the hoof downwards. In this position in 1450 BC, the Big Dipper would have been seen through all the portals on the north side of the Satet temple.[151]

The "oxleg" or bull's thigh/foreleg is, of course, the Mesekhtiu constellation of the ancient Egyptians, our modern Big Dipper. It is, as a matter of fact, the only known constellation that the ancient Egyptians accurately drew with all its seven distinctive stars, as can be seen on the lids of wooden coffins dated to the Middle Kingdom (c. 2000 BC) and belonging to the 9th and 10th Dynasties found at Assiut between 1893 and 1903.

Lid of a wooden coffin from Assiut c. 2000 BC.

The astronomer Alexander Pogo, chief librarian of Mount Wilson and the Palomar Observatories, examined these coffin lids in 1932. Pogo, a Russian who immigrated to America, obtained his degree in astronomy at the University of Chicago in 1928 and later joined the teaching staff at Harvard University. In the early 1950s, he worked as a senior astronomer at the Mount Wilson and Palomar Observatories. Dr. Pogo knew his astronomy.

Regarding the coffin lids of Assiut, Pogo easily recognized the Big Dipper/Ursa Major in the scene that is depicted on the underside of the lids. This scene shows the Big Dipper on one half of the upper lid, and Orion and Canis Major (Pogo still accepted *spdt* as being Sirius) on the other side. Pogo also correctly deduced that Sirius was marking the New Year, which is when it rose heliacally and coincided with the start of the flood season.[152] It was clearly desirable for the Egyptians to have this particular celestial imagery depicted over the body of the dead person inside the coffin.

Astronomical ceilings of New Kingdom tombs. Some show the northern sky; others show the eastern sky with Sirius/Canis Major and Orion.

It is interesting that this scene, with more elaboration on the details, is also depicted on the many so-called astronomical ceilings of the New Kingdom tombs of kings and nobles—the oldest example being the astronomical ceiling in the tomb of Senmut, the vizier (some say also lover) of Queen Hatschepsut. In these cases, the ceiling of the sepulcher chamber serves as a "lid." It is obvious that these astronomical scenes freeze, as it were, the moment of rebirth, when the heliacal rising of Sirius took place in the east and the Big Dipper appeared upright in the north.

Mesekhtiu/Big Dipper, also mentioned in the Pyramid Texts (c. 2300 BC), was in all probability known from prehistoric times. Indeed, Belmonte seems to think that it was used to align a Predynastic structure at Hierokonpolis.[153]

Astral Rebirth—Becoming an Akh

In our previous books, *The Egypt Code* and *Black Genesis,* we showed how the ancient Egyptians used the stars of the Mesekhtiu constellation as a "clock" or marker to tell the time of the rising of Sirius—and, more specifically, the heliacal rising of this star, which, in their minds, defined the ideal moment of rebirth for the king.[154] Using StarryNight Pro set for the latitude of Elephantine Island and for the date 3100 BC, the rising of Sirius at altitude 11° (to breach over the eastern hills) would have occurred when Mesekhtiu was in full view over the Nile. By noting and fixing the position of one of its stars, then noting each day when this star reached this position told the time that Sirius would rise. This method would work for one generation or so, but would, after that, need a minor adjustment due to the precession shift of the stars. But what proof is there that this is what the ancient astronomer-priests did during the rebirth rituals for the king?

Dendera

We do know with certainty that the beautiful temple of the goddess Hathor at Dendera is aligned to a star in the Big Dipper at the moment of the heliacal rising of Sirius. As at Elephantine Island, Dendera's great antiquity is attested to by archaeological evidence, even though the temple we see today was built in relatively late times during the reign of Ptolemy XII

Auletes in 54 BC.[155] French astronomer Karine Gadre used astronomical software to investigate this date and concluded this:

> The use of the software allowing us to determine the day of helical rising of any star visible with the naked eye effectively reveals that Sirius made its heliacal rising on July 16, 54 BC, at Dendara. No other Egyptian location fulfills this condition, which proves that the temple of Hathor was founded on the day Sirius made its reappearance at dawn.[156]

It is known, for example, that there once existed here an older temple built by Tuthmoses III c.1450 BC. But a far greater antiquity is claimed by an inscription in one of the crypts of the temple:

> King Tuthmoses (III) has caused this building to be erected in memory of his mother, the goddess Hathor, the Lady of Dendera, the Eye of the Sun, the Heavenly Queen of the Gods. The ground plan was found in the city of Dendera in an archaic drawing on a leather roll of the time of the Shemsu-Hor (Followers of Horus); it was (also) found in the interior of a brick wall in the south side of the temple in the reign of King Pepi.[157]

The Hathor temple has its entrance and axis 18.5° toward the northeast. Attached to the rear of the temple is a small shrine known as the Birth of Isis Temple, whose entrance and axis is also 18.5° toward the northeast. Oddly, however, another axis is directed 18.5° toward the southeast. Until the early 1890s, no Egyptologists had wondered why, let alone considered an astronomical reason for these axial directions.

It was Norman Lockyer who first proposed that the temples of Dendera were aligned toward stars important to the religious beliefs of the Egyptians, and for good reason.[158] In 1891, Lockyer, who was then teaching astronomy in London, developed an interest in ancient history and especially ancient Egypt. It was while consulting the works of French Egyptologist Auguste Mariette that his attention was drawn to a statement Mariette had made regarding the small temple known as the Birth of Isis:

> [The temple Birth of Isis which] is to the south-west of the temple of Hathor has its portal turned to the east, and the sun shines on the portal when it rises to illuminate the world.

The ancient text that had inspired Mariette to write these words was even more revealing: "She (Sothis/Sirius) shines into her temple on New Year's Day, and she mingles her light with that of her Father Ra on the horizon."[159]

In these early days of Egyptology, however, scholars had not yet understood that this reddish glow (birth blood?) in the east that appears an hour or so before sunrise was called *akhet* by the ancient Egyptians, and was regarded as a sort of cosmic "combustion chamber"—or, better still, a rebirth chamber that the dead celestial bodies passed through on their way out of the underworld, taking on new life as they emerged into the light of day. The akhet, according to American Egyptologist James P. Allen, an expert on this issue, is not the horizon *per se*, as many have supposed, but rather a region below it. Allen calls this zone the "*Akh*ifier," as it was there that the dead sun and stars were regenerated and rebirthed as *akhs*—spiritualized beings or light spirits.

To become an *akh*, then, was the ultimate purpose of the elaborate rebirth rituals described in the various funerary texts of the Egyptians. Allen thus correctly concludes that the pyramids or the funerary temples and tombs were, in a real sense, the "hardware" needed to achieve this objective.[160] As Allen puts it:

> Though usually translated "horizon," the Akhet is in fact a region below the visible horizon, rather than a dividing line between night and day: it is the region through which the sun passes in the hour between its emergence from the Duat [underworld] at first light and its appearance in the sky at dawn. . . . As the king's *ba* [soul] proceeds from the sarcophagus chamber to the antechamber [of the pyramid], it emerges from the Duat. . . . The Akhet is more than a zone of passage, however: it is literally the "place of becoming *akh*" where the deceased's ba and the sun together are transformed into a newly effective (*akh*) mode of existence. In the antechamber [of the pyramid] the king "becomes *akh* in the Akhet". . . . This process of transformation is reflected in the generic term often applied to spells such as those in the Pyramid Texts: *s3hw*, literally "*akh*ifiers". . . . The New Kingdom "Book of Night" describes the sun rising "from the mouth of the Akhet door" into the day-sky at the first hour of daylight:

"In possession of your akh; emerge from the Akhet

Emergent in this day in the proper form of a living akh."[161]

In his article *Reading a Pyramid,* from which we have just quoted, Allen does not mention the stars at all. This is most bizarre, because the Pyramid Texts make it abundantly clear that the *ba* (soul) of the departed king is a star that is reborn in the east at dawn after a protracted period of invisibility—seventy days in the Duat (i.e., the starry underworld). This period of invisibility of the ba-star in the Duat is given as seventy days in the Carlsberg I papyrus, the content of which dates from c. 1300–1100 BC.[162] In the so-called Dramatic Texts that are from the cenotaph of Seti I at Abydos, the stellar rebirth of the ba is made explicit, at least to the trained eye of an astronomer:

> The *bas* (souls) go forth and they travel in the sky at night.... The rising of stars: . . . when the *ba* is seen by the living, it is indeed a star . . . the people do not see it by day; one sees that this is how the *ba* lives there. You see it shining forth in the sky [at night].[163]

In the Pyramid Texts of Unas (c. 2300 BC), it is also clear which stars are being specially observed when they are being reborn at dawn in the Akhet:

> Orion (Sah) is enveloped in the dawn-light, when the Living One bathes in the Akhet. Canis Major (Spdt) is enveloped in the dawn-light, when the Living One bathes in the Akhet. This King Unas is enveloped in the dawn-light, when the Living One bathes in the Akhet.[164]

Any astronomer, even an amateur, quickly realizes that the rebirth cycle described in the ancient texts is actually observable, because the non-circumpolar stars—like, for example, those of Orion, Leo, and Canis Major (containing Sirius)—do in fact disappear into the western horizon (into the underworld). Visually, the star "disappears" because the sky is too bright with daylight; it cannot be seen the whole time it is passing above the horizon. After seventy days or so, it emerges again in the east just before sunrise (in the Akhet). It is evident that, at dawn, after enduring seventy days in the tenebrous Duat-underworld, the star's light mingles with the red glow of the dawn-light (the light of the not yet risen sun) and is now deemed to be in the Akhet, where it undergoes the transformation or rebirth into an akh and emerges into the day sky—i.e., the world of the living.

Looking again at the text that Lockyer fell upon back in 1890 in Mariette's publications, it is now easy to understand how, as an astronomer, he immediately realized that the text was describing the heliacal rising of Sirius, when that star rises for the first time at dawn and mingles its light with the dawn light an hour or so before the sun breaks over the horizon.

From maps provided in Mariette's publication, Lockyer ascertained that the axis of the small temple at Dendera was directed 18° 30' south-of-east (azimuth 108° 30', which we verified with GPS). Lockyer's hunch proved correct: This was the very place where Sirius would have risen when the small temple was built. In Lockyer's own words: "The temple of Isis at Denderah was built to watch it (Sirius)."

There were other inscriptions at Dendera, however, relating to the Stretching of the Cord ceremony that confirmed that the axis of the larger Hathor temple was aligned toward something called *āk* in the Big Dipper:

> The living god (the king) . . . stretches the cord with joy. With his glance toward the *āk* of the bull's thigh (Big Dipper) constellation, he establishes the temple-house of the mistress of Dendera (Hathor), as took place there before.

> Looking to the sky at the course of the rising stars (and) recognizing the *āk* of the bull's thigh constellation (Big Dipper), (the king) establishes the corners of the temple of Her Majesty (Hathor).[165]

Lockyer wondered what the mysterious *āk* was, and had a hunch that it might be one of the seven stars in the Big Dipper:

> The inscriptions state that the king while stretching the cord has his glance directed to the *āk* of the constellation of the thigh [Big Dipper]. . . . Here, then, we have more evidence of the stretching of the cord towards a star. . . . But it may suggest that the word *āk*, used in relation to the king's observation, most probably refers to the brightest star, Dubhe (Alpha Ursa Major) in the asterism, or the "middle point" of the constellation.[166]

Much later, in 1981, Krupp, then director of the Griffith Observatory in Los Angeles, did not quite agree with Lockyer that the mysterious āk was a star, but rather felt differently:

> [T]he texts mention the āk in the Big Dipper, but we don't know what the āk means. Most likely it refers to a particular position and orientation of the Big Dipper in its circular course around the Pole.[167]

In 2004, Belmonte, in collaboration with Egyptian astronomer Mossalam Shaltout, was commissioned by the Supreme Council of Egyptian Antiquities (SCA) to establish the astronomical alignments of temples in Upper Egypt. Regarding the Dendera temple, they concluded:

> [T]he inscriptions in the Hathor temple are crystal clear and, according to them, the astronomical target observed to lay down its main axis, and thus presumably the plan of the whole complex . . . was the constellation of the bull's foreleg, *Mesekhtiu*, today the Plough [Big Dipper]. In the text accompanying one of the stretching of the cord ceremony scenes, we can read: "The king stretches the rope in joy. With his glance towards the Ax [āk] of *msxt* [Mesekhtiu], he establishes the temple of the Lady of Dendera, as took place there before." Here the texts mention the *Ax* of the Plough [Big Dipper]. The term *Ax*, plural *Akhu* (*Axw*) is mentioned since the Pyramid Texts and has been translated as "Spirit," "Brilliant," or "Blessed." Hence we might translate it as "the brilliant (star) of the Plough [Big Dipper]." However, bearing in mind that the seven stars are most of the same brightness (only Megrez, Uma, is slightly fainter), Krupp has suggested that *Ax* [āk] "most likely refers to a particular position and orientation of the Big Dipper in its circular course around the Pole."

Belmonte and Shaltout, however, were not convinced by Krupp's conclusions. Like Lockyer, they were of the opinion that the āk was a star in the Big Dipper:

> However, our current hypothesis would be a different version of the same idea. In 54 BC, at an azimuth 18°, Alkaid (in Ursa Major), the conspicuous star at the end of the handle of the Plough

The star we call Alkaid was catalogued by Egyptian astronomer Claudius Ptolemy, writing in Greek c. 150 CE, as #35 of 1022 stars. He described it as "the third, on the end of the tail" in the constellation Ursa Major. Ptolemy's star catalogue, *The Almagest*, is the earliest comprehensive stellar directory known to be continuously in use until today. It gave us many of the constellation names we still use, including Ursa Major. Persian astronomer 'Abd al-Raḥmān al-Ṣūfī (903–986 CE) succeeded Ptolemy with the next major comprehensive and updated star catalogue, *The Book of Fixed Stars*. Al Sufi used The Almagest as his basis and combined Greek, Arabic, and Bedouin star lore—all of which drew from much earlier traditions, likely including Ancient Egypt—to give many of the Arabic individual star names we use today, including Alkaid. In Arabic it is Al qā'id, which means "the leader," and is specifically from the phrase (qā'id bināt na'sh), "the leader of the daughters of the bier." The daughters of the bier are the handle stars of the Big Dipper, and the bier (stand or frame for a corpse or coffin) is the bowl stars of the Big Dipper. (Note that, although this word sounds similar to the name of the international terrorist group Al Qaeda, happily in Arabic that is an entirely different unrelated word that means "the base.")

If in Old Kingdom Egyptian times Alkaid was thought of as "the leader" of the constellation of the Bull's Thigh, and Alkaid was the āk referred to in the inscription at Dendera, then what puzzled the Egyptologists makes clear sense as "the leader of the constellation of the Thigh"—that is, the hoof. And even Al Sufi's identification of the Bull's Thigh constellation as "the bier" resonates with the ancient Egyptian notion of it being the place where the soul from the king's corpse metamorphoses into an eternal being.

The possibility of such a carryover of bits of star lore from earliest Egyptian times should not be dismissed. While it is clear that modern European scholars had no clue how to decipher Egyptian hieroglyphics until Champollion translated the Rosetta Stone c. 1822, some Islamic (or Sufi) scholars of esoteric traditions may well have maintained some knowledge of the meaning of ancient hieroglyphs into modern times.[168]

[Big Dipper], was first visible when rising at an angular height of about 2°. This star was perhaps already pinpointed in the ceiling of the tomb of Senmut (where) the constellation of Mesekhtyu is represented in such a way that the last star of what might be the handle of the Plough [Big Dipper] is signaled with a red symbol. This perhaps indicates that Alkaid played a differential role within the star of this important circumpolar constellation. Consequently, we must agree with the Egyptians that the temple was orientated towards a conspicuous star of Meskhetiu (Big Dipper).[169]

We wholeheartedly agree with Belmonte and Shaltout regarding the importance of the star Alkaid. The word āk, however, does not mean *akh* (brilliant spirit) in this context, as mistakenly assumed by Belmonte. It is not written with the crested Ibis, which denotes the akh spirit, but rather with different symbols.[170] Moreover, we agree with him about the role it played in the alignment of the temple at Dendera—but, as we shall see in chapter 4, for quite a different reasons.

Meanwhile, we need to discuss the alignment of another important temple in Upper Egypt that had a direct connection with Dendera, even though it was located 135 kilometers farther south. This is the great temple of Horus at Edfu. Each year, in September, an effigy of Hathor was taken by boat from Dendera to Edfu, to be placed for fourteen days in the *naos*, the Holy of Holies, inside the temple of Horus. This was the so-called union (marriage) of the two deities, symbolic of the king and his queen.

Edfu

There is a relief at the temple of Horus at Edfu depicting the Stretching of the Cord that is accompanied by an inscription that has the king stating:

> I have grasped the rod and the mallet; I hold the rope with Seshat, my glance follows the course of the stars; my eye is on the Big Dipper. . . . I establish the corners of the temple . . .

> I have grasped the rod and the mallet; I hold the rope with Seshat; I direct my face toward the course of the rising stars; I let my glance enter the constellation of the Big Dipper. . . . I establish the four corners of the temple.

But here's the problem: Of all the temples along the Nile that have known astronomical alignments, the only one that has a north-south alignment is the temple of Horus at Edfu. To be more specific, the axis of the temple is at azimuth 1° 58', making the temple axis nearly parallel to its longitudinal position. Now, if the meridian had been the target, then either the ancient astronomer made an uncharacteristic error or, as we are inclined to think, he *intentionally* aligned the temple 1° 58' to something in the Big Dipper. But what could that something have been?

The Edfu temple as we see it today dates from the Ptolemaic era. It was started c. 237 BC by Ptolemy III and was completed in 142 BC by Ptolemy VIII. The alignment of the axis is azimuth 1° 58' (measured by Google Earth). Using StarryNight Pro to reconstruct the sky at that date, and taking the location of Edfu at 24° 58' N; 32° 52' E, we can see that none of the seven stars of the Big Dipper would rise anywhere near azimuth 1° 58'. At that time, six of the seven stars of the Big Dipper were circumpolar—i.e., they never rose or set—the exception being Alkaid, the "handle" star (or "hoof" star of the bull's leg). But Alkaid rose at nearly azimuth 16° 30', which is about 14° to the east of the temple's axis. Something was not quite right. Had the ancient scribes and artists who carved the inscriptions and the scene of the Stretching of the Cord made a mistake? Or did the ancient astronomer-priest come up with an alignment that was way off target? Or, more likely, did modern Egyptologists interpret the inscription wrongly?

Let's look at the inscription more closely. The king clearly states that his glance "follows the course of the stars" and that his "eye is on the Big Dipper." He also states that he directed his "face toward the course of the rising stars" and that he also lets his "glance enter the constellation of the Big Dipper." The impression that we get is that the king is watching the rising of stars in one direction, but also keeping his glance toward the Big Dipper in the north. Also, it is more practical for the ceremony to involve the sighting of a star already up in the sky and visible, simultaneous with the rising of another star not yet visible. We show later in this chapter how this is precisely what the astronomer-priests did three millennia earlier when the Saqqara complex was aligned.

Assuming that this hypothesis is correct, which star rising was the king observing while at the same time glancing at the Big Dipper? Sirius is, of course, the most likely candidate. In 237 BC, Sirius rose at azimuth 108°

30' as seen from Edfu; but then turning north, there are no stars of the Big Dipper that have an azimuth of 1° 58'. Alioth is a little more than 2° to the east. And as we have seen, the stars of the Bull's Thigh/Big Dipper that are of primary ritual importance are Dubhe on the top of the thigh and Alkaid, the hoof. So this date does not work. Was there another date, therefore, when it would work?

The temple of Edfu has long been known to be standing on hallowed ground that was used for ritual in a much earlier epoch. Indeed, it was quite common for the Ptolemaic kings, who were very keen to show the Egyptians that they had adopted their old religion, to lavishly restore or rebuild temples, or to use sacred sites that dated from much earlier epochs. Note that the Ptolemaic astronomer-priests claimed that they had performed the Stretching of the Cord "as took place there before." Could it not perhaps mean, to quote the very perceptive astronomer Norman Lockyer, that these Ptolemaic astronomers "carried forward the account of an older foundation"?[171] Such a practice was quite common in ancient Egypt, and Egyptologists have long been aware of it.[172]

More recently, in 2004, commenting on the Ptolemaic architecture of the Edfu temple, Italian Egyptologist Corinna Rossi observed:

> In the Ptolemaic Period many temples were rebuilt above pre-existing temples, but it is not easy to reconstruct the appearance of these earlier sanctuaries. At Edfu, for instance, in order to make room for the larger Ptolemaic temple, the New Kingdom stone temple was completely demolished apart from one of its pylons which was retained as a secondary entrance to the first courtyard. All we know is that the New Kingdom temple was laid at 90° to the Ptolemaic temple . . . and that it was probably surrounded by an enclosure wall.[173]

The practice of using older sacred grounds was indeed common from earliest times, as we noted earlier and will see later in this chapter. Archaeological investigation in the 1900s showed that there is an ancient portal at Edfu facing east that was part of a temple built by Ramses III c. 1200 BC, nearly 1,000 years before the Ptolemaic intervention. But in more recent years, the Oriental Institute of the University of Chicago has excavated in the vicinity of the Edfu temple and found foundation walls immediately west of the Ptolemaic temple that date to the 4th

Dynasty, c. 2500 BC. According to Nadine Moeller, director of the Tell Edfu Project of the Oriental Institute, on the west side of the enclosure wall of the Ptolemaic temple they discovered during the 2008 season, there was "a large wall of the enclosure wall of the Old Kingdom running north-south . . . [which] surrounded the Old Kingdom town during the 5th and 6th Dynasties."

In the 2010 season, another wall was found dated from the 4th to the 6th Dynasty. According to Moeller:

> Pottery samples we have found so far in this area date back to the 4th to 6th Dynasties but it is very likely that we will discover remains that date even further back than that. The presence of a Third Dynasty step pyramid in the vicinity and the relief in the Djoser complex mentioning the shrine of Edfu, provide some indication that the town of Edfu already existed back then . . . a large concentration of sherds dating to the Third to Early Fouth Dynasty was found along the northern and eastern side.[174]

A small step pyramid was discovered some five kilometers southwest of Edfu at the village of el-Gnonameya. It has been dated to the reign of Huni, last king of the 3rd Dynasty. The step pyramid in its current ruined state has sides of eighteen meters, and is about five meters high. It is thought to be marking the site of a royal cult active in the region.

In view of all this evidence, we set StarryNight Pro to the date of the 4th Dynasty (c. 2500 BC) to view the northern sky at the moment of the heliacal rising of Sirius. This event took place in 2500 BC on July 11 Julian at azimuth 113° 36'. Looking north at that exact moment, we could see that the star Alkaid, the "hoof" star of the bull's leg (or thigh), was at azimuth 1° 55' in almost perfect alignment with the axis of the Edfu temple. Surely coincidence had to be ruled out.

We now had determined, accepting the interpretation by Belmonte and Shaltout that the Hathor temple at Dendera was aligned to the rising of Alkaid in 54 BC, that the twin temples of Dendera and Edfu each have their main axis aligned to the same star, Alkaid, but 2,450 years apart. There is, however, a flaw in this interpretation, for, although it is true that Alkaid would have been seen rising almost in alignment with the axis of the temple at Dendera in 54 BC, the same star could not have been seen at the time of the heliacal rising of Sirius, because it would have risen almost four hours *after* sunrise, in broad daylight. And all the ancient ritual texts say that the star in the Bull's Thigh was sighted simultaneously with the rising of Sirius.

So we need to consider an older date for the alignment at Dendera, when Alkaid was seen at the moment of the heliacal rising of Sirius.

Dendera Revisted

As noted, Lockyer deduced that the axis of the Hathor temple at Dendera is directed at azimuth 18° 30'. And it is clear that the inscriptions in the Hathor temple say that the king was gazing at the āk of the Big Dipper, and the āk is the star Alkaid. So, let us look back in time to find when Alkaid would have been at azimuth 18° 30' and visible at the time of Sirius's heliacal rising.

If we go to 54 BC and the latitude of the location (26° 08' N; 32° 40' E), we can "see" with StarryNight Pro what the astronomer-priest at Dendera saw on the day of the heliacal rising of Sirius, which we know occurred on July 16 Julian. At the precise moment when Sirius was seen, however, about 1° over the horizon, Alkaid had not even risen yet and was still about 4° west-of-north. So could the alignment of the Dendera temple have been made at an earlier epoch when there was a star of the Big Dipper, possibly Alkaid as at Edfu, in alignment with the axis at the moment of the heliacal rising of Sirius?

There is much archaeological evidence that the Dendera site had been used since at least the Old Kingdom.[175] There are also inscriptions inside the Ptolemaic temple that refer to "earlier plans" of the temple:

> One inscription states that the great ground plan (*senti*) of Ant (Dendera) was found in old writing on parchments of the time of the *Followers of Horus*, preserved in the reign of King Pepi [Old Kingdom, 6th Dynasty].[176]

The inscriptions further attest that "the ground plan . . . was found in the interior of a brick wall in the south side of the temple during the reign of King Pepi."[177] Commenting on these ancient records, the eminent German Egyptologist Heinrich Brugsch wrote:

> In spite of the brevity of these words it appears to be certain that first Pepi, and after him Tehuti-mes [Thotmoses III], undertook

to re-build the ancient temple of the goddess. In the time of the Ptolemies it had again fallen into decay, and those princes re-built it from the very foundations.[178]

Egyptologists, however, tend to discount these texts as some kind of pharaonic fiction writing by the Ptolemaic priests. But Lockyer, like Brugsch, felt otherwise, for he wrote: "I, for one, believe in these old records more and more." We feel the same way—not because of the inscriptions *per se*, but because the astronomical evidence corroborates the statement that the alignment or ground plan was made in the "time of the Followers of Horus."

To the ancient Egyptians, the Followers of Horus were historical ancestors who had been present at the origins of their civilization. Most modern Egyptologists, on the other hand, regard them as mythical ancestors. However, there has been a tendency in recent years for less-blinkered researchers to be open to the idea that the Followers of Horus were actual historical ancestors in some Predynastic epoch. Bearing this in mind, there is another inscription at Dendera that implies a simultaneous sighting toward the heliacal rising of Sirius in the southeast and the Big Dipper in the north that occurred in a remote epoch:

> The great goddess Seshat brings the writings that relate to your [Sirius] rising . . . and to the rising of Ra [dawn]. . . . The king joyously stretches the cord, having cast his gaze toward the Big Dipper and thus establishes the temple as *took place there before.*[179]

We decided to use StarryNight Pro to check the heliacal rising for Dendera for various epochs to see if and when Alkaid, the prominent star of the Big Dipper, would match the azimuth 18° 30' of the axis of the Hathor temple. But going back even to the 1st Dynasty at c. 3100 BC, Alkaid was not close to that azimuth when the heliacal rising of Sirius took place. Here was one of those moments in such investigations when a leap of faith was required. So, bypassing the opinion of Egyptologists that the Followers of Horus were mythical ancestors, we pushed our date to earlier epochs: 4000 BC; 5000 BC; 6000 BC. To our astonishment, the star Alkaid got closer and closer to this specific azimuth—and hit the 18° 30' azimuth around 6100 to 6000 BC! At this time, Alkaid was at an altitude of about 26°, which is also the latitude of Dendera. This meant that it was at its longest eastern elongation/amplitude; in layman's terms, it was at the same altitude as the celestial pole.

It was hard to assume that this could be due to coincidence. Ironically, back in 1894, Lockyer had actually suspected that the mysterious āk star in the Big Dipper (which we believe to be Alkaid) might have been at the maximum eastern elongation:

> We may consider another interpretation of the word *āk*. The amplitude of the temple . . . shows conclusively that we cannot be dealing with the meridian, but may we be dealing with the most *eastern elongation* of the star in its journey around the pole?[180]

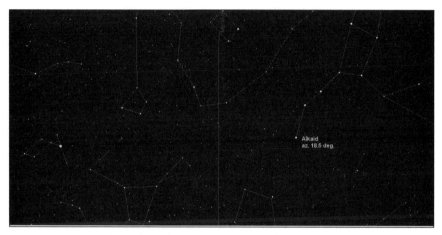

The northern sky in 6100 BC as seen from Dendera.

Yet so convinced was he that the alignments of temples were taken to the rising locations of stars that he brushed aside the idea. Recently, however, a clue that this idea may after all be correct was hinted at by Egyptologist Richard H. Wilkinson.

Upon carefully examining the Senmut diagrams, Wilkinson came to the conclusion that the ancient astronomer-priest may have observed Alkaid when it was in line with the tip of a tall rod with a pointed end, thus when the star was high up in the northern sky. This astronomical ceiling, as we noted earlier, is considered to be the oldest sky map in the world, dating to c. 1450 BC. This would make it contemporary with the pharaoh Thotmoses III, who had made use of an older ground plan from the "time of the Followers of Horus" for the temple of Hathor at Dendera. In the Senmut scene, the tip of the tall rod clearly marks the position of Alkaid, which was marked by a dot by the ancient artist—surely to indicate this star's special importance.

The Senmut scene from the Hathor temple at Dendera. The ceiling shows the northern sky. Note the dot that represents the "star" Alkaid.

The idea that Alkaid of the Mesekhtiu/Bull's Thigh constellation was of importance to the ancient Egyptians was, in fact, first put forth in 1902 by French astronomer A. Romieu, who also pointed out that "the lower culmination of the star η of the Big Bear, i.e. Alkaid (η Ursa Major), coincided with the rising of Sirius at Thebes (Luxor) in 1800 BC."[181] In 1953, Zaba also noted the long rod in the Senmut scene, "the tip of which coincides with the last star of Mesekhtiu highlighted by a small red disc inside a circle."[182] Belmonte, like Lockyer before him, was fixated on finding a star *rising at the horizon*, and thus misunderstood the way that the Stretching of the Cord was executed by the ancient astronomers. From the Senmut scene, as well as from many other examples in tombs

The main Hathor temple is, of course, famous for having housed the so-called round zodiac of Dendera (as well as a lesser-known rectangular zodiac that is on the ceiling of the first hypostyle hall). The round zodiac is not so much a zodiac as it is a planisphere or sky map that shows the whole celestial landscape with the north celestial pole near its center. The actual zodiac, which was fixed on the ceiling of a chapel on the upper floor of the temple, is made up of the twelve familiar Babylonian-Greek astrological signs scattered in a rough loop around the celestial pole. In a larger loop, the thirty-six decans of ancient Egypt that were used for time-keeping and rebirth rites (since they contain Orion and Sirius) are strewn.

The decans were known from at least the Pyramid Age, which suggests, if not proves, that the Dendera planisphere has incorporated in it elements of great antiquity. Here Orion-Osiris is represented by a striding man wearing the royal crown, while Sirius-Isis is shown as a recumbent cow with a five-pointed star above her horns. Behind the Isis-Sirius cow is the figure of a woman holding a bow and arrow, almost certainly Satis of Elephantine. Very near the center of the zodiac is the familiar bull's thigh that represents the Big Dipper. Dendera may indeed have been a center for astronomical observations that harked back thousands of years, perhaps even to the time of the legendary Shemsu-Hor, those Followers of Horus who tracked Sirius across the ages.

with astronomical ceilings, it is evident that the Big Dipper was sighted when the constellation was high up in the sky and "upright." If Alkaid was sighted when it was 26° above the horizon, this would explain the long rod in the Senmut scene of the northern sky.

So here again we have astronomy confirming the veracity of an inscription claiming a remote origin for a temple—in this case, at "the time of the Followers of Horus," which works out to be c. 6100 BC. But what archaeological evidence was there at Dendera—or, for that matter, anywhere else in Egypt—that indicates that the Followers of Horus might indeed have left an astronomical legacy dating as far back as 6100 BC? We return to this intriguing question in the next chapter.

Remote Ancestors

Meanwhile, it would seem appropriate, in view of our findings so far, not to ignore the possibility that the Step Pyramid Complex is sited over a temple built by remote ancestors. Indeed, there are many indications that this may be the case.

Take, for example, the so-called Western Massif that runs along the west side of the Step Pyramid Complex. Some Egyptologists have begun to suspect that it, and the strange subterranean galleries within it, may long predate Netjerykhet, possibly to the Early Dynastic period or perhaps even earlier. There is also the area known as the North Court, which has subterranean storerooms that may be from a far older epoch as well. But we don't want to get ahead of ourselves by moving too fast. So let us hold these thoughts for now, and return to the Famine Stele for a closer look.

Thanking Satet

At the top of the Famine Stele, there is a scene showing a king wearing the double crown of Lower and Upper Egypt. He is paying homage and giving thanks to three divinities, one of which, not surprisingly, is Satet, goddess of the Nile flood. The other two deities are Khnum and Anuket who, with Satet, formed the triad of Elephantine Island. Anuket, also identified with the Nile flood, was either the daughter of Satet and Khnum, or the latter's concubine. The depiction clearly indicates that this king

King Netjerykhet/Djoser receiving homage from Khnum, Satet, and Anukhet, as shown on the Famine Stele.

was particularly grateful to this goddess and her kin for having brought forth a "good flood" and thus saved Egypt from the devastation, blight, and famine caused by the previous seven years of drought.

The cartouche name and Horus name over the king confirm that he is Netjerykhet/Djoser. Thus this scene, which presumably takes place in a temple dedicated to either Satet or her kin (the gods Khnum and Anukhet)—whether real or invented—was set in the time of the 3rd Dynasty, c. 2650 BC. On the island of Elephantine, literally a stone's throw from the Famine Stele, are very ancient temples dedicated to these divinities. So, could there be truth in the story narrated in the stele? Let's examine some evidence.

First, let's look at the lowest temple under the existing Temple of Satet on Elephantine Island. Although this mysterious shrine is labeled as Early Dynastic or Archaic by Egyptologists, its construction is surprisingly crude compared with the standard seen elsewhere, even for this remote epoch. At any rate, this temple or shrine makes use of two natural rock outcroppings that form a U-shaped niche, which, apparently by the 3rd Dynasty, was expanded outward using mud bricks. Today, it is some seven meters below the level of the floor of the existing 18th-Dynasty temple. There are no markings on the rocks or elsewhere at that bottom level, although many votive objects were found there that are now displayed in the small museum on Elephantine Island. Interestingly, some of the pottery fragments found there also dated to the Predynastic era. Moreover, archaeological evidence has shown that this archaic shrine was used for rituals well into the Old Kingdom and, therefore, was still active at the time of Imhotep.

Immediately to the east of the Satet temple is the Nilometer by which the level of the rising flood waters was measured in late June. This structure consists of steps descending to the river's waterline, with graduations on the side of the walls for measuring the level of the river. A "good flood" had to be around seven meters above the normal level of the river. A flood that was much below or much above this optimum level would result in either famine or destructive flooding for riverside dwellers. The deities who watched over the First Cataract and the source of the Nile's flood were, understandably, regarded as crucially important to the welfare, even to the very survival, of Egypt.

A Water Purification Ritual

The goddess Satet was especially associated with the mystical islands of Elephantine and Sehel, which were believed to harbor the deep caverns from which the flood emerged. According to another belief, it was the "tears of Isis" that brought the flood, and some of this life-giving, rejuvenating, and almost divine elixir was collected in jars by Satet. From earliest times, as attested in the Pyramid Texts, jars or pots were filled with this precious water in order to purify and refresh the bodies of kings prior to their entrance through the gates of heaven and their journey into the Afterworld. Wilkinson comments on the antiquity of this ritual and Satet:

> Her [Satet's] links with the upper reaches of the Nile perhaps caused her to be associated with the annual inundation and with Elephantine in the area of Aswan which Egyptian mythology sometimes identified as the source of the Nile. Her name is first attested in stone jars found beneath the Step Pyramid at Saqqara (3rd Dynasty), and by the 6th Dynasty she is mentioned in the Pyramid Texts as purifying the deceased king with four jars of water from Elephantine.[183]

When all these compelling clues are put together—Satet's connection with the Nile flood, her temple on Elephantine Island aligned to the star Sirius, the first mention of this goddess on a stone jar found underneath the Step Pyramid at Saqqara, Sirius being the star of Horus, and the Step Pyramid Complex being named Horus Is the Star at the Head of the Sky—it is tempting to conclude that the story reported on the Famine Stele is, after all, true.

Who or What Controls the Flood?

The ultimate purpose of the king's role as the guardian and controller of *Maat*, the cosmic order, was to ensure that the proper rituals, sacrifices, and other religious activities were done in order to please or appease the celestial powers and thus assure a good flood each year. Nothing preoccupied the monarchy, the priesthood, and the population at large more than the coming of a yearly "good flood" to ensure the regeneration of crops and fauna, bringing a comfortable year for all.

The actual hydraulics that cause the yearly inundation of the Nile of course were, and still are, the torrential monsoon rainfalls in early summer in the highlands of Ethiopia and the low plains of the Sudd in central Africa. These yearly monsoons gorge the great lakes of Tana in Ethiopia, and Albert Nyanza and Victoria in Uganda, and cause them to overflow, spilling billions of cubic meters of excess water into the tributaries of the Blue and White Niles. But this source and the cause of the yearly inundation were not known to Europeans until the mid-19th century, let alone to the ancient Egyptians. Not only were they totally mystified about the origins of the river, they were totally confounded by the bigger mystery of why the yearly inundation came in summer when you'd expect the level of the river to ebb, not rise! As we noted in chapter 1, the ancient Egyptians connected their observations of the sky's yearly cycle with the cycle of the Nile, and they saw in the heliacal rising of Sirius the herald, perhaps even the cause, of the yearly inundation. The rejuvenating waters of the flood, and their highly refreshing quality, were used for important rituals and libations. As Nathalie Beaux explains:

> [The Pyramid Texts] allude to the heliacal rising of Sirius, herald of the inundation of the Nile and promise of an abundant harvest. After seventy days of invisibility, the star appears in the bosom of the constellation of Canis Major, as if carried, given "birth" bathed in the first light of dawn which tints the sky red, the color of wine. The dawn and its celestial harvest give birth on this day to the sunrise and the star that announces the earthly harvest. . . . When the stars reappear briefly for the first time, the day of their heliacal rising, before becoming invisible in the solar glare, they seem to scintillate in these luminous waters, as if they came out washed, purified, and even more bright. The water in the Duat can "envelop" a star and make it disappear, but it can also "give it birth". . . . From the Pyramid Texts: "O (king) Merenre, may the sky become pregnant with you and Orion, may the dawn give you birth like Orion."[184]

The belief that these special waters came from within the bowels of the earth, as witnessed also in the eastern horizon in the Akhet, may explain Satet's "four jars," specified in the Pyramid Texts, which she brought from Elephantine to refresh the corpse of the dead king. The passage in the

Pyramid Texts clearly proclaims that "Satet washes him [the king] with the water which is in her four jars in Elephantine (Island)."[185]

In 1926, when Lauer and Quibell explored the subterranean galleries of the Step Pyramid Complex at Saqqara, they discovered thousands of vases or jars—many with the names of 1st- and 2nd-Dynasty kings, but none, oddly enough, with the name of Netjerykhet/Djoser.[186] There was even one jar that had the name of Satet on it—apparently the very first time that her name is found in Egyptian texts. Some of the jars are believed to have contained beer and food offerings. But were these jars perhaps brought down from Elephantine filled with the sacred water of the inundation? And were they placed in the subterranean parts of the Step Pyramid Complex to mimic or symbolize their underworld source? And if so, by whom? And when?

The evidence suggests that they may indeed have been brought to Saqqara in Early Dynastic times, probably originally placed in the royal mastabas that are north of the Step Pyramid Complex.

Lauer and other Egyptologists (Michel Baud, for one) seem to think that these jars were originally placed in these Early Dynastic mastabas, but then later moved to the subterranean galleries of the Step Pyramid by the priests of Netjerykhet. This conclusion was arrived at by Lauer because he had found some cloth sacks, apparently to transport the jars, sealed with the names of Netjerykhet and Kheseskhemy.[187] Baud, however, claims that only one of the seals was of Netjerykhet.[188] Could these sacks, then, be a later addition to the haul of jars? Egyptologist Ilona Regulski, who wrote her thesis on these vases and jars, does not think so:

> [T]he archaeological context of the subterranean galleries, which also contained seal impressions of Netjerykhet, indicates that this king was indeed responsible for the deposition of the vessels.[189]

We are not so convinced about this. We remain open to the possibility that the subterranean galleries of the Step Pyramid may indeed be of the Early Dynastic period. In any case, why would Netjerykhet want to take the vases and jars belonging to his predecessors only to place them underneath his own funerary complex? Would that not be seen as a terrible sacrilege on his part? On the other hand, if he knew that there were subterranean galleries from the Early Dynastic period, and if he also suspected that the jars from the Early Dynastic royal mastabas would be safer in these subterranean galleries, then the presence of Early Dynastic royal names on the jars as well as the seal inscriptions of Netjerykhet on the sacks makes more sense.

We strongly suspect that Imhotep developed his architectural masterpiece on older hallowed ground that already contained the mastaba as well as the galleries directly underneath it.

Let us see why this may indeed be the case.

Right Man, Right Place, Right Time

First, we can examine the archaeological evidence. We saw in chapter 2 how the Saqqara site had been used as early as the 1st Dynasty (c. 3100 BC)—that is, at least four centuries before Imhotep. The evidence, of course, is the many Early Dynastic mastabas that are found at Saqqara. Many of these mastabas belonged to nobles and a few others to kings of the 1st Dynasty.[190] Furthermore, according to the eminent Egyptologist Alexander Badawy: "Students of Egyptian religion are agreed that the conception of the stellar destiny preceded that of the Osirian destiny, itself earlier than the idea of the solar destiny."[191] Indeed, in one of his landmark articles published in the *Journal of Near Eastern Studies* (JNES), Badawy discussed "the ideology of the superstructure of the mastaba–tomb in Egypt," and demonstrated that the mastaabas were orientated by sighting to circumpolar stars in the north.[192]

We encountered the work of this eminent Egyptian scholar back in the early 1990s, when we investigated the stellar religion in the Pyramid Texts and, especially, the stellar alignments of the shafts inside the Great Pyramid. It was back in 1963 that Badawy, then a professor of Art Design and Art History at UCLA specializing in ancient Egyptian architecture, collaborated with the young astronomer Virginia Trimble and published with her a new finding on the symbolic meaning or function of the shafts in the Great Pyramid. Badawy and Trimble showed that they were aligned to stars crucially important to the rebirth rituals for the ancient pyramid kings, with particular reference to Orion's belt and the circumpolar stars.[193]

In his discussions on Early Dynastic mastabas, Badawy showed how the axis of this type of funerary monument, which was directed toward the north, was almost certainly meant to "ascend" toward the circumpolar

Alexander Badawy (1913–1986) had the ideal combination of training to understand ancient Egyptian religious monuments. He received three degrees from the University of Cairo—in engineering, architecture, and archaeology—as well as a Ph.D. He has held professorships at the Universities of Cairo and Alexandria, as well as at the School of Engineering and Architecture at the University of Kansas and at UCLA. It was there that he befriended Virginia Trimble, who inspired him to look into the astronomical alignments of ancient Egyptian temples, mastabas, and pyramids.

Trimble, who became vice president of the International Astronomical Union, spoke very highly and affectionately of Badawy and their collaboration at UCLA. In the mid-1960s, Badawy had devoted much time to studying the layout plans and wall decorations of the many tombs at Saqqara and Giza. These studies were published in three volumes titled *History of Egyptian Architecture*. Edwards paid great homage to Badawy, recognizing that "he had a deep understanding of the mentality of the ancient Egyptians and of the conventions which they observed. His articles on the so-called air shafts of the Great Pyramid paved the way to the final elucidation of these features—so long a puzzle to students."[194]

region of the sky where the imperishable stars were found. Badawy also showed that the sign for the words "to ascend" and "to cause to ascend" (to the sky) in the Pyramid Texts formed the outline of a stepped mastaba. He concluded:

> The aim of this ascension was to reach the circumpolar stars, which the deceased should lead, or be in their forefront and command. This was the royal destiny as pictured in the stellar religion . . . it seems that the original ascension . . . served as a model to that of the king by means of the mastaba.[195]

The idea that the axes of mastabas were set deliberately north–south had been advanced earlier, in 1887, by Gaston Maspero, who wrote: "It was intended that the mastabas should be correctly orientated, the four sides to the four cardinal points, and the greater axis stretching from north and south."[196]

Mastaba of the Early Dynastic period north of the Saqqara complex.

The Saqqara site contains dozens of Early Dynastic mastabas, mostly located in the northern part of the plateau. All of them, as far as we can tell, face north, although few are close to facing true north. Most are several degrees east or west of the meridian; the majority are aligned between azimuths 330° and 350°—i.e., between 10° to 30° west-of-north, which is within the boundaries of the circumpolar region containing the Big Dipper.

This, and the fact that the Stretching of the Cord ceremony is attested from the 1st Dynasty, strongly implies that the mastabas were ritualistically aligned to the circumpolar stars, almost certainly a star in the Big Dipper. The precise northerly direction, however, varies from mastaba to mastaba. This, perhaps, was because they may have been generally aligned to the Big Dipper at different times as the constellation rotated around the north celestial pole, reaching maximum easterly and westerly elongations every twelve hours. Due to the unsettled political situation in Egypt and the difficulty of getting exploration permits, we have not had the opportunity to measure the alignments of these mastabas accurately. Clearly a detailed study is now warranted.

According to Christian Jacq, at least one of these mastabas—a large one labeled No. 3517—has the same orientation as the Step Pyramid.[197] This is further evidence, if not proof, that the original orientation of the mastaba upon which the Step Pyramid was built may date from the Early Dynastic period. Furthermore, the numerous mastabas in north Saqqara oriented west-of-north are curiously reminiscent of the dozens of complex structures or shrines of megalithic blocks found at the center of the Predynastic/prehistoric site at Nabta Playa, all of which had their long axes oriented similarly, several degrees west-of-north. In the next chapter, we describe the amazing continuity of symbology and evident ceremonialism from Nabta Playa to Dynastic Eygpt, especially Imhotep's Step Pyramid Complex at Saqqara.

Let's therefore test this hypothesis empirically, with precise astronomical measurements.

The Great Trench or Dry Moat

In August 26, 1985, Egyptian archaeologist Nabil Swelim announced that he had discovered a giant trench that completely surrounded the Step Pyramid Complex boundary wall. Swelim had come across aerial photographs from the 1920s that showed the outlines of a massive trench or moat going around the Step Pyramid Complex. Eventually, Swelim's claim was vindicated by further investigation and by the work of a Polish expedition in the 1990s. It is now generally accepted that the Step Pyramid Complex was indeed surrounded by a massive trench, forty meters wide and twenty-five meters deep, that has the same orientation of azimuth 4° 35′ as the complex itself. This trench or moat was, by any standard, a huge engineering project. It has a total length of nearly three kilometers and, assuming the width and depth to be uniform throughout, some 3 million tons of debris must have been removed to create it—six times the volume removed for the Step Pyramid itself. Oddly, the massive volume of rock that was excavated to create this engineering structure was apparently never found.

According to Swelim: "The similarity of the great dry moat and the much smaller trenches surrounding the royal tombs and open courts of Dynasty 1 (in which are found subsidiary burials) is striking." So could the Dry Moat/Great Trench also date from the 1st Dynasty? Further investigation showed that the walls of the moat were originally outfitted with niches. We suspect that this trench was a sort of royal enclosure to protect underground galleries that had been there since the Early Dynastic period. The mystery, however, is far from solved. Unfortunately, it is now almost impossible to conduct further investigation of the Dry Moat due to the huge cost involved and also because nearly all of it is now covered by rubble and sand.[198]

In the Manner of Ancient Times

With sloping entrances in the north side, the mastabas at Saqqara clearly were meant to face the northern sky at an altitude of between 20° to 30°, smack into the circumpolar region. We noted in chapter 2 that the Stretching of the Cord ritual was extremely ancient, going back to at least the 1st Dynasty. We have also seen how, in this ritual, the king was assisted by a priestess impersonating the goddess Seshat, and how together they aligned the axis of the temple, tomb, or pyramid toward the Big Dipper.

The symbol of Seshat was a seven-pointed star or flower (a rosette) that was held by a long stem attached to a tiara the goddess wore on her head. As G. A. Wainwright pointed out, this symbol appears on the Narmer palette (1st Dynasty) and the Scorpion palette (Zero Dynasty), which suggests that the goddess, and consequently the Stretching of the Cord ritual, was known in those remote times.[199] Seshat and her priesthood are, in any case, mentioned on the famous Palermo stone in the annals of the 1st Dynasty. According to Spence, an expert on stellar alignments of the Old Kingdom:

> Seshat was a divinity of some importance in the beginning of the historical era in Egypt, as is clear from a record of a First Dynasty ceremony involving one of her priests inscribed on the Palermo Stone (a set of annals for Egypt's earliest kings) as well as the creation of a statue of the goddess during the same reign.[200]

Toby Wilkinson, Spence's colleague at Cambridge and an expert on the Palermo stone and its fragments, agrees:

> A temple foundation ceremony involving a priest of Seshat is recorded for year x+7 of Den's reign [a 1st-Dynasty king]. A granite block of Khasekhemy [2nd Dynasty] from the temple area at Hierakonpolis shows the king "stetching the cord" assisted by Seshat. A similar scene appears on a relief block from the temple of Hathor at Gebelein, dated stylistically to the Second or early Third Dynasty. A fragment of a diorite cup from beneath the Step Pyramid gives a theophorous name which may be compounded with the goddess Seshat.[201]

Although Spence admits that there is no textual confirmation before Ptolemaic times that explicitly state that the Stretching of the Cord ceremony involved stellar observations, knowing how conservative the ancients were and how important it was for them to adhere to the correct rituals and understanding of Maat, there is little reason to doubt that the sighting of stars—and, more specifically, the Big Dipper and Sirius—was also practiced at the temple foundation ceremony in the Early Dynastic period and perhaps even before. As we already observed, the astronomer-priest performing the ritual makes a statement that strongly implies the simultaneous observation of Sirius and the Big Dipper, which, according to the inscriptions at Dendera, was done according to the "manner of ancient times."

Could this manner of aligning also have been applied to the Step Pyramid Complex at Saqqara?

The Hoof of Mesekhtiu

We have established that the orientation and inclination of the serdab of the Step Pyramid—and consequently the whole complex to which it is attached—are:

Azimuth 4° 35'

Altitude over horizon line 16° 30'

As noted earlier, when Lauer examined the inner core of the Step Pyramid, he concluded that there was originally a square mastaba that was eventually extended to become the pyramid. According to Lauer, this square mastaba, which had almost vertical walls, was first enlarged and then further extended and its walls made to slant at 16° 30'. In further extensions, the walls were made to extend upward in a series of six graduated steps, but retaining the angle of 16° 30' for each step, creating the Step Pyramid that we see today.

There are two descending passages in the north face of the pyramid: one with steps starting at the midpoint, and another very much cruder passage farther to the west. Could this latter passage be older? It is entirely possible that, when Imhotep started his own architectural work, the square mastaba was already there, and that its orientation and inclination were retained. And if, as we now suspect, the square mastaba was from the Early Dynastic period, as were the vases and jars found in the galleries directly underneath it, we needed to examine the sky at the rising of Sirius in 3100 BC, circa the start of the 1st Dynasty.

Using our StaryNight Pro astronomy software, we focused on the latitude of Saqqara (29° 52' N, 31° 13' E), the year 3100 BC, and the time one hour before sunrise. Allowing 1° altitude for Sirius with the sun at -10° 37' altitude (below horizon line), we found that the heliacal rising of Sirius occurred on the day of the Summer Solstice, July 19 Julian. A similar date, within a hundred years, was calculated by Austrian astronomer Theodor von Oppolzer:

> We find that the Heliacal Rising of Sothis (Sirius), the Summer Solstice, and the annual rise of the river Nile coincided in the year 3000 BC Julian in the latitude of Memphis on July 18 Julian.[202]

Richard Parker, an expert on the ancient Egyptian calendar, gives a date of 2937 BC.[203] M. F. Ingham calculated 2769 BC for a first day of Thoth-Sirius heliacal rising.[204]

In an appendix to our book *Black Genesis,* we review the calculation of Sothic Cycles, and note that, in this epoch, the heliacal rising of Sirius generally took place near the day of the Summer Solstice. We could not be precise as to the specific year, because exactly how far beneath the horizon the sun needs to be in order to sight the star Sirius is not definite, although it is generally held to be when the sun is about 10° beneath the horizon when the star is 1° altitude. But because Sirius is very bright, it is possible that it could be sighted when the sky was even brighter. In *Black Genesis*, we noted that a Summer Solstice heliacal rising of Sirius could plausibly be considered as late as 2781 BC, when the sun was 8° 28' beneath the horizon—two calculated Sothic Cycles (of 1,460 years) before Censorinus's anchor date of 139 CE.

In the ancient Egyptian calendar, this was New Year's Day—also called the 1st of Thoth, or 1 Akhet I. It was at this time of year, of course, that the Nile inundation began. The sun would have been in the constellation of Leo in 3100 BC. One hour before sunrise, the "head" of Leo would have been visible in the northeast at the spot on the horizon where the sun would soon rise. Surely this must have been the imagery of the ancient Heliopolitan god Atum in his lion form emerging/born out of the Primeval Ocean.[205]

According to Richard Wilkinson:

> An important mythological aspect of the solar god in the heavens is found in his identity as a cosmic lion . . . the stellar constellation now known as Leo was also recognized by the Egyptians as being in the form of a recumbent lion . . . the constellation was directly associated with the sun god.[206]

Recall how Karol Mysliwiec demonstrated that the Egyptians believed that the world began when Atum came forth as the Primeval Mound at Heliopolis, and that it was said that a lion had been the first creature to populate the world. Given what was actually *seen* in the eastern sky on this day of cosmic birth, it seems obvious to associate the birth of Atum as the solar lion and the birth of Horus as the star Sirius, with both merging in the dawn light of the Akhet in the form of Ra-Horakhti, the sun god/ Horus of the Horizon.

The observation of these celestial figures in the red glow of the pre-dawn eastern sky on the day of the Summer Solstice would surely have provided a powerful visual "unification" between the celestial lion (Leo), Ra (the sun), and Horus (Sirius), all being reborn in the Akhet on this special day that marked the beginning of the flood season, also called Akhet. Turning toward the north, an observer would have seen the Big Dipper upright, with the hoof of Mesekhtiu/oxleg—the star Alkaid, the leader—at azimuth 4° 51' and altitude 16° 42'. And that is the spot in the northern sky toward which the statue of Netjerykhet in the sedab is positioned to gaze!

At this point, it is instructive to consider this alignment in more detail, because this mysterious serdab is almost unique in the study of archaeoastronomy. Think back to the basics of aligning something with a star. If we have only a single alignment—say, a line of stones on the ground—that alone is not considered very meaningful, because many stars, at any given date, will rise (or set) near such a direction to the horizon. If there is an independent reason to think that the alignment was intended for a specific star, then a single alignment may be more meaningful. The serdab, however, gazes at a specific point in the sky. And, as we have documented, it is believed to have gazed toward some star that was at a single point *at a very specific time*—when another star, Sirius, rose above the horizon. That allows for a very precise determination of which possible star, and when.

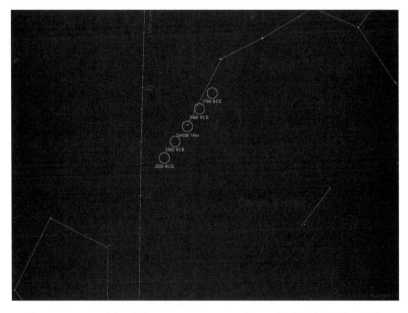

Screen capture of the sky from our astronomy software for 3100 BC. The circle labeled "serdab view" shows a 1° field of view; the circles chart the changing location of Alkaid over time.

The sky image shown here is taken for 3100 BC, precisely when Sirius in the southeast has risen above the horizon to 1° (considered the heliacal-rising height). Inside the serdab field of view, practically in the middle, is the star Alkaid. The path that Alkaid is following as the minutes pass is parallel to the curved lines—that is, it is traveling around the celestial pole every twenty-four hours. The four other small circles, marked with dates, show the location of Alkaid simultaneous with Sirius rising in increments of 300 years from 3100 BC. As one can see, it is a very rare alignment. In fact, Alkaid is the *only* bright named star that lands in the serdab view circle for many centuries, probably millennia, before or after that time. Only Mizar, the next star in the Bull's Thigh/ Big Dipper comes close, at c. 2000 BC. But this specific, unambiguous date determination comes out to 3100 BC, about 400 years before the conventional dating of King Netjerykhet/Djoser.

So what are we to make of this date difference? Maybe the statue in the serdab is not of King Djoser, but of an earlier king. But the statue inscription says it is Netjerykhet, and there is other strong evidence that Netjerykhet was Djoser. Maybe the serdab orientation was not so precise. Perhaps the builders were aiming at where Alkaid would be c. 2700 BC, and they were a bit off. But both the angle of orientation and the inclination apply to the whole Step Pyramid itself, and Old Kingdom pyramid builders are known for their mania for precise orientations.

We are drawn to a third probability. The orientation to Alkaid was established c. 3100 BC with the original 1st-Dynasty mastaba for an earlier king—possibly the first great unifier of Upper and Lower Egypt—who employed the "method of ancient times," the methods brought in from the Western Desert. Imhotep then later built the magnificent Calendar Wall monumental enclosure, finished the Step Pyramid and other buildings, and ensconced King Djoser's statue in the serdab gazing where his great ancestor king had gazed before him. Perhaps these developments served the dual purpose of connecting Djoser to the origin of his earlier kingly lineage and also symbolically launched his soul to the generally correct region of sky. Possibly the "soul-launching technology" had advanced so much that Djoser no longer needed the actual stone to align precisely to Alkaid and could travel there by symbolic means.

The Cosmic Connection

We have previously indicated that the name of the Step Pyramid Complex was Horus Is the Star at the Head of the Sky—almost certainly a reference to Sirius. There are many such "domains" from the Early Dynasties that use the name Horus that also relate this god to a star.[207]

The name Horus Is the Star at the Head of the Sky may imply the culmination of Sirius near the south meridian. In 3100 BC, Sirius had a declination of -22° 50', and culminated south at an altitude of 37° 18' as seen from Saqqara. An observer standing on the north side of the Step Pyramid (if part of it was there at the time) and looking at the southern sky would not be able to see Sirius at culmination because the pyramid, with a slope of about 52°, would block the view. The observer would need to walk several paces from the pyramid in order to see the star. On the north side of the pyramid is a wide open courtyard. At its far end, almost in line with the axis of the pyramid, is a stone platform shaped from a natural outcrop of rock measuring fifteen meters square. Egyptologists call it the North Altar.[208] No one knows for sure what its function was, although various theories have been proposed.

Rainer Stadelmann suggested it was a sun temple, but his colleague Dr. Altenmuller believed it was the podium for an obelisk. Zahi Hawass asserted that it was for offering purposes. In view of the intense astronomical concerns evident in the funerary rites and the conspicuous position of the altar, it may have served as a platform for astronomical observations related to the rebirth rituals. This idea was suggested to us by Egyptologist David Rohl. Preliminary boreholes have shown that the area near the North Altar and the carved stairway leading up to it could be older than the Step Pyramid Complex itself.

We also note that, in the late 1870s, French Egyptologist August Mariette found near the North Altar a sculpted alabaster block decorated on its sides with two lions—the so-called Lion Altar—which he dated to the 2nd Dynasty. In our opinion, the way that the North Altar is positioned to face the Step Pyramid is ideal for observations of the southern sky, using the profile of the Step Pyramid as a template. Someone sitting or standing on the North Altar at night would have a 180° view of the starry sky and be able to observe Sirius sailing from east to west in an arched pathway over the monument. When Sirius was aligned with the axis of the Step Pyramid, it would be at azimuth 4° 35' (west-of-south). Turning around to face north, an observer could not avoid noting that the star Alkaid—the "hoof" of the Big Dipper—would now be right above the holy city of Heliopolis (at azimuth 16° 30' and some twenty-four kilometers to the northeast). There is no other place in the region where this cosmic connection could be made with Heliopolis. Only Saqqara would do. But are we dealing with a series of coincidences, or with a clever plan to integrate the Step Pyramid Complex permanently into the working of the Big Dipper and Sirius?

A Model of the Sky

Today, visitors come to Saqqara by the busload. Arriving at the parking lot on the east side of the Step Pyramid Complex, some 200 meters from the original entrance, is like arriving at Grand Central Station at rush hour.

Crowds jostle through the narrow entrance and walk single-file along the colonnade, while another file of tourists passes them in the opposite direction on the way out, their guides holding up umbrellas or little flags and shouting in English, Spanish, German, Russian, and even Chinese. Finally, they emerge into the open courtyard, only to be encircled and hounded by boys selling postcards and sunhats. Chased by these grinning salesmen, who do not stop shouting "only five Egyptian pounds!" and simply refuse to take "no" for an answer, they are finally relieved by a tourist policeman who comes to their rescue and shoos them all off—and then asks for a *bakshish*.

To be fair, it's not always like that, and many visitors quickly learn to ignore the vendors and the corrupt tourist police, and enjoy their stopover. The point we want to make, however, is that—whether good or bad—a visit to this most holy of places where high rituals involving the stars and the rebirth of kings took place in the most solemn of conditions was definitely not meant to be experienced in such a chaotic and mundane way.

In ancient times, during the New Kingdom, when the Step Pyramid Complex was already hoary with age, conditions were very different for the occasional visitors. Pilgrims came here, not to take photographs or listen to local guides parroting what they'd learned from textbooks, but rather to pay respect and homage to their illustrious ancestors, and to marvel at the splendor of this extraordinary place. Some of them left graffiti—not the ugly type we have today, but touching mementos praising the ancestor-king who bequeathed to Egypt such a glorious legacy. One such memento, neatly written in hieroglyphs, declares: "The scribe Iahmes, son of Lyptah, has come to see this temple of Djoser. He found it beautiful as if the sky was within it."[209]

According to Hans Goedicke, these ancient Egyptian visitors considered the Step Pyramid Complex literally to be the "sky" *(pt),* or more likely, a model of the sky on earth.[210] Christian Jacq also reminds us that a school of "magicians" (astrologers?) was set up at Saqqara under the aegis of Imhotep, where "he taught the movement of the stars and the *decans* [constellations]."[211] In other words, the Step Pyramid Complex was also a place where sacred astronomy was taught to adepts and neophytes entering the priesthood.

In a deeply perceptive thesis, Florence Friedman seriously considered that the ancient Egyptians did, in fact, regard the Step Pyramid Complex as a model of the sky. Friedman pointed out that the hieroglyphic sign (Gardiner N1) for pt, the "sky"—a flat rectangular slab ▭ imagined to rest above the earth—was uncannily similar to the rectangular boundary wall of the Step Pyramid Complex. Friedman imagined the sky being like a giant lid or cover over the complex and sandwiching it, as it were, with another, inverted sky believed to be under the earth, in which the stars traveled after setting from west to east.[212]

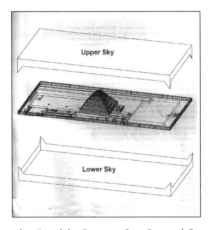

The "two skies" and the Saqqara Step Pyramid Complex, as imagined by Florence D. Friedman.

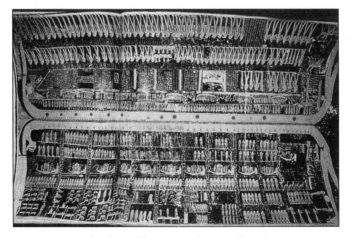

The sky goddess Nut as the "two skies."

If she is correct in her basic premise that the Step Pyramid Complex, and more specifically its rectangular boundary wall, was a model of the sky and a "notion of cosmos," then we ought to find in its design and dimensions evidence for this view, especially involving the star Sirius.

The Womb of the Sky

In chapter 2, we observed that the great boundary wall of the Step Pyramid Complex is composed of bastions, panels, and so-called false doors. The conception, design, and construction of this 1.5-kilometer ten-meter-high wall were in themselves major architectural and engineering feats. The complexity and scale of the design is simply stunning: 196 huge bastions each three meters deep and three meters wide; fifteen false doors three meters deep and nine meters wide; one massive entrance bastion five meters deep and nine meters wide; and, most impressive of all, 1,722 recessed panels that are 0.25 meters deep, 0.5 meters wide, and nine meters high. When we add the panel count to the recesses and the protrusions they create, we get a staggering 4,363 panels! Furthermore, the recesses for creating those panels were actually carved into the wall *in situ*. And so perfectly straight are they edged that today we would be hard-pressed to achieve this quality of stonemasonry without using machine cutting tools. It is extremely hard to imagine that this type of high architectural aptitude and this high level of workmanship were directed by one man, Imhotep, even though he may well have been a genius.

At any rate, and notwithstanding the dramatic decorative effect of this architectural design, a nagging question arises: Why such complexity, precision, symmetry, and huge effort for a mere boundary wall?

Seeing Is Believing

On more than one occasion, we have had the privilege of seeing the Step Pyramid Complex without the hindrance of the chaotic daily tourist crowds. On one such visit, Italian photographer Sandro Mainardi came with us. Equipped with a good-quality digital SLR camera, Sandro took a series of photographs of the southeast part of the boundary wall that contains the entrance bastion. As we stood near the huge structure, we felt completely dwarfed by its scale, as if it had not been designed for mere mortals, but for giants. The monumental size and the superb quality of workmanship baffles the mind—especially when you realize it's been here for 4,700 years or more. You are somehow forced to consider that this amazing boundary wall must have been of paramount importance to the ancients who built it, and that it must contain some lofty knowledge or purpose cyphered into its design.

The first signs of the structure's meaning are the fourteen false doors, a number that immediately brings to mind the phases of the moon and the so-called fourteen pieces of Osiris's body, which, according to popular Egyptian mythology, Isis collected from all over the land of Egypt. Using magical rituals, Isis put these pieces back together to reconstitute Osiris's body and bring him back to life so that she could become pregnant and bear him a son–successor, Horus. Here again is the relevant passage in the Pyramid Texts:

> O Osiris the king, arise, lift yourself up. . . . Your sister (wife) Isis comes to you rejoicing for love of you. You have placed her on your phallus and your seed issues into her, she being ready as Spdt (Canis Major), and Horus–Spd (Sirius) has come forth from you as "Horus who is in Spdt."

Each of the four sides of the rectangular boundary wall faces a cardinal astronomical direction. The east and west sides are about 545 meters long; the south and north sides are about 277 meters—making a total of some 1,644 meters.[213] But when we take into account the 121 bastions, the length

Other clues of a sacred astronomy in the design of the complex are the two parallel rows of columns along the fifty-four-meter colonnade, each having twenty plus four extra columns, making a total of twenty-four for each row. We know that, early on, the ancient Egyptians divided the day into twenty-four hours; so here, too, there may be a connection to the daily cycle of the sun and stars. What is intriguing is the number of niches that these column rows make: 11 + 7 on the south row; 11 + 7 on the north row, giving a total of thirty-six. Again, the number is conspicuously "astronomical," since there were thirty-six decans (weeks of ten days) in the Egyptian sky calendar. The decans were star clusters or asterisms. Also, in the so-called Jubilee Court, there are twelve pavilions, the *per-nou*, along the east side, implying the twelve months of the year.

expands to over 2,600 meters![214] Regarding the rectangular design of the boundary wall, we feel that Florence Friedman's proposal that it may be a 3-D model of the hieroglyphic sign for the sky is very plausible.

It has never been properly understood by Egyptologists why, in some interpretations, the ancient Egyptians imagined the sky, not as a vault or hemisphere, but rather as a gigantic flat rectangular slab possibly made of iron. Actually, this strange idea that the sky's "floor" was a rectangular flat iron slab can be explained by the fact that the only solid matter that falls from the sky are meteorites—which are often solid iron and black in color. (Iron meteorites are much more common and easier to find and collect than the rarer stony meteorites because of the magnetic properties of the iron.) This "iron from the sky," called bja by the ancient Egyptians, may also have been confused or associated with very hard black or dark igneous rocks like granite, basalt, and diorite—which is implied by the term *bja-kam*, "iron stone," used for black basalt. It may also explain why the plan of Egyptian temples was rectangular and often paved with black granite or basalt, and also why these sanctuaries were imagined as microcosms—i.e., models of the sky.[215]

The rectangular "sky of iron" was also imagined to have four supports or pillars, as Wallis Budge explained:

> According to one myth the floor of heaven was made of a vast, rectangular plate of iron, the four corners of which rested upon four pillars which served to mark the cardinal points.[216]

The pillars or supports of the sky are often mentioned in the Pyramid Texts, for example:

> O you four gods who stand at the supports of the sky, my father Osiris the King has not died in death, for my father Osiris the King possesses a spirit in the Akhet. (pyr. 56)

> O Re-Atum, this King comes to you, an Imperishable Spirit, Lord of the affairs of the place of the Four Pillars. (part of Ut. 217)

The Egyptians also believed that the goddess Nut, wife of the earth god Geb and mother of Osiris and Isis, was the personification of the sky. Many depictions of Nut exist, mostly on the ceilings of temples, tombs, and coffin lids. Nut is always shown stretching over the earth with her feet on the eastern horizon and her hands on the western horizon, with the sun and stars "sailing" through her body. Her elongated body, from hips to shoulders, is not arched, as often described, but rigid and flat—very much like a slab—with her feet and hands being the four pillars. It does not require much imagination to see how a stylized representation of Nut can be seen in the pt sky-sign, which is also an elongated rectangle with four corners. This sign is very reminiscent of the lids of rectangular sarcophagi, and is further attested to in the Pyramid Texts, where it is said that the dead king goes to Nut (sky) "in her name of 'sarcophagus'" and "embraces her in her name of 'coffin.'"[217]

A vivid example of this can be seen in the sarcophagus of King Psussenes I (c. 1000 BC), where Nut is shown as a woman with arms and feet outstretched surrounded by five-pointed stars on the underside of the rectangular granite lid covering the sarcophagus, which once contained the embalmed corpse of the king. In the Valley of the Kings in Upper Egypt, many of the royal tombs have the sarcophagus placed under a decorated ceiling showing the starry sky—and more specifically, the eastern sky (with Orion and Sirius) and the northern sky (with the Big Dipper and other circumpolar stars). The same idea is expressed in the Great Pyramid using the shafts, where one set of shafts was directed to Orion and Sirius, and another directed to the circumpolar constellations. It seems logical to assume, therefore, that the rectangular roof of mastabas of the Early Dynastic period may, indeed, be like sarcophagus lids representing the sky. The idea is clearly seen at the mastaba of King Shepseskaf of the 4th Dynasty, who built his tomb, known locally as Mastaba Fara'un, in the form of a giant sarcophagus at Saqqara.[218]

The question, therefore, cannot be avoided: Did Imhotep, as both Chief Astronomer and high priest of Heliopolis, conceive the Step Pyramid Complex as a giant sarcophagus whose lid would be the real sky—a sort of giant open-air sarcophagus with a canopy of real constellations above it?

Strange Synchronicity

Sometimes, there is a strange synchronicity that creeps into the tedious, although rewarding, labor of library research. It happened to us in 1983 when we spotted an aerial photograph of the Giza pyramids and noted the anomalistic offset of the smaller pyramid. Twenty years later, while searching on the bookshelf marked "Pyramid Studies" on the first floor of the Sackler Library at Oxford, we came across a book by an obscure French author. As we opened to a page at random, we saw a diagram of the boundary wall of the Step Pyramid Complex with various numbers around it. The number 1,461 was placed on the west side of the wall. The proverbial alarm bell went off in our heads, for this number, we well knew from our studies of ancient Egyptian astronomy, was the calculated value of the Sothic Cycle—the long-term cycle of 1,461 years created by the ancient Egyptians in their calendric computations.

In chapter 1, we explained that this number represented the return of the New Year in the 365-day calendar to the heliacal rising of Sirius. But this number was arrived at by assuming an exact ¼ day to add to the 365-day calendar and simply multiplying by four. In other words, this Sothic Cycle was not observed, but calculated. The true or *actual* length of the Sothic Cycle for the period beginning c. 4226 BC and ending c. 2767 BC was, in fact, worked out by British astronomer M. F. Ingham, a fellow of the Royal Astronomical Society. Ingham, who was of course well aware that the length of the Sothic Cycle would change slightly due to the precession of Sirius and the Proper Motion of the star, worked out that the "Sothic *year*" (the days it took between two heliacal risings of Sirius) would have been 365.25025 days in that epoch, giving an actual Sothic Cycle of 1,458.5—that is, between 1,458 and 1,459 years, which Ingham rounded to 1,458.[219] And on that fateful day in 2003 at the Sackler Library, we looked at the diagram once again and saw the numbers 1,458 and 1,459 printed next to the east side of the boundary wall.

Intrigued by what we were contemplating, we looked at the diagram more closely and saw that, next to the two other sides of the boundary wall—the south and north sides—were the numbers 366 x 2 = 732. Again, this was extraordinary, since we also knew that 366 was the number of days in the leap year when the heliacal rising of Sirius would re-synchronize with the solar year. It was from the knowledge of this extra day every four years that the Egyptians had derived the Sothic Cycle. In *Black Genesis*, we independently calculated the actual Sothic Cycles in that epoch and found that Ingham was correct, although we stated that the east side may be interpreted as having either 1,458 panels or 1,459 if the main entrance door is counted as one.

But from where did the author of this curious book obtain these values? How did he come up with the numbers 1461, 1458, 1459, and 366? And, more intriguingly, why did he put them on a diagram of the boundary wall of the Step Pyramid Complex?

Panels

As we studied the diagram, we saw that the author had cleverly thought of counting the tall panels on the boundary wall—not only the inserts, but also the protrusions created by this architectural detail. It was a sort of image inside a symbol—an effect that so often eludes people until someone actually "sees" it and it becomes obvious to all. If his count of the panels was correct, then the numbers he derived were simply mind-boggling, for they gave a completely different meaning to the boundary wall. Perhaps the wall was not a mere enclosure, as Egyptologists had thought. But of course, we had to make doubly sure.

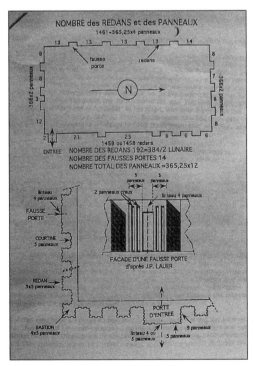

Diagram of the boundary wall of the Step Pyramid Complex.

Using the same ingenious way of counting the panels, we consulted all the plans of the boundary wall that had been made: those of Firth and Lauer, and the latest by Mark Lehner. We carefully counted the panels and found that the numbers were the same as those in the diagram:

- West side, 1,461 panels

- East side, 1,458 panels

- South side, 732 panels (366 x 2)

- North side, 732 panels (366 x 2)

It was clear that we were on to something here.

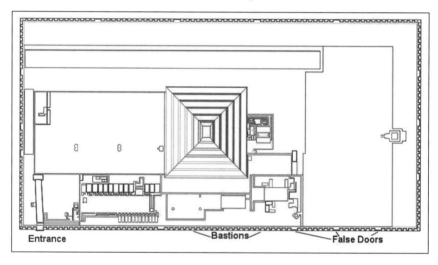

Plan of the Step Pyramid Complex showing bastions and false doors.

Ratios and Numbers

The first thing to notice is that the rectangle has the ratio 1,461:732, which is close to 2:1. This ratio creates the angle of 26° 30' used in the slope of the ascending/descending passages of mastabas and pyramids. If a rectangle is drawn within a circle representing the horizon, such that the corners of the rectangle denote the azimuths of the rising and setting sun at the solstices, then it will have the same nearly 2:1 ratio. From a metaphoric viewpoint, the rectangle would represent the domain of the sun. The boundary wall of the Step Pyramid Complex is a rectangle that has the ratio 545:277, or 1.97:1—also nearly 2:1. The number 732, which is 366 x 2, found on the south and north sides of the wall, thus four times, is reminiscent of the leap year of 366 days that occurs every four years.

Although the ancient Egyptians knew this, they nonetheless kept their calendar year at 365 days without a leap year. By keeping the calendar to 365 days, they created, whether intentionally or not, the Sothic Cycle of 1,461 years, which is the calculated number of years for the calendar to return to its original position in the true astronomical year, taking the heliacal rising of Sirius as the starting point—hence the term "Sothic" (pertaining to Sirius) Cycle.[220] The non-adjustment of the 365-day calendar had immense repercussions for the way the Egyptians perceived time and the order of the universe. It would very much seem that the numerical/astronomical message incorporated in the boundary wall is that the panels on the north and south sides are to be counted as *days*, whereas the west and east sides are to be counted as *years*. The latter, then, would give us a total of 1,461 + 1,458 = 2,919 years.

If we take the date of 3100 BC for the boundary wall's alignment, then it is logical to consider the date 6019 BC as a kind of starting point. This date is the same as the best fit to when Alkaid matched the ancient axis of the Hathor temple at Dendera—about 6020 BC. Although we find meaning in the coincidence of these dates, matching the star alignments at that epoch in time, this matching may well be coincidental. Why would 6019 BC have been used as a starting point?? Did something important happen at that remote date? And if so, what did it have to do with the heliacal rising of Sirius and the constellation of the Big Dipper?

We knew, however, that the answers to these questions were encapsulated in two words: Nabta Playa.

Chapter Four

THE STAR TEMPLE
OF THE SAHARA

The king joyously . . . casts his gaze toward the Big Dipper and thus establishes the temple in the manner of ancient times.

Temple Inscription at Dendera[221]

The paleo-astronomer J. McKim Malville determined that the line of megaliths . . . aimed at the point where the brightest star of the Big Dipper, Alpha Ursa Major (Dubhe), rose between c. 6700 and 6000 years ago . . . [One of the] alignments points to the rising position of Sirius.

Fred Wendorf and Romuald Schild[222]

Two years ago when we wrote *Black Genesis,* little did we know that our search for Imhotep would take us back to the very place where our quest for the source of Egyptian civilization truly began: the enigmatic site of Nabta Playa.

Our first visit to Nabta Playa was in 2003; since then, we have been back three times. The last time was in April 2008, when we also visited the distant places in the deep Sahara of Gebel Uwainat and Gilf Kebir. These are uninhabited mountain ranges in the extreme southwest of Egypt only discovered by Europeans in the early 1920s. They remain largely unexplored due to their remoteness and super-aridity. In December

General view of Nabta Playa, with stone fragments in the foreground.

Pharaonic inscriptions at Gebel Uwainat.

2007, Mark Borda and Mahmoud Marai, a chemistry teacher from Cairo, reported seeing pharaonic inscriptions on a boulder on the south side of the Uwainat plateau. The inscriptions, which we also saw during our own expedition of April 2008, confirmed that, since the late Old Kingdom and most likely before, envoys were sent by pharaohs to meet with the "People of Yam" and the "People of Tekhebet."

Many modern researchers, including us, are convinced that it is the ancestors of these mysterious Saharan peoples who came into the Nile Valley in the 4th millennium BC and kick-started the Egyptian civilization. In chapter 5, we examine the archaeological evidence that confirms the points of contact these ancestors had in Upper Egypt and Nubia. Suffice it to point out now that, according to anthropologist Michael Hoffman, a specialist in Predynastic Egypt:

> [T]he link between the Predynastic cultures of the [Nile] Valley and the prehistoric rock drawings of the Libyan Desert [Egyptian Sahara] . . . [must be] attributed to a nomadic desert society . . . called the *Saharan culture* . . . [with] puzzling similarity shared by . . . [Upper Egyptian] Predynastic inhabitants and the faraway prehistoric peoples of Gebel Uwainat and Gilf Kebir.[223]

Indeed, some anthropologists are now even open to the possibility that the legendary founder of Dynastic Egypt, King Narmer (Menes), could have himself been a Nubian from this ancestral stock.[224] In a similar vein, American Egyptologist W. A. Fairservis, Jr., a member of the Hierakonpolis Project, wrote:

> It should be noted that the Nubian origins of leaders such as Narmer is entirely possible. Indeed, there is no reason why critical motifs in the Narmer palette's iconography could not have been of Nubian origins.[225]

A Proto-Temple in the Desert

The unique archaeological site of Nabta Playa had been investigated since the 1970s by the Combined Prehistoric Expedition (CPE) headed by Wendorf and Schild. Since 2007, however, Nabta Playa has been abandoned by the CPE. Many of the megaliths have been tampered with by illegal visitors, and some of the important artifacts have been taken to the Nubian Museum at Aswan (see Appendix 3 in *Black Genesis*). Although the CPE originally focused primarily on the archaeological and anthropological aspects of Nabta Playa, the bombshell came in 1997 when they brought American paleoastronomer Kim Malville to the site. After carefully studying the many strange stone alignments the CPE had found there, Malville, Wendorf, and Schild concluded that Nabta Playa was a prehistoric astronomical or astro-ceremonial complex. Not only that, but carbon 14 dating made it the oldest of its kind in the world, predating Stonehenge and the Giza pyramids by at least 2,000 years!

It is known that the Sahara experienced cycles of humid wet periods that periodically converted this vast region into a fertile savannah. These periods, which lasted several millennia, were regularly followed by equally long periods of dryness that brought the region back to being an extremely arid desert. The last of these periods occurred after the breakup of the Ice Age c. 10,500 BC. This was when the southwestern desert of Egypt began to be inhabited by pastoralists coming from the south, probably from the Tibesti-Ennedi Mountains in the area that is now Chad, known to be geologically linked to the Uwainat and Gilf Kebir massifs. It was these people who, from about 9000 to about 3500 BC, serviced the mysterious ceremonial complex of Nabta Playa. (For a full description of Nabta Playa, see Appendix IV.) Here, we will concern ourselves with only the following structures at the site: the long lines of megaliths aligned to stars; the stone Calendar Circle; the cow burials; and the so-called "cow stone" megalithic sculpture.

Richard Wilkinson states:

> While the carefully arranged stones of this site seem to have served as a simple calendric observatory, Nabta Playa is also believed to have had symbolic and ceremonial functions. It may thus have integrated the temporal cycles of the sun with the recurrent cycles of the life-giving waters as a kind of cosmic clock tied to the underlying principles of life and death. As such, the site might even be called a proto-temple. . . . these same factors of life and death, water and the sun certainly lie at the symbolic core of all later Egyptian temples.[226]

Today, Wilkinson is not the only scholar who sees a bridge across time and space between the prehistoric people of the Sahara and the early Egyptians of the Nile Valley. Egyptologist Salima Ikram, who recently visited the Egyptian Sahara and saw the evidence for herself, concurs:

> In about 4000 BC there seems to have been a change in climate. The whole rain cycle changed and therefore people started moving away from the Sahara and into more dependable water sources here in Egypt—that would have been the Nile Valley. As the people from the desert converged into the Nile Valley, you can see them taking their ideas and belief systems there, and these have gradually transformed into what we have and what we know as "Egypt."[227]

During our visit to Nabta Playa in November 2007, we had the pleasure of meeting Nicole Douek, an Egyptologist from the University of London who was on her way to Gilf Kebir and Gebel Uwainat with a group of visitors. She, too, was of the opinion that the astronomy at Nabta Playa was clear evidence of a connection between the prehistoric people of the Sahara and the people of the Nile Valley civilization. Dr. Douek readily listened to our views on the possible astronomical connections between Nabta Playa and the pyramid and temple builders of Egypt, and then told us this:

> [T]here are connections . . . of course there are, and they are very, very important connections, because there are no other answers, for the moment anyway, and this is as good as any . . . better![228]

We totally concur with Wilkinson, Ikram, and Douek, but we have found that the scant archaeological evidence confirming these connections is heavily buttressed by the more precise astronomical evidence that we have assembled. This evidence shows the intellectual and cultural bridge between the stargazers of Nabta Playa and the early astronomer-priests of the Nile Valley.

Coordinates and Directions

In 2003, we traveled to Nabta Playa to record with GPS the individual coordinates of the many megaliths. For an initial measure of the megalith locations and in order to double-check our results, we commissioned high-resolution photographs to be taken from space, directly over the site, by the Quickbird Satellite on December 31, 2002.[229] On the 2003 trip, we used that satellite imagery to find the megaliths in the vast unmarked desert, and then to measure their locations independently with a handheld GPS device on the ground. Satisfied that the coordinates we obtained were as precise as the circumstances and the best technology available permitted, we felt totally confident that we could determine the alignments of the megalith lines with the highest possible degree of accuracy.

Strange Polemics

Previously, the only set of coordinates available for the Nabta Playa megaliths were those taken by the CPE and published in their 2001 report.[230] And although now, with hindsight, we know that the CPE coordinates were basically accurate and matched our own taken in 2003, the azimuths—i.e., directions calculated from these coordinates by the CPE and also published in their 2001 report—were surprisingly incorrect. As a result, it was impossible to untangle from the CPE report whether they had made errors in measuring the megalith locations and/or errors in calculating the astronomy (see Appendix IV for a complete description). That is why we had to make our own independent measurements of the megaliths. In one case, the CPE had made the classic error of taking due east as azimuth 100° instead of azimuth 90°, and thus all their azimuths were out by 10°. When we finally resolved those errors, we were able to establish a completely new set of dates for the six rows of megaliths A1, A2, A3 and B1, B2, and C1.

Most significant was the alignment of C1 for the rising of Sirius, which our calculations now placed at c. 6091 BC. Consequently, we proposed that 6100 BC (plus or minus 200 years) was the correct average epoch for many of the stellar alignments at Nabta Playa. The CPE acknowledged their computing errors but, most oddly, rejected our date of c. 6100 BC because they claimed that some of the megaliths on the playa sediment were placed in c. 5100 BC and that, in any case, the date of 6100 BC was "about 1,500 years earlier than our best estimates for the Terminal Neolithic [cultural era]."[231]

Notwithstanding that what they now claimed was a contradiction in terms, and even though some of the megaliths may have been placed *after* the

Satellite image of the megalith lines of
Nabta Playa.

Satellite image showing the stellar alignments to
the Big Dipper and Sirius in 6100 BC.

sedimentation of the playa's basin, the CPE themselves claimed, in the same
2007 article, that the point from which all the stone alignments emanated,
which they called Complex Structure A, was "part of the symbolic landscape
of the Middle Neolithic and became significant *before* the establishment of the
complex ceremonial center [and] perhaps their locations had been marked
by rock cairns before gradual burial by playa sediments."[232] Furthermore,
much of the radiocarbon dating obtained at Nabta Playa clustered around
6000 BC, which all but confirmed that our own dating of 6100 BC was
likely correct. Based on the data and the corrected azimuths for the megalith lines, it had to be concluded that some of the megaliths—and certainly
those within the vicinity of Complex Structure A—predated the Terminal
Neolithic, since this part of the ceremonial complex, by the CPE's own
reckoning, was created *before* that epoch.

Alignments to Sirius and the Big Dipper

There are at least nine megaliths that form the three lines A1, A2, and A3 that point northeast. There are also at least six megaliths that form lines B1 and B2 pointing southeast. All the megalith lines radiate out from the centerpiece, Complex Structure A. Seen together from altitude, they seem to form a huge right angle, a sort of gigantic set square made of stone. According to the CPE's 2001 report, all these megalith lines had stellar alignments. The CPE presented a table giving the GPS coordinates of all the megalithic stones that formed the lines, and then claimed:

> According to our analysis, these lines coincide with the rising positions of three prominent stars during the period 4800–3700 BC (calendrical years): Sirius (the brightest star of the night sky), Dubhe (the brightest star in Ursa Major [Big Dipper], and stars in the belt of Orion.[233]

Malville was more specific, claiming that the three lines labeled A1, A2, and A3 were aimed at Dubhe in the Big Dipper, tracking it over time from a period between c. 4742 BC (line A1), 4423 BC (line A2), and 4199 BC (line A3).

Malville also claimed that a line labeled C1 was aligned to Sirius in c. 4820 BC.[234] As for the purpose of these megalithic star lines, the CPE postulated:

> [T]he rising of Sirius in the dawn, coupled with the northernmost excursion of the sun at summer solstice, may have been viewed as the harbingers of the summer rains. . . . [T]he megalithic alignments may have commemorated a perceived connection between heaven and earth, which was especially vital at the time of summer solstice and the monsoon rains. . . . [The Nabta lines serviced] astronomical ceremonies to induce rains.[235]

When we read these statements, especially now that the corrected azimuths for the megalith lines indicate an average date of 6100 BC, we were immediately reminded of the same date of c. 6100 BC for the alignment of the temple of Hathor at Dendera. As we saw in chapter 3, our analysis of the textual, archaeological, and astronomical data indicated that the astronomer-priests of Dendera aligned the axis of

IMHOTEP: THE AFRICAN

the temple on a much older ground plan from the "time of the Followers of Horus."

Our conclusion was that the axis was aimed at the star Alkaid in the Big Dipper at the moment of the heliacal rising of Sirius in 6100 BC. We are, of course, acutely aware that the date of 6100 BC radically opposes the consensus by Egyptologists that Egyptian civilization began in 3100 BC. But to paraphrase our friend and colleague Robert Schoch: We do not follow Egyptologists; we follow the science. And the hard science of astronomy corroborates the ancient texts inscribed on the walls of the Hathor temple.

To be fair, the idea that there may have indeed been a connection between the astronomy of Nabta Playa and Dendera was also sensed by the CPE, for, in their 2001 report, they cautiously proposed this:

> It is interesting to note that this is not the only time that Dubhe [in the Big Dipper] had been implicated as a target star in the stones of Egypt. The temple of Dendera has an alignment of 18.5° east-of-north, the same azimuth as alignment A2 [at Nabta Playa]. In 1894 Lockyer suggested that although the temple was constructed several millennia later, it may have marked the earlier alignment as a commemoration of past time.... Our evidence of attention to the prominent stars, Sirius, Dubhe, and those of the belt of Orion, coupled with the recurrent symbolism of cattle on the earth and in the sky, suggests cultural connection across both space and time in Southern Egypt. The astronomical tradition at Nabta may have been part of the inheritance of the nomadic cultures that was passed to populations of the Nile Valley.[236]

As the CPE noted, Lockyer had indeed made such a claim in 1894, namely that the temple of Dendera may have had a much earlier alignment to the star Dubhe in the Big Dipper. Lockyer calculated that the star Dubhe would rise in the direction of the temple's axis in c. 5000 BC. But we believe, as we showed in chapter 3, that it is not the star Dubhe, but rather Alkaid, that was the target for the axis of the Hathor temple. We believe that both Lockyer in 1894 and the CPE in 2001 were right in principle about a possible older alignment for Dendera, but wrong in their choice of stellar target. We readily agree with them that the astronomical tradition begun at Nabta Playa could have been passed down to the populations of the Nile Valley. And if so, could not the Stretching of the Cord ritual be as ancient as Nabta Playa and also have been passed on to the populations of the Nile Valley?

At this point, it is instructive to consider what was going on simultaneously with the northerly constellations and the circumpolar stars as Sirius rose in the southeast. As Sirius rose, the Bull's Thigh constellation was clearly visible in the northeast sky, with "hoof" star Alkaid at azimuth about 18.5° and altitude about 22°. The rest of the thigh angled up and to the east to Dubhe at the top at azimuth about 39° and altitude about 41°. So the megalith lines A1, A2, A3 pointed toward the center of the Bull's Thigh from Alioth to Megrez (two of the seven bright stars that make up the Bull's Thigh/Big Dipper constellation). Also, a little less than four hours earlier, the Bull's Thigh constellation as a whole would have just risen above the horizon and been laid out horizontally from Alkaid in the north at azimuth 9° with stars Phecda and Merak breaking one degree above the horizon at azimuths 26.5° and 34.5°, such that Phecda rose near megalith line A3 and Dubhe rose near megalith line A1.

Furthermore, Alkaid had just become an "eternal" or "imperishable" circumpolar star that never passes beneath the horizon in the north and is visible every night of the year whenever the sky is dark. As mentioned in chapter 3, modern star lore calls Alkaid "the leader" of the Bull's Thigh constellation ("the sisters of the bier"). In the centuries before 6100 BC, Alkaid was observed to be leading the constellation in becoming circumpolar imperishable stars. Before about 7000 BC, none of the Bull's Thigh stars were imperishable circumpolar stars. Alkaid became the first one, so that, by 6100 BC, Alkaid skimmed down to about 5° above the horizon at due north.

Also c. 6100 BC, there was no "north star" like our Polaris today. So it is natural that the people of the time became highly attuned to the importance of Alkaid, the leader of the Bull's Thigh, especially as they were establishing their cattle cult and the importance of the constellation. As the first "imperishable" circumpolar star, with no north star, Alkaid could be relied on to be available for navigation and time-keeping—and, in a sense, it was the only star that could serve that purpose. Recall also that the megaliths in lines A1, A2, A3 as found today are set into playa sediments that were yet to be deposited from 6100 to 5000 BC. And the construction at the center point of all the megalith lines (Complex Structure A) was initiated beneath those sediments at an earlier time and somehow maintained over the centuries.

The sequence of events during one year at Nabta Playa would have been this. Alkaid was visible at night all year, serving as a "clock" for the astronomer-priest observers. The top of the thigh (including stars Phecda, Merak, and Dubhe) became visible again (rose heliacally) about a month before the Spring Equinox. Then about a month after the Spring Equinox, two months before the Summer Solstice, Orion's belt reappeared and rose heliacally. About one month before the Summer Solstice, several things happened: The sun moved far enough north that it passed directly over-head at noon so that standing stones cast no shadow; Sirius re-appeared rising heliacally; and (as we shall see) the rains came to fill up the playa. All of this was predictable by tracking the circumpolar Bull's Thigh/Big Dipper stars as clocks, led by Alkaid.

So the sequence of events we are suggesting is that, c. 6100 BC and the centuries leading up to then, the Bull's Thigh constellation stars and especially Alkaid were tracked and marked with megaliths aligned in the general northeasterly direction where lines A1, A2, and A3 are today. Also during this time, the ability to use the circumpolar constellation stars as "clocks" by sighting their location in the sky became more refined, so that they could be used at altitude in the sky, not only when rising on the horizon. Thus the consistent 90° right-angle relationship between Sirius and Dubhe became important and was noted. Then, after the playa sedimentation stopped c. 5000 BC, the ritual Stretching of the Cord ceremony developed and was monumentalized in the two sets of 90° megalith lines simultaneously marking rising Sirius with Dubhe in the sky on the dates 4500 BC and 3500 BC. Hence the megaliths we can still find today—except for the fact that some of them have been bulldozed and removed in recent years.

In the CPE's 2001 report, Malville mistakenly stated that the megalithic line A2 had the same azimuth as the axis of the Hathor temple at Dendera, namely 18.5°. The azimuth of line A2 is actually closer to 28°, as corrected by Brophy and Rosen in 2005 using GPS coordinates and high-resolution imagery taken by the Quickbird Sattelite. However, at the time we wrote *Black Genesis*, we unfortunately referred to Malville's value of 18.5°. Thus we mistakenly said that line A2 aligned with Alkaid. We apologize for this lapse of concentration. However, the general thrust of our argument showing a connection between the sacred astronomy of Nabta Playa and that of Imhotep at the Step Pyramid Complex is not affected.

So why would the prehistoric people of the Sahara have gone to such lengths to fix the rising point of these stars c. 6100 BC?

Cattle Cult

The double alignment of Nabta Playa to Sirius and the Big Dipper is strikingly similar to that at the Hathor temple at Dendera. Considering the possible connection of the 6100 BC dating, we need to consider another obvious thing these two places have in common: cattle or, to be more specific, a cattle cult related to a cow goddess associated with the star Sirius.

Two of the most mysterious aspects of the Nabta Playa complex are the cluster of tumuli and the complex structures that were excavated in the 1970s and 1980s by the CPE. These tumuli, about twelve of them, look like flattened igloos of rock and sand debris covered with slabs. When

The skeleton of a young cow found under a tumulus at Nabta Playa; its spine
is oriented north-south with its head to the south.

they were excavated, the CPE was perplexed to find the skeletal remains
of cows in some of them. And in one of them—the largest, excavated
in the 1994 season—there was the full skeleton of a young cow, which
strongly suggests a ceremonial burial and, therefore, a cattle cult. The spine
of the cow was oriented north-south with its head to the south, implying
a ritual involving some sort of sacred astronomy:

> The placement of the animal, lying on its left side and oriented
> north to south with its head to the south, appears to enhance the
> north-to-south orientation of other features within the Nabta
> ceremonial complex.[239]

The area containing the tumuli, a wadi that would have served to supply
water to the playa on the north side, was christened the Valley of Sacrifices
by the CPE, and radiocarbon indicates a date of c. 5500 BC.

Not far from the tumuli, in the playa on its west side and surrounding
the central hub from which the lines of megaliths radiate, is another area
containing a score or more of what the CPE called "complex structures"
that were made from large, megalithic stone slabs placed in oval shapes
on the sand. The long axes of these megalithic ovals were oriented a few
degrees west-of-north, like the axes of the 1st Dynasty and Predynastic
mastabas at Saqqara. When some of these structures were excavated, they
were found to cover rock outcrops on the bedrock under about four

meters of playa sediment. Below ground level, these appear to have been partially sculpted by human hands. The largest of these structures, Complex Structure A, was found to contain a sculptured megalith that has some resemblance to a cow.

> It was standing upright with its base 2 m below the surface, and its long axis was oriented a few degrees west-of-north. The rock had been blocked into place by two smaller slabs. Farther beneath it, at a depth of 4 m [about 13 feet], the shaped table (bed) rock had a similar northward orientation.[240]

The "cow stone," as this was called, was eventually brought out from its 8,000-year-old burial by local Egyptian laborers from Abu Simbel and Aswan using a small steel hand-operated winch.

The cow stone of Nabta Playa, as it is now at the Nubian Museum at Aswan, repaired and reconstructed after being broken during transport from the desert.

Unfortunately, the cow stone was broken into two pieces and parts of its features shattered during transport to the Nubian Museum at Aswan, where it was shown to us in 2003 by the director. The stone is now repaired and exhibited in the courtyard of the museum, where we saw it again in 2011. The stone is definitely fashioned by human hands and, depending on the angle from which it is observed, it can be seen to resemble the stylized contours of a cow. The sculpture also has a smoothed "almost polished" outer surface with some strangely sharp-edged geometric features (see

Appendix IV for more discussion of the cow stone sculpture). Dated to at least 4800 BC by the CPE, it is the oldest known sculpture in Egypt. Wendorf, leader of the CPE excavation, speculated that this sculpture "may represent the origin of Egyptians' fascination for working large stones." In our opinion, however, Complex Structure A as a whole, and probably the cow stone that was under it, must be dated to 6100 BC, because it is from this precise spot that the various megalithic lines of stones that have been astronomically dated to 6100 BC emanated.

But why mingle the symbolism and rituals of a cattle cult with the stars of the Big Dipper and Sirius?

For nomadic pastoralists in the open Sahara, which was then a savanah with a seasonal monsoon, the dominant preoccupation would have been the survival of their cattle, which totally depended on the rains that came in early summer—"water from the sky" that was a matter of life and death for both people and cattle. Not only did these cattle herders have somehow to ensure that the rains did come, but also—and perhaps more important—they needed to be able to predict the time of their coming. In other words, they needed magical rituals for the former and practical astronomical knowledge for the latter.

The monsoon rains, of course, came from farther south in central Africa, where these heavy downpours, in prehistoric times, drifted to Lower Nubia and the adjacent desert and created temporary lakes, Nabta Playa being one. The CPE investigation at Nabta Playa demonstrated that the prehistoric pastoralists came to this temporary lake every year during the rainy season, when the lake's basin was refilled with water. The temporary lake provided water for a few months, after which the people left. This to-and-fro migration started around 11,000 BC and ended about 6100 BC, when the nomadic pastoralists realized they could dig deep wells into the Nabta Playa basin from which water could be extracted all year round. It was then that they changed from nomadic to sedentary cattle farmers.

The long-held practical knowledge of astronomy of the people of Nabta Playa, which previously was needed for navigating in the open desert and calculating the coming of the monsoon rains, now acquired a religious purpose. And although they still carried out the same astronomical observations of the stars, these were now used for ritualistic purposes—to induce the favors of the gods to send them the precious life-giving waters from the sky—and probably also for what we now call "scientific" purposes—to investigate how their world operated. In this context, Complex Structure A, with its cow stone and its megalith alignments that shoot out northward and then eastward, can be regarded as a proto-temple dedicated to a very ancient cow goddess associated with the sky.

Recall that the special interest and reverence paid by the ancient Egyptians of the Nile Valley to the heliacal rising of Sirius was principally because this star was considered the harbinger of the crucial annual flood of the Nile. The events narrated on the Famine Stele, as we saw in chapter 3, drive home this point with poignancy. Since the formation of the Nile in deep prehistory, the annual flood always occurred (and still does) around the time of the Summer Solstice—that is, at the end of June Gregorian. The root cause of this annual hydraulic "gift from the sky gods" is the sun's growing heat as it heads to its zenith in midsummer, which provokes the monsoons in central Africa, which in turn gorge the great lakes that then overflow into the tributaries of the Nile to create the annual flood. We noted that c. 3000 BC, the heliacal rising of Sirius coincided with the Summer Solstice when observed at the latitude of Memphis at latitude 30° N. But the heliacal rising of Sirius occurs later or earlier depending on where exactly along the 1,000 kilometers of the Egyptian Nile it is observed. An approximate rule of thumb is to deduct one day for one degree latitude south of Memphis. Thus in 3000 BC at 22.5° N, which is the latitude of Nabta Playa, the heliacal rising of Sirius occurred some seven to eight days before the Summer Solstice.

The heliacal rising of Sirius is also affected by precession over long periods of time, however, as the star changes its azimuth at rising. Here, the difference in days is more complicated to work out. A very approximate rule of thumb, however, is to add about ten days every millennium from the Summer Solstice if you are considering an epoch *after* 3000 BC, and deduct about ten days every millennium from the Summer Solstice if you are considering an epoch *before* 3000 BC. Rigorous calculations show that, in 6100 BC, the heliacal rising of Sirius occurred at Nabta Playa some thirty-three days *before* the Summer Solstice—that is, about the middle of May Gregorian.

So if we are correct in thinking that it was the heliacal rising of Sirius that was of paramount importance to the prehistoric people of Nabta

Playa in 6100 BC, what could possibly have impressed them so much at that time of the year—i.e., around May 15 Gregorian?

Water from the Sky

The precious water on which the prehistoric people of the Sahara depended did not, of course, come from the Nile flood, but from the "water falling from the sky"—rains. And although the water from the sky was, in fact, the very same water from the monsoon rains that also caused the Nile inundation, the ancients did not know this. The monsoon rains were even more crucial to the Saharan people than to those who lived along the banks of the Nile, for the latter had the permanently flowing river to survive should the flood fail to come. Indeed, the extreme importance of the monsoon rains to these desert people was made evident in modern times by the dramatic events that happened in the Sahel on the southern rim of the Sahara. The monsoon rains that normally come in early summer to the Sahel usually transform this extremely arid region into a temporary lush grassland ideal for grazing cattle. But in the late 1960s, the monsoons started to fail and the areas in northern Sahel dried up. The desperate nomadic herdsmen were forced to search for grassland and water, causing an exodus during which thousands died. It was not until 1974–1975 that the monsoon returned to the northern Sahel. In the six years that the monsoon had failed to come, the area endured a massive famine with heavy loss of life.

Climatologists have worked out that, from 150,000 to 130,000 years ago, the African continent experienced short alternate cold and arid phases. About 130,000 years ago, a warm, moist phase began that lasted 5,000 years. During that period, the deserts were almost completely covered with vegetation. Subsequent cooling and drying of the climate led to an aridity maximum about 70,000 years ago, followed by a slight moderation of climate, and finally a second aridity maximum around 22,000 to 13,000 years ago. After that, conditions became warmer and moister, which led to what anthropologists call the Holocene era, with vegetation covering most of the southern and middle Sahara. Then, around 5000 BC, the Sahara Desert started to become dryer, until around 3500 BC, with precise dates varying by location, it reached the super-aridity that we see today. When the prehistoric pastoralists started coming regularly to Nabta Plata, possibly from 11,000 BC, they had to make sure that the basin that formed the temporary lake would have water. Arriving there at the right time was imperative.

According to modern meteorological data, the monsoon rains in the so-called Greater Horn of Africa (GHA) show strong seasonality:

> In the southern GHA (Kenya, Uganda, Tanzania, and Somalia) the rainy seasons come during the boreal spring (from March to May) and in the fall (October–November). The spring season is referred to as the long rains, while the fall season is referred to as the short rains. In the northern areas of the GHA (Ethiopia, Djibouti, and Eritrea) the primary rainy seasons are in the spring (*belg*) and summer (*kiremt*) with a dry period (*bega*) in the winter. Belg rains make possible crops such as wheat and barley that are harvested in June or July.[241]

It is likely that, in 6100 BC, it was the Ethiopian *belg* spring rains of April–May that reached the Nubian regions. The constellation of Orion, followed by the heliacal rising of Sirius, would re-appear in the dawn sky around that time of year. The astronomy of Nabta Playa correlates with this dramatic cosmic signal, surely observed by these avid stargazers of the desert. It is our contention that, when they settled in the areas around Nabta Playa from around 6100 BC, they established a megalith proto-temple dedicated to a proto-Hathorian cow goddess identified with Canis Major and Sirius. From the stone alignments of this proto-temple, they could monitor the stars of the Big Dipper and Sirius that would tell them when to expect the seasonal "water from the sky."

The earliest recorded evidence of a cow cult in the Nile Valley can be traced back at least as far as the 1st Dynasty. A sacred cow appears on the top of the Narmer palette, and there is a similar sacred cow on a 1st-Dynasty tablet belonging to King Djer, both thought to represent a primitive cow goddess known as Sekhet-Hor.[242] British Egyptologist Carolyn Graves-Brown wrote:

> One of the early proponents of the Egyptian fertility goddess was a pioneering Egyptologist, Elise Baumgartel, who cited the evi-

dence of the female form on some pottery vessels and so-called "cow amulets." More recently the respected Egyptologist, Fekri Hassan, argued for the importance of a mother goddess, usually taking cow form, in Predynastic Egypt, extending the idea of a mothering cow goddess back to 7000 BC. . . . [H]e (Hassan) sees the location and the economy of Egypt as being critical to the importance of the female cow goddess—the life-giving importance of the woman, milk and water in an increasingly desert environment. The idea of a predynastic goddess is also supported by other Egyptologists.[243]

Graves-Brown gives numerous examples of Predynastic and Early Dynastic artifacts:

[T]he Naqada II First Dynasty depiction of a bovine head shown facing forward in conjunction with five stars, one on each horn, and one on top of the head . . . three particular depictions of a Predynastic bovine head with stars are commonly cited. . .the most famous depiction with stars is a Naqada II oversized palette from Gerza. . . . Another bovine occurs on a black and white porphyry bowl from Hierakonpolis . . . the third is on a seal impression of the Naqada II period from a burial at Abydos.

Nagada II, a 1st-Dynasty depiction of a
Predynastic cow goddess with stars.

The Narmer palette is sometimes called the "earliest historical document." Its standard interpretation is that it depicts King Narmer (perhaps the same person as Menes) leading an army from southern Egypt to conquer northern Egypt, unifying the two. The king is shown wearing the crowns of both regions. However, if we look at the overall iconography of the palette, we can also see evidence of the cattle cult that permeated the unification of the two lands.

Both the front and back of the palette are topped by the dual images of the Hathor-like cow god, flanking Narmer's name. And the front of the palette features a falcon/Horus god subjugating a man with papyrus reeds growing out of his back—suggesting "the river people." The bottom front scene of the palette shows the king in the form of a bull god simultaneously vanquishing a warrior and destroying the walls of a city. The back bottom scene shows dead enemies with a glyph representing walled towns. Also, the back center scene features two Nubian-looking fellows harnessing two intertwined mythical wild beasts symbolizing Upper and Lower Egypt. These images seem to portray the pastoralist cattle culture mastering the Upper and Lower river cultures as they domesticated actual cattle many centuries earlier.

The CPE's anthropological and zoological research at Nabta Playa shows that the domestication of cattle probably occurred first in this part of the world at c. 7500 BC or, at the very least, independently from other parts of the world.[244] Indeed, all one has to do to be convinced of the huge importance of cattle to the prehistoric people of the Sahara is to see the rock art at Gebel Uwainat and Gilf Kebir, where hundreds of scenes depict domesticated cattle, some even showing cows in paddocks.

All these interconnecting clues—astronomical alignments to stars associated to sacred cows (Hathor and Isis) or to a bull's (or cow's) thigh/foreleg constellation; cow cults; multi-ton sculpted boulders; and a meteorological phenomenon with a common source (monsoons)—strongly suggest that the ceremonial complex of Nabta Playa must be seen as a bovine/star/goddess temple and regional ceremonial center, as well as the precursor of the star-aligned temples in the Nile Valley dedicated to bovine star goddesses like Hathor and Isis at Dendera and Satet at Elephantine Island. Evidence of a cow cult related to the northern

A cow goddess, probably a proto-Hathor deity called
Sekhet-Hor, with a "star" (dot) over her head.

Domesticated cattle in the prehistoric rock art at Gebel Uwainat. Note the strange
zoomorphic, possibly cow-shaped, heads of the humans, suggesting very early
Hathor-like imagery.

circumpolar stars can also be seen at Saqqara on a 1st–Dynasty mastaba, where model heads of cattle were placed all around the monument.

Model cattle heads on a 1st-Dynasty mastaba at Saqqara.

At this point in our investigation, we are compelled to ask: Was Imhotep heir to knowledge and rituals of astral rebirth devised long ago by the prehistoric African stargazers of the Sahara? Could Imhotep even have been their descendant?

Chapter Five

BLACK-SKINNED ANCESTORS

The importance of Garstang's findings was that he demonstrated a very real stratigraphic relationship between an archaic monument [Khamesekmy's "Fort"] and its prehistoric predecessors—a relationship that, thanks to more recent work in the vicinity, can be extended back through the Predynastic era well into the Palaeolithic times.

MICHAEL A. HOFFMAN[245]

A few years ago, ex-Minister of Egyptian Antiquities Zahi Hawass made an extraordinary statement. He claimed, in all seriousness, that "Egyptians are not Africans." This bizarre proclamation was not made because Hawass failed to consult a world map, but because he regarded "African" as being synonymous with "black." In our book *Black Genesis,* we not only showed that the fount of the pharaonic civilization was a sub-Saharan people, but also that they were, indeed, *black* Africans who had their roots in central Africa. We now intend to show that Imhotep himself may well have come from this culture. And although the smoking-gun evidence can only be found if and when Imhotep's tomb and mummy turn up so his DNA can be examined, nonetheless the circumstantial evidence that we present in this final chapter is strongly in favor of this possibility.

The Search for Imhotep's Tomb

The discovery of Imhotep's tomb is widely regarded as "the holy grail of Egyptology," likely to spark a worldwide media frenzy of interest in ancient Egypt akin to the 1922 discovery of Tutankhamun by Howard Carter. In 2007, Scottish Egyptologist and archaeologist Ian Mathiesen, director of the Saqqara Geophysical Survey Project, who had been producing a map of the underground structures at Saqqara for over fifteen years, made a major announcement. He revealed that ground-penetrating scanning technology had located two immense underground structures, possibly tombs, in the region of Saqqara thought most likely to contain Imhotep's tomb. The next step, Mathieson said, would be an excavation to look for Imhotep. But, he lamented:

> The official line is that there's an excavation ban in the area for the next five years, primarily because it is so sensitive. Also, as soon as work begins on a major discovery like this treasure hunters pour into the area to pillage the sites. At the moment the Egyptian authorities say they simply don't have enough guards to look after these sites. But who knows? These revelations could change their minds.[246]

Curiously, in August 2008, a German Egyptoloy forum, *Isis and Osiris*, interviewed Zahi Hawass about the find, asking whether Mathieson had actually discovered Imhotep's tomb in Saqqara. Hawass answered:

> What Mathieson has found is a mud brick structure that probably dates to the 5th Dynasty, much later than the lifetime of Imhotep. This shows how easy it is for the wrong information to get out concerning archaeological discoveries—people were eager to jump to the conclusion that it was the long-sought tomb of the great architect. In order to avoid such misunderstandings and the negative publicity that follows, we require excavators to inform the SCA of their discoveries and verify all of their information before announcing them to the public. Violation of this policy is grounds for the revocation of an archaeologist's permission to work in Egypt.[247]

Sadly, Ian Mathieson passed away in 2010 at the age of eighty-three, and the leadership of the survey project moved to Egyptologist Campbell

Price. Currently, the project's official website still says the following about Mathieson's find:

> In 2005 and 2006 our geophysical survey was extended to the north and east where we hoped to link our work with the existing 1st and 2nd Dynasty tombs excavated by J E Quibell and W B Emery during 1912 to 1958. The survey proved to be very rewarding in that many previously unrecorded mastaba tombs were found. They extended across the site, linking up with the above excavations.
>
> It was during this survey that the two largest structures yet discovered in the Saqqara Necropolis were recorded. The largest unit appears to be a mud brick enclosure which measures approximately 90 metres in length and 40 metres in width. It has walls over five metres thick, with an entrance in the south east corner of the east wall.
>
> There appears to have been a mound in the centre, where it can be seen there has been an attempt at excavation. Otherwise, the remainder of the structure appears untouched, almost a copy of the Step Pyramid enclosure.
>
> The second large enclosure lies some 20 metres to the east and is approximately 70 metres in length and 50 metres wide. It has very thick walls and a complicated internal structure which could point to a temple or courtyard with columns. An attempt at excavation is apparent in the north central area.
>
> Someone of the standing of Imhotep would command the artisans and labour needed to build such imposing structures and it is surely time we carried out further exploration.
>
> Due to the sensitive nature of the area, there is a ban on excavation work until 2013.[248]

It is our hope that, whatever is actually at the site of Mathieson's important find, it is indeed being protected from looting and theft. And perhaps in

the near future, one of the most important finds of modern Egyptology—
Imhotep's tomb—just may emerge.

The Armant Expedition

In the mid-1930s, just a few years after Hassanein Bey discovered Gebel
Uwainat and reported his finding of prehistoric rock art, another scientific expedition to Armant in Upper Egypt was sponsored by philan-
thropist Robert Mond. Sir Robert was an extremely wealthy British
chemist who also happened to be a very keen student of Egyptian
archaeology. He financed the Armant Expedition, which was headed
by British archaeologist Oliver H. Myers and his assistant, German art
historian and Egyptologist Hans Winkler.[249] The expedition was supported by a huge cohort of experts in mineralogy, metallurgy, botany,
entomology, petrology, pathology, paleontology, zoology, and epigraphy.
Myers and his team soon discovered rudimentary prehistoric artifacts
that would be seen as:

> . . . a link between the Predynastic cultures of the [Nile] Valley
> and the prehistoric rock drawing of the Libyan Desert [Western
> Desert] . . . that he [Myers] attributed to a nomadic desert society
> which he called the *Saharan culture* . . . [with] puzzling similarity
> shared by Armant's Predynastic inhabitants and the faraway pre-
> historic peoples of Gebel Uwainat and Gilf Kebir.[250]

The Predynastic pottery and rock drawings that Myers found in the
vicinity of Armant prompted him to conclude that "the true connections of this culture [Predynastic Egyptians] are to be found in the
Sahara, and the Nubian resemblances must be attributed to infiltration
from that area."[251]

Another important region a little to the north of Lower Nubia that
the prehistoric black-skinned people occupied was Gebelein (ancient
Inerty), located some thirty kilometers south of modern Luxor. A further
location was the nearby town of Hierakonpolis, ancient Nekhen.

Although most Egyptologists assert that Imhotep was native to
Memphis in northern Egypt, there are a few who oppose this view and

think that he may be from Upper Egypt, probably Gebelein. In his book *Egypt Before the Pharaohs,* British scholar Michael Rice commented on the possibility that Imhotep's father was an Upper Egyptian called Kanefer who held the title Director of (Building) Works, and, therefore, that "there may have been a family tradition to account for Imhotep's architectural genius."[252] If Imhotep was from Upper Egypt, then the regions of Gebelein and Hierakonpolis do indeed seem likely locations. This is supported by one of the official titles held by Imhotep that was found printed on a clay wall at Saqqara: *medjeh Nekhen,* Master Builder of Nekhen, which clearly gives credence to his likely Upper Egyptian origin. Indeed, Lauer himself called Imhotep "the builder of Nekhen, from the town of Nekhen, which is Hierakonpolis."[253]

According to Michel Baud, referring to his colleague Luc Pfisch, the term *medjeh Nekhen,* rather than meaning the builder of Nekhen, was a title of Imhotep related to the personal service of the king regarding food offerings and the furniture of the palace and tomb. Yet the title (which Baud translates as Chief of Nekhen) implies an architect, builder, or master sculptor, since the sign *(medjeh)* is a builder's adze or cutting tool (see Gardiner T7). In any case, this term is also used for another title of Imhotep on the plinth of the contemporary statue of Netjerykhet, where he is called *medjeh genouty (ou),* which Baud himself translates as Master of the Sculptors and Masons.[254]

There are also the various stories told about Imhotep, albeit from much later times, one of which says that his mother was a beautiful singer called Kheredu-ankh and a daughter of the god Banebjedet, the so-called Ram of Mendes.[255] It was also said that Imhotep was the son of the creator god Ptah,[256] making the lioness goddess of Upper Egypt—Sekhmet, Ptah's consort—his stepmother. But a more down-to-earth claim was that Imhotep was the son of the Upper Egyptian architect Kanefer. One comes to learn, when studying ancient Egypt in depth and with an open mind, that many alleged legends transmit a kernel of truth. At any rate, what seems fairly clear is that there was a desire among Egyptians of the Late Period to "dualize" Imhotep's parentage so that one family was connected to Upper Egypt and the other to Lower Egypt.

The Souls of Nekhen

From earliest times, perhaps even far back into prehistory, the ancient Egyptians called their royal ancestors the Souls of Nekhen and the Souls of Pe. Nekhen—modern Kom el Ahmar, classical Hierakonpolis—is an Upper Egyptian town some eighty kilometers south of Luxor; Pe—classical Buto and modern Tell el Fara'in—is a town in Lower Egypt in the Delta, some 140 kilometers north of Cairo. In ancient times, Nekhen was considered the capital of Upper Egypt and Pe the capital of Lower Egypt. Nekhen, however, was probably the older settlement and the original capital of Egypt before the so-called Unification of the Two Kingdoms or Two Lands. In the Pyramid Texts and other religious texts, it is made clear that "the Souls (*Baui*) of Nekhen and Pe" was a designation for divine ancestors. Those of Nekhen were depicted as jackal-headed men, while those of Pe were depicted as falcon-headed men. Both were often shown kneeling in the so-called *huna* position, with their left hands raised with clenched fists and their right hands against their chests, also with clenched fists. This kneeling position and the gesture with the hands and clenched fists were displayed during the king's *heb-sed*, or royal jubilee. Jubilation was displayed by the performers apparently beating their chests in order to make a gurgling sound while singing.

The Souls of Nekhen and the Souls of Pe.

The town of Nekhen—Hierakonpolis, meaning "falcon city" in Greek—was sacred to the falcon god Horus, yet, oddly, the Souls of Nekhen were depicted as jackal-headed men, while it was the Souls of Pe who were shown as falcon-headed men. Jackals were animals that roamed the adjacent desert; hence the depiction suggests that the original ancestors of Nekhen—and thus of all Egyptians—had come from the desert. The god of Nekhen was Horus of Nekhen, clearly regarded as the very first ancestor of the lineage of Horus kings that were to follow. The falcon god Horus was also venerated at Pe and so they too were known as the Followers of Horus and sometimes also as the Souls of Heliopolis. Although Nekhen is possibly older and therefore the home of these original divine ancestors, the association with Pe and Heliopolis was perhaps a political and/or religious reform that occurred when Upper and Lower Egypt were unified.[257]

Be that as it may, since Imhotep's father was from Upper Egypt where Nekhen was the capital and Imhotep's name meant He Who Comes in Peace, then his title *medjeh Nekhen* strongly implies that he was also from this city.[258]

Greater Nubia

Archaeologists and anthropologists have a tendency to segregate regions, even small sites, into parts to facilitate their work. This is understandable; but it can also sometimes make matters complicated when studying the development of events in prehistory—before Dynastic Egypt began—because it can give a distorted view of how the ancient Egyptians themselves regarded their land and geography. Open any book on Egyptian prehistory and you will spend more time trying to remember the various names of cultures and settlements than anything else. All one has to do is read the Introduction to Hoffman's excellent book, *Egypt Before the Pharaohs* (Ark Books, 1984), to realize how hopelessly complex and, as he himself admits, boringly dull anthropologists have made this otherwise fascinating subject. In Hoffman's own words:

> All too often we either bore our audiences with laundry lists of countless archeological sites or preach to them like modern Savonarolas, denouncing or ignoring all that has gone before in

the name of a narrowly based conception of scientific rigor. Perhaps this is why it is painful to read, let alone understand many contemporary prehistorians.[259]

We have no intention, therefore, of reviewing the laundry list of archaeological prehistoric sites, let alone explaining their names here. Were we to do so, it would require another book at the very least. Suffice it to say that the Nile Valley in Egypt was inhabited by New Stone Age (Neolithic) people in the region today known as Lower Nubia, when a highly sophisticated black-skinned people—bringing along their domesticated cattle, their astronomical know-how, and their sky-oriented religious beliefs—came in from the adjacent Western Desert around the middle of the 4th millennium BC. It is almost certainly these newcomers who moved northward and unified the whole Egyptian Nile Valley into a united kingdom. What we need to focus on now, however, is the strong possibility that Imhotep was not just an Upper Egyptian, but also a direct descendant of these black-skinned ancestors who eventually became the Egyptians. Was Imhotep the "keeper," or high priest, of their esoteric and scientific knowledge?

The Land of the Black Egyptians

The region of Upper or southern Egypt of today that runs from Qena to Aswan, and the region of Lower Nubia of today that runs between Aswan and Abu Simbel, together cover some 450 kilometers of the Nile Valley. As everywhere along the Nile, the valley is flanked by desert on both sides. Recent evidence, as presented in detail in our previous book *Black Genesis*, strongly suggests that "civilization" first entered the Nile Valley in this 450-kilometer strip from the Western Desert (the Sahara).[260] Excavations over the last century conducted from Qena (Naqada) to Aswan have revealed a wealth of prehistoric artifacts that leave absolutely no doubt that civilization in Egypt took root first in that region and then, a bit later, intertwined with other cultures entering the Nile Valley from the east, the Levant, and the Mediterranean coastline to create the Egyptians of the Dynastic Era.

Nekhen, the original capital of Upper Egypt, was first excavated by the British in the 1890s, first by James Quibell (whom we have already encountered at Saqqara in chapter 2) and by another British Egyptologist,

F. W. Green. Green joined the newly created Geological Survey of Egypt in 1896 and made several expeditions into the Eastern and Western Deserts. He excavated under many eminent archaeologists, including Somers Clarke, George Reisner, and Flinders Petrie. His main work, however, was with Quibell at Nekhen from 1897 to 1899. Green was present during the spectacular find of the Narmer palette and the beautiful Predynastic Tomb 100 with its decorated walls. It was not far from Nekhen, at Gebelein, that several Predynastic desiccated corpses were unearthed from the hot

The earliest human remains that have been found in large quantities are from the Predynastic era of the so-called Badarian culture of Upper Egypt, which is dated to c. 4400 BC. A much older cemetery, however, has been discovered at Gebel Sahaba in Upper Nubia, dating from the Late Stone Age roughly 12,000 to 10,000 years ago. This cemetery contained some sixty skeletal remains of men, women, and children. According to anthropologists, these skeletons may have belonged to an early type of Homo sapiens like the Cro-Magnons, as they do not share the same physical features as Predynastic Egyptians, which demonstrates that "the latter were the product of further genetic modifications."[261]

In our book Black Genesis, we reported the find of another cemetery at Gebel Ramlah, some twenty kilometers from Nabta Playa, thus well within Egyptian territory and hardly 100 kilometers west of Lower Nubia.[262] This cemetery was dated to the Neolithic period and showed the dominant presence of sub-Saharan or black people alongside Mediterranean-type populations. In Appendix IV, we review evidence strongly linking the teeth from the Gebel Ramlah cemeteries to later Nile Valley populations.[263]

From this and other evidence, and from geographical considerations, it seems logical to conclude that the earliest migration into Egypt was from the southwest by a black-skinned African population, followed by another wave, also black-skinned, from the Sahara carrying the rudiments and ingredients of civilization—domesticated cattle, sophisticated religious ceremonies, astronomy, and even perhaps an early primitive form of stone building and large-stone sculpting. These newcomers entered the Nile Valley in the 4th millennium BC and, as the evidence strongly suggests, kick-started what modern scholars call Egyptian civilization.

sand, some so well preserved that it is hard to imagine them being nearly 5,000 years old—like the one nicknamed Ginger that is now at the British Museum.

When Quibell and Green arrived at Nekhen in December 1897, the area was relatively untouched by modern treasure hunters and vandals. The dams at Aswan, which would eventually control the natural flood, had not yet been built, nor had the deep canals that can be seen today at Kom el Ahmar (modern Nekhen). Within the walls of ancient Nekhen were the remains of ancient burials and a mysterious stone mound that, to this day, has not been explained.[264] A large wadi (dry river bed) ran along the northwest side of the town. On its western bank were the remains of a Predynastic cemetery, on top of which stood the ruins of a massive mud-brick fortress built by the pharaoh Khasekhemwy, last king of the 2nd Dynasty and the presumed father of King Netjerykhet/Djoser, the builder of the Step Pyramid Complex.

This fortress, which Hoffman calls the "last enigma associated to Khasekhemwy," was first explored scientifically by an English architect turned Egyptologist, Somers Clarke, who had worked there with Quibell and Green in the late 1890s, and later, in 1905, by British archaeologist John Garstang. Today, most Egyptologists believe that this fortress was probably a temple, perhaps a mortuary monument for Khasekhemwy. Unfortunately, these early archaeologists were more interested in Predynastic graves (some 188 graves were opened according to Garstang), and didn't much bother to record, let alone publish, the architectural details of this enigmatic structure properly. Sadly, because of the modern canals built in the area, the fortress and huge walls of the Early Dynastic town, some of which were virtually intact in 1897, have now been reduced to shapeless heaps in a mere three-quarters of a century by the moisture coming from the canals.

From Clarke's scant records and from what remains of this building today, however, Egyptologists were able to deduce that there was an outer wall some ten meters high and 2.34 meters thick, as well as an inner wall; the two were separated by a narrow space of about 2.3 meters. The outer wall was plain, whereas the inner wall was built in panels, very reminiscent of the boundary wall of the Step Pyramid Complex at Saqqara.

Had this fortress or tomb or temple of Khasekhemy at Hierakonpolis been designed and constructed by Imhotep's architect father, Kanefer?

And was it because of this that Imhotep was to become an architect himself, and eventually join the court of Netjerykhet/Djoser at Memphis?

Point of Contact

Just beyond Nekhen is the open Western Desert, or Sahara. The vast sandy, dusty area adjacent to Nekhen is filled with debris from the largest Predynastic settlement in Egypt.[265] In that region, there was also a red sandstone mound that, as elsewhere in this desert, contained debris and artifacts from the Neolithic era. Typical of 19th-century archaeologists, Quibell and Green ignored both the Predynastic and Neolithic evidence and focused on the more sensational Dynastic artifacts, which, after all, were more lucrative for museums and private collectors in those days. Quibell and Green did, however, made some amazing discoveries at Nekhen, not the least of which was the Narmer palette and other valuable artifacts like the so-called Two Dog palette, which dated to 3200 BC and is now in the Ashmolean Museum in Oxford.

The hunting dogs are the dominant feature in this fascinating artifact. During a recent visit at the newly refurbished Ashmolean Museum, however, our attention was drawn to the reverse side of the palette, which depicts, among many other figures, a strange human-bodied creature with the head of an animal with long ears and pointed snout. It is often described as a donkey or fox playing the flute. But the latest interpretation by British Egyptologist Barry Kemp is probably closer to the truth. Kemp observes that the scene "...portrays life allegorically as an unequal conflict between the strong and the weak, seemingly animated by the flute-playing presence of the Seth-like figure in the bottom left corner."[266] Another interpretation, from Geoffrey W. Bromiley, suggests that it depicts "a fox playing an end-blown flute, accompanied by a dancing giraffe and ibex."[267]

The identification of this Seth-headed mythical creature that appears to be playing the flute is most interesting. According to Wilkinson:

[The god Seth] seems to have been originally a desert deity who early came to represent the forces of disturbance and confusion in the world. He is attested from the earliest periods and survived until late in the dynastic age. . . . An ivory artefact [sic] carved in his distinctive form is known from Naqada I Period (4000–3500

BC) and the god appears on standards carved on the mace-head of the Protodynastic ruler Scorpion indicating that he was certainly well established by this time.[268]

Michael Rice, who published an extensive thesis on Egypt's Predynastic era, not only concords with this view, he also feels that there was originally a "Sethian clan" and a "Falcon clan" that, at some point during the 2nd Dynasty, clashed. In Rice's words:

> As the Second Dynasty unfolded it is evident that some of the ancient influences in the Valley, dormant or repressed during the First Dynasty, began to stir. Some sort of reaction against the Falcon clan seems to have occurred and this found its focus evidently in the deep-routed honours paid by the southern people to the god Set(h).[269]

Recall from chapter 2 that, even though all of the kings of Egypt from earliest times had the falcon (Horus) symbol over their serekh, there were nonetheless two exceptions, namely King Peribsen and King Khasekhemwy of the 2nd Dynasty—the immediate predecessors of King Netjerykhet/Djoser, who probably was the son of the latter. Peribsen's serekh had the Seth dog on it, whereas Khasekhemwy had both the Seth dog *and* the Horus falcon. The distinct impression one gets is that some sort of rebellion against the Followers of Horus took place during the 2nd Dynasty by the Followers of Seth, perhaps a much older clan of black-skinned people originally from the Western Desert who had been subdued forcefully and integrated into the Horus clan by the 1st-Dynasty King Narmer.

This rebellion—a sort of archaic Tahrir Revolution—seems to have been led by Peribsen and to have succeeded—at least for a while. In the reign of his successor, Khasekhemy, however, some sort of truce took place leading to a merger of the gods Horus and Seth into the person of the divine king, as attested on his serekh. This, too, was short-lived, for Khasekhemy's son/successor, Netjerykhet/Djoser, not only removed the Seth symbol and used only the Horus symbol, but also moved his court to the North at Memphis and chose nearby Saqqara, not Nekhen, for his revolutionary funerary complex.

This historical sequence of events seems to be confirmed by an elaborate historical text inscribed in the temple of Edfu dedicated to the falcon god Horus. This text narrates how the now-deified Imhotep informs King Netjerykhet/Djoser how the god Horus, upon returning to Egypt after a military campaign abroad, finds that his brother Seth has usurped his kingdom. Another inscription at Edfu claims that the plan of the temple was culled from "the book that fell from the sky north of Memphis" and that it was built using a construction manual that was written by Imhotep himself. From all these archaeological and textual clues, we are compelled to think that the Followers of Seth were originally from the Paleolithic culture of the Sahara. After becoming Followers of Horus, these people temporarily reasserted their authority in the 2nd Dynasty, but then lost it again—or were assimilated—in the reign of Netjerykhet/Djoser.

Was the Seth animal, therefore, originally a Saharan symbol? In chapter 2, we saw how Belgian anthropologist Pierre de Maret argued that this dog-like animal was actually an aardvark. We also saw how Mark Borda found rock art depicting an aardvark in the region of Gebel Arkenu near Gilf Kebir, precisely where the black-skinned prehistoric/Neolithic people were living prior to coming into the Nile Valley. And we have seen that it was already common for the same Neolithic-era people in the Gebel Uwainat–Gilf Kebir region to depict humans with zoomorphic, often cow-like, heads similar to Seth's. All this evidence, together with the Sethian symbolism of the Two Dog palette found at Nekhen and the fortress there where evidence of Neolithic presence was found, strongly implies that Imhotep's ancestors were black-skinned Africans from the extreme southwest of Egypt. This may explain why the Souls of Nekhen, the divine ancestors, were depicted with jackal heads in a region where the falcon god Horus was venerated. It may also explain the combined Seth and Horus symbolism on the serekh of Khasemkhemwy. According to Wilkinson:

> [A]t the beginning of his reign, the last king of the Second Dynasty adopted the Horus name of Khasekhem, "the power has arrived." Later, however, he added the Seth-animal to the top of his serekh, and changed his name accordingly to the dual form Khasekhemy, "the two powers have appeared," together with the additional epithet *nbwy htp im=f,* "the two lords are at peace in him. . . . " In the early part of his reign Khasekhem seems to have shown particular interest in, and reverence for, Hierakonpolis

[Nekhen], the Predynastic capital in the far south of the country. ... the Horus-falcon atop of the king's serekh wears only the white crown associated with Upper Egypt.[271]

The symbolism of Khasekhemwy's serekh would also imply that some sort of political compromise took place between the Followers of Horus and the Followers of Seth, which then explains the name of Imhotep— He Who Comes in Peace, i.e., a Seth follower perhaps coming in peace to Memphis to join the court of the Horus king, Netjerykhet/Djoser. Wilkinson, among others, sees in the serekh of Khasekhemy the possibility of a conflict between north and south similar to the conflict of Seth and Horus in the so-called Creation Myth.

The "north" in this context, however, may not imply the Delta region of Lower Egypt, but rather the region of Abydos, which is 150 kilometers north of Hierakonpolis/Nekhen. This may be why Khasekhemy chose Abydos to build the structures of his mortuary complex, which, according to Wilkinson, are truly impressive:

> In their design and symbolism they point the way towards the Step Pyramid complex of Netjerykhet a generation later. The burial chamber of *Khasekhemy's* tomb was lined with blocks of dressed limestone.[272]

The connection between Abydos and the Step Pyramid Complex is also attested by dozens of seals found at Abydos in the precinct and tomb of Khasekhemwy that bear the name of his son, Netjerykhet.[273] Considering all the evidence, it is not unreasonable to suppose that Imhotep's father was the architect of Khasekhemy at Nekhen, and that his title of *medjeh* (master mason-sculptor) was inherited by Imhotep, hence his title of *medjeh Nekhen* inscribed under the Step Pyramid at Saqqara.

There is, however, one more point to consider. And it involves other creatures that once roamed the Sahara—one of them, especially, in the rugged mountainous regions of the southwest of Egypt.

Giraffes, Lions, Cattle, and Barbary Sheep

Returning to the Two Dogs palette, we can easily identify several lions, Barbary sheep, cattle, gazelles, and even a giraffe. These animals are not native to Egypt, not even in Early Dynastic times—with the possible exceptions of the lion and the gazelle, which are known to have inhabited the deserts bordering the Nile until fairly recently. But the giraffe, which today lives in the wild at least 1,000 kilometers farther to the south of Egypt, is prolifically depicted in the rock art at Gebel Uwainat and also in the rock art of the southern part of the Eastern Desert, showing that this animal was quite common in prehistoric times in Egypt's deserts near its southern border. The *waddan,* or Barbary sheep, still exist today in Egypt, but only in the mountain regions of Gilf Kebir and Gebel Uwainat.

Robert Bauval holding the bones of a modern waddan that we found in Uwainat in 2008.

We can vouch for this, because we came across the fresh skeleton of a waddan at Gebel Uwainat during our 2008 expedition, and we were told by our guide that the Bedouin, who occasionally come to this remote region, still hunt the waddan for food.[274] The Two Dogs palette also shows the long-horned eland that today exists only in the sub-Sahara. Interestingly, in the Uwainat inscriptions discovered by Mark Borda in late 2007, a man from Tekhebet, a yet unknown location, is depicted offering a long-horned eland to King Mentuhotep II.

There is also evidence of prehistoric astronomy at Hierakonpolis/ Nekhen that is tantalizingly similar to evidence we found at Gebel Uwainat. James O. Mills, an archaeologist who was working at Hierakonpolis in the 1990s, reported that he and an Egyptian colleague, Ahmed Radwan, discovered "a complex geometric design etched and pecked into the bedrock" near the crest of a hill in the vicinity of Hierakonpolis. It also contained typical petroglyphs showing fauna like "elephants, a giraffe, and . . . a large cat, probably a lion." Here is how Mills described the complex geometric design:

> The glyph lies level with the slope of the hill, which faces the flood plain. 12 or 13 pecked divots form a bulging "V" shape which points eastwards. 2 and possibly 3 additional divots form a horizontal row within the "V." The divots are superimposed over an earlier series of short parallel incised marks along the left arm of the "V" across its center. In addition, a series of incisions above the "V" are arranged in an arch. This petroglyph is a totally unique representation. The glyph's symmetry and repetition of form suggest that it may have been used for Pneumonic or orientation purposes. Its bilateral symmetry along an east–west axis presented the question of its being a record or device for astronomical observations.[275]

In brief, Mills suspected that the V-shaped petroglyph and the various markings around it may have indicated the directions of the two solstices at rising, since the angle the V formed was very close to the angle the solstices form, about 52°.

Unfortunately, Mills was not sure if the rock on which the glyph was carved had been moved, thus shedding doubt on his suggestion.

Petroglyphs at Karkur Tahl in Gebel Uwainat, suspected to be astronomical markers.

Yet, if what Mills suspected is correct, it adds even more support to the thesis that prehistoric people at Hierakopolis/Nekhen may have been the ones who also created the astronomical alignment to the Summer Solstice at Nabta Playa's Calendar Circle. In addition, when we were at Gebel Uwainat in 2008 exploring petroglyphs in Karkur Tahl, we came across some strange markings, engravings on a stony hill, that are very reminiscent of those found by Mills at Hierakonpolis. Like Mills, we suspected that they were solar markers. And sure enough, when we returned with our electronic compass, we found the central engraved arrow pointing toward the Summer Solstice sunset.

The Two Dogs palette and other similar palettes of the Early Dynastic period found in Upper Egypt and Nubia certainly indicate, if not prove, that the Predynastic and Early Dynastic Egyptians are none other than the black-skinned people depicted on the rock art in southwestern Egypt. And if so, could these ancestors have been the Souls of Nekhen—the elusive ancestors also called the Followers of Horus and/or Seth?

Nubia Today

When we take foreign visitors to Aswan today, we make sure to visit the Nubian village that is near the First Cataract on the west side of the Nile. The journey is usually made by local *felluca* boats; visitors sail slowly upriver past the lovely Elephantine Island and through the gentle rapids of the cataract flanked with tall reeds and glistening outcrops of granite boulders. There are fine sand beaches along the way, and they sometimes swim in the cool, refreshing waters of the upper Nile. It is on these occasions that you can sense how the ancient Egyptians lived along this sacred river and why they developed such a great respect and veneration for it and the nature nearby. Seeing the black Nubian children playing and swimming, you are struck by a sense of timelessness as you contemplate the descendants of the black-African Egyptians of thousands of years ago.

There is now a small modern concrete jetty at the edge of the ancient Nubian village for disembarking. From there, you go up a wide concrete stairway to be greeted by dozens of Nubian women and young girls selling handmade wooden dolls and bead necklaces. Black-skinned and with gleaming white teeth, the Nubians are a very beautiful people, inside and out. Walking along the single unpaved road that runs through the village, you pass rows of shops selling colorful scarfs, handmade vases, and the usual imitation pharaonic statuettes and amulets, as well as exotic herbs and spices. Near the south end of the village is the local teahouse where you can relax and get some respite from the oppressive heat. Here, the owner will bring you mint tea with homemade unleavened bread served with thick dark palm honey.

Sometimes, in this very Nubian context, we are coaxed into telling the strange story of the so-called *Ta-seti* controversy, which concerns an ancient site discovered in the early 1960s near the city of Qustul in Upper Nubia, about thirty kilometers south of Abu Simbel, just before the region was totally flooded after completion of the High Dam. Qustul is now submerged, lost forever like a mini-Atlantis beneath the artificially created Lake Nasser.

The first archaeologist to excavate at Qustul was Keith Seele in 1962–1964. He was lucky to be in time to examine a series of large tombs before the High Dam was completed. The large size of the tombs and the wealthy artifacts they contained indicate that they were used for royalty. Later, in the early 1980s, Professor Bruce B. Williams of the Oriental Institute Nubian Expedition was to write of these tombs that "the range of these and other fragments from the plundered cemetery [at Qustul] began to indicate a wealth and complexity that could only be called royal." This led Williams to claim that this ancient burial site, now termed "A-Group of Cemetery L," indicated that Qustul Nubian kings predated by some 300 years the 1st Dynasty of Egyptian kings.

The consensus among Egyptologists, however, was that this conclusion was unlikely, if not impossible. So Williams's work was treated with the intellectual catatonia that seems to plague modern Egyptology. At any rate, hieroglyphs found at a nearby site provided a name for this "lost Nubian kingdom": *Ta-seti*, Land of the Bow, so named for the prowess of Nubian archers. In February 1987, the Oriental Institute organized an exhibition titled *Nubia—Its Glory and Its People*. Concerning the A-Group, which was called "An Early Kingdom in the Land of the Bow" and dated to 3800–3100 BC, the brochure of the exhibition asserted:

> Most surprising, evidence that early Pharaohs ruled in A-Group
> Nubia was discovered by the Oriental Institute at Qustul, almost

at the modern Sudanese border. A cemetery of large tombs containing evidence of wealth and representations of the rulers and their victories. Other representations and monuments could then be identified, and in the process, a lost kingdom, or Land of the Bow, was discovered. In fact, the cemetery at Qustul leads directly to the first great royal monuments of Egypt in a progression. Qustul in Nubia could well have been the seat of Egypt's founding dynasty.[276]

It is our opinion that there has been much bias, unwarranted caution, and a form of academic denial and perhaps even racism in the handling of this discovery—not to mention the unfortunate fact that the archaeological evidence at Qustul is now dozens of meters under Lake Nasser. This has obstructed the emergence of an important truth about Egypt's origins—or, at very least, has diluted the huge importance of Keith Seele's findings and conclusions. Today, the issue is lost in unsavory verbiage between those who support and those who reject the likelihood that the A-Group Nubians were Predynastic Nubian kings of Egypt. Certainly, the matter is far from being settled.

The Oriental Institute was part of the international salvage excavation project headed by Seele under UNESCO inside the reservoir area of the High Dam at Aswan between 1960 and 1964. When Seele died in 1971, the Institute began a new project to complete the publication of data from the Nubian Expedition under the directorship of Dr. Bruce Williams, a graduate in Egyptology from the University of Chicago. Williams devoted his whole academic career to the Nubian publications project. Apparently some data still remains to be published. The same UNESCO preservation effort created in response to the building of the Aswan High Dam created the Combined Prehistoric Expedition to survey the desert region west of Aswan. This expedition, headed by Fred Wendorf, eventually discovered Nabta Playa.

Conclusion

Throughout this book, we have shown evidence of a black prehistoric people that developed a high knowledge of astronomy and methods of cattle domestication and breeding, and began a cult with complex rituals related to the stars and seasonal rhythms of the rainfalls in the open Sahara. These mysterious people also developed the social sophistication and knowledge to move huge stones, shape or sculpt them, and place them to mark the rising points of special stars and constellations to indicate the yearly cycle of the sun. The evidence is overwhelming that they made contact with the Nile Valley at the very time and place of the origin of the pharaonic civilization and, more pertinent to our quest, where Imhotep started his life and acquired his amazing knowledge. An intellectual and spiritual bridge was thus created whereby the knowledge acquired by these prehistoric black-African forefathers could legitimately be transmitted into the Nile Valley, allowing us to see Imhotep, not just as an Egyptian, but also as an African who first carried that ancient knowledge and the memory from whence it came to the plan of Saqqara to ensure its survival in the Great Step Pyramid Complex.

With all the evidence and clues that we have investigated in this book, we have reached a point where we must, at least for now, pause in our search for the real Imhotep and his black-African ancestry. From now on, we will always think of him above all else as African—a sage among the greatest of all sages, immensely wise and learned, and constructively influential in the development of humanity. It is a testimony to his name that his legacy at Saqqara is still universally admired after more than 4,500 years. All Africans, be they on the mother continent or in the West among the diaspora of African Americans and Afro-Europeans, should be proud of such an illustrious ancestor—one known to the ages as He Who Comes in Peace.

Imhotep is rightly regarded today as Father of Architecture, Inventor of Medicine, and Inventor of the Calendar. His magnificent Temple of the Stars at Saqqara still awes and thrills visitors from all over the world. With this present book, however, it is our hope that a new epithet be added to his name:

Imhotep the African, Architect of the Cosmos.

THE ORIGINS OF THE BENBEN STONE

ADAPTED FROM "INVESTIGATION ON THE ORIGINS OF THE BENBEN STONE"
BY ROBERT G. BAUVAL[279]

The prevailing theory on the design of monumental true pyramids is that their shape was modeled on the benben—a conical-shaped stone venerated in the Mansion of the Phoenix at Heliopolis.[280] The Mansion of the Phoenix was presumably within the precinct of the Great Sun Temple of Heliopolis, but there is evidence that the benben was worshipped there well before the sun cult of Ra.[281] The stone was probably originally associated to Atum, a much older deity who was mainly identified with the act of creation via his masturbation.[282]

Atum was later assimilated to Ra, as Ra-Atum. Though it is often recognized that the older, stepped pyramid design is the product of a predominant star cult,[283] it is nevertheless widely advocated that the "true pyramid" design that succeeded the stepped design reflects the solar ideas induced by the powerful sun cult favored in the Pyramid Age. The solar ideas supposedly dominated the stellar and Osirian cults from the 4th Dynasty, when the true pyramid design was introduced.[284] Many have therefore claimed that the benben stone was symbolic of the sun. James Breasted, an instigator of such claims, noted the similarity of the word *benben* with the word *benbenet* (the pyramid-shaped apex of an obelisk)

Figure A1. Atum masturbating and creating the stars and humans.

and accordingly declared that "an obelisk is simply a pyramid upon a lofty base which has become a shaft." Breasted also speculated that, because "the obelisk, as is commonly known, is a symbol sacred to the Sun-god ... [it followed that] the king was buried under the very symbol of the Sun-god which stood in the holy of holies in the Sun-temple at Heliopolis."[285]

This, perhaps too hasty, conclusion inevitably extended the solar symbolism to the whole bulk of the monument below the pyramidion/ capstone. Breasted's ideas were later supported and expanded by Edwards, who also proposed that the occasional sight of an immaterial triangle afforded by the sun's rays striking downward through the clouds at sunset could have been the origin of the benben's shape "and its architectural derivative, the true Pyramid." Edwards looked for textual evidence in the Pyramid Texts, and quoted passages 1108 and 1231:

> "I have laid down for myself this sunshine of yours as a stairway under my feet ... " and: "May the sky make the sunlight strong for you, may you rise up to the sky ... " (I have used R. O. Faulkner's more recent translation here).

Edwards thus added that "the temptation to regard the true Pyramid as a material representation of the sun's rays and consequently as a means whereby the dead king could ascend to heaven seems irresistible." True, the sun's rays are said to be a means for the dead pharaoh to ascend to the sky; but several other "means" for precisely the same purpose are also mentioned in the Pyramid Texts—on a ladder: "The king climbs to the sky on a ladder" (Ut. 304); on the wind: "the king is bound for the sky on the wind" (pyr. 309); on a storm cloud/thunderbolt: "The king is a flame (moving) before the wind . . . there is brought to him a way of ascent to the sky" (Ut. 261); on a hailstorm: "the hailstorms of the sky have taken me" (pyr. 336); on a reed float/boat: "the reed-floats of the sky are set in place for me . . . I am ferried over to the eastern sky" (Ut. 263); by climbing a rope: "set the rope aright, cross the Milky Way" (Ut. 254); and on the thighs of Isis: "I ascend [to the sky] upon the thighs of Isis" (pyr. 379).

Evidently, climbing on the sun's rays was not the only means, but just another cosmic means made available for the celestial ascent of the departed king. Giving preference to any one of them for having influenced the shape of the true pyramid/benben is unwarranted, especially when neither is specifically mentioned in the passage in question.

There is, however, a passage that does directly equate the pyramid construction to Osiris: "This king is Osiris, this pyramid of the king is Osiris, this construction of his is Osiris, betake yourself to it, do not be far from it in its name of pyramid" (pyr. 1657). Osiris in the Old Kingdom was primarily a star god, whose soul was identified to the constellation of Orion: "Behold Osiris has come as Orion" (pyr. 820). Furthermore, the dead king was mostly identified with Osiris, and his star soul is usually paired with Orion: "O king, you are this Great Star, the companion of Orion" (pyr. 882). On account of this, it would seem apt to examine the possibility of a stellar symbolism for the benben and, consequently, the true pyramid's shape.

Though the Mansion of the Phoenix in which the benben stood may have been linked to the sun temple of Ra in the latter part of the Pyramid Age, an association of the benben with the sun does not necessarily follow. For one thing, no satisfactory explanation has yet been given for why a conical stone would be venerated as a solar symbol (usually depicted as a disc). Supporters of the benben's solar symbolism offer as one explanation that the benben was representative of the Primeval Mound on which the first sunrise took place. This would imply that the pyramid also had a similar correlation.

This hypothesis is justifiably rejected by Edwards,[287] for though the Primeval Mound is perhaps indirectly linked to the much older mastaba tomb structure of the first three Dynasties, extending this association to the pyramidal tomb is certainly stretching this possible correlation too far. In any case, the mastaba tomb ideology may not be exclusively solar, for Badawy seems to have found strong stellar symbolism in its orientation and design.[288] The radical change of the tomb design into monumental pyramids is likely grounded in a new interpretation by the clergy of the skyward ascent of the departed pharaoh, and possibly in new evidence of his posthumous form, which was, for some hitherto unexplained reason, now believed to be conical or pyramidal.

It is also often argued that the phoenix, a mythical bird that was said to appear at dawn perched on a pole extending from a benben, was representative of the sun god's self-creating power.[289] But the phoenix's cosmic identification was by no means exclusive to the sun. In the Middle Kingdom, for example, the phoenix was also said to be the soul of Osiris, as well as the moon and sometimes the morning star—i.e., Venus.[290] The phoenix thus was symbolic of the rebirth at dawn, not only of the sun god, but also of cosmic beings in general. In the Book of the Dead (chapter 83, "Spell for Becoming the Phoenix (Bennu) Bird"), the phoenix claims: "I am the seed corn of every god."[291] His power of self-creation clearly symbolized the emerging (rebirth) of celestial bodies (gods) at dawn from the underworld, the tenebrous land of the dead below the horizon.

It is known that a sacred pillar was worshipped at Heliopolis before the benben.[292] The phallic symbolism of a pillar is, of course, obvious, and its association to the phallus of Atum seems almost a certainty, for in the Pyramid Texts we read:

> Atum is he who once came into being, who masturbated in On (Heliopolis). He took his phallus in his grasp that he might create orgasm by means of it . . . (pyr. 1248)

> O Atum-khoprer (as the Beetle or rising sun), you became high on the heights (pillar/mound?), you rose as the Benben stone in the Mansion Of The Phoenix in On . . . (pyr. 1652)

Frankfort suggested that the combination of the benben with a pillar—later stylized perhaps into an obelisk with a benbenet—may thus represent the

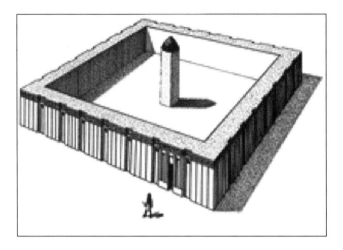

Figure A2. Artist's impression of the Temple of the Phoenix at Heliopolis.

semen or seed being ejaculated from a cosmic phallus associated to Atum.[293] Later, this fetish was probably considered sacred to Ra or Atum-Ra. In the Pyramid Texts, it is said:

> O Ra, make the womb of Nut pregnant with the seed of the spirit which is in her. (pyr. 990)

> Pressure is in your womb, O Nut, through the seed of the god which is in you; it is I [the king] who am the seed of the god which is in you ... (pyr. 1416–1417)

> ... the king is an imperishable star, son of the sky-goddess. . . (pyr. 1469)

> The king was fashioned by his father Atum ... (pyr.1466)

> O Ra-Atum, this king comes to you, an imperishable spirit (star?) ... your son comes to you, this king comes to you. (pyr.152)

Judging from these passages, it is evident that Nut was imagined to be the mother of the king in his star form, the latter sired by Ra/Atum. A pillar surging skyward, atop of which is placed a fetish representing a star seed and offered to the sky goddess for gestation in her womb, very much appears to be the intended symbolic function of the pillar/benben combined fetish at Heliopolis. In consideration of the above, it is indeed significant to note that the word *benben* means "to copulate" (to seed a womb?) when followed by the determinative of an erect phallus ejaculating semen.[294] Several words containing the root *ben* also have sexual meanings.[295]

In the Pyramid Texts, the astronomical/mythological scenario that must be considered is that the departed pharaoh becomes a "seed" to be reborn as a star. This seed is sired by Ra/Atum and gestated in the womb of Nut:

The king is your seed, O Ra. (pyr. 1508)

the king comes to you, O mother of the king, he has come to Nut, that you may bring the sky to the king and hang the stars for him . . . (pyr. 1516)

the sky conceives you with Orion . . . (pyr. 820)

Recitation by Nut, the greatly beneficent: the king is my eldest son who splits open my womb . . . (pyr. 1)

O King, you are this Great Star, the companion of Orion . . . the sky has borne you with Orion . . . (pyr. 882–883)

The King is a star brilliant . . . the King appears as a star . . . (pyr. 262–263)

For you belong to the stars that surround Ra. (pyr. 412)

You [Nut] have set this King as an imperishable Star who is in you . . . (pyr. 782)

The King is a star. (pyr. 1470)

The King is a star in the sky among the gods. (pyr. 1583)

I [the king] am a soul . . . a star of gold . . . (pyr. 887–889)

I sit among you, you stars of the Netherworld. (pyr. 953)

I am a star which illumines the sky . . . (pyr. 1455)

I am a nhh-star, the companion of nhh-star, I become a nhh-star
... (pyr. 909)

O Ra, for which you have said, O Ra, O for a Son! ... he having
a soul and being mighty and strong ... Here I am, O Ra; I am
your Son, I am a soul ... I row Ra when traversing the sky, even
I a star of gold. (pyr. 886–889)

I row Ra to the West ... I am a Nhh-Star. (pyr. Ut. 469)

my star is set on high with Ra ... (pyr. 698)

Figure A3. The earth god Geb with phallus erect toward the sky goddess Nut.

In consideration of this, it is justified to assume that the predominant symbolism for the pyramid would be stellar, for this monument undoubtedly
was considered the agency of the king's astral rebirth. The contemporary
names of several monumental pyramids indeed attest to such a stellar
symbolism: "Djedefra is a Sehetu star"; "Nebka is a star"; "The soul (*ba*) of
Sahura gleams"; "Sneferu gleams"; "Neferirkare has become a soul (*ba*)."[296]

The compounding of the pharaoh's name with that of his pyramid is
also significant, for it implies that the monument (or mainly its capstone,
as we shall later see) was regarded as being the transfigured form of the
departed pharaoh—viz., a star soul. Retaining the hypothesis that the
benben did inspire the designers of the true pyramid, in what manner can
this sacred stone's conical shape be related to the imagined shape of a star?

Taking into account the stellar destiny of the dead pharaoh and his astral "iron bones" (see below), the benben stone's supposedly cosmic origin, and most particularly its conical shape, it is justified to conjecture that this sacred stone was an "oriented" (conical) iron meteorite.

The idea in antiquity that meteorites were shooting or falling stars needs no further emphasis. Factually, meteorites are debris from space—mostly from broken-up asteroids—that fall on our planet and that can be recovered (as opposed to meteors, which completely burn up during atmospheric transit). Meteorites are classified into three main groups: iron meteorites (usually 90 percent iron and 10 to12 percent nickel), stony/iron meteorites, and stone meteorites. The largest known are the iron meteorites, as these tend to survive their impact with the ground more easily than the others for obvious reasons.

Most meteorites are, in fact, very small. Occasionally, however, a large meteorite enters our atmosphere. If it is very large (the famous 1.2-kilometers-wide Arizona meteor crater was caused by a lump of iron twenty-five meters across), it will retain most of its original velocity and usually explodes with dramatic effect just before hitting the ground, its mass breaking up into thousands of minute fragments. (The Arizona meteor caused a blast equivalent to a four-megaton nuclear explosion). Not all large meteorites, however, break up so easily. The largest single known meteoritic mass is the Hoba iron meteorite, which still lies in the place where it fell near Grootfontein farm in Southwest Africa.

Figure A4. The Hoba meteorite in Namibia.

This meteorite is estimated to be a sixty-ton chunk of iron. Most meteorites with a mass of 1,000 to 15,000 kilograms have their velocity dampened by the atmosphere, causing them to free-fall for the last twenty kilometers and thus strike the earth at about 0.1 kilometers per second. In the case of an iron meteorite, the odds of survival with minimal damage in such cases is good. Also, many meteorites retain their orientation in the direction of flight; this causes the front part to melt and flow toward the rear. The result—especially for the iron variety—is a meteorite having the characteristic shape of a rough cone. These are known as "oriented" meteorites.

Several oriented iron meteorites weighing from five to fifteen tons are known.[297] The best examples are the Morito meteorite (ten tons) and the Willamette meteorite (fourteen tons)—the names are usually taken from the places the meteorites were found. Morito is a well-preserved conical iron meteorite that is displayed in Mexico City. It measures about 110

Figure A5. The Willamette meteorite.

Figure A6. The Morito meteorite.

centimeters in height, while the base is about 150 centimeters. Indeed, it does look eerily like a pyramidal cone. Willamette is displayed in the American Museum of Natural History in New York.

There was a widespread belief among ancient Mediterranean people—including the Egyptians—that iron actually came from heaven, clearly an allusion to its meteoritic origin. Today, the average number of meteorite finds is only five per year—in spite of our sophisticated communication systems and greater scientific interest. However, a low number like this could hardly have caused the widespread belief in antiquity that iron came from the sky. Many scientists are of the opinion, therefore, that meteorite falls occurred more frequently in the past—a hypothesis apparently supported by astrophysics research.

The probability, therefore, of observing the fall of a large iron meteorite and also recovering it was higher in our remote past than it is today. Indeed, many sacred stones that were believed to have "fallen from heaven," and were accordingly worshipped in temples or shrines, were surely meteorites. The Ephesians (Acts 19:35), for example, are said to have worshipped in the temple of Diana "that symbol of her which fell from heaven." In the temple of Apollo in Delphi, a stone[298] probably shaped like an ovoid/cone (later to be replaced by the well-known Omphalos) was believed to have come from Cronnos, the sky god, and was the object of much veneration. This "stone of Cronnos" was most likely a meteorite.[299] A conical iron meteorite is also said to have been worshipped by the Phrygians in the 7th century BC.[300] The conical black stone known as Elagalabus was worshipped in Emessa and was a meteorite.[301] Not far from Emessa, in the temple of Heliopolis-Baalbek, black conical stones were venerated.[302] The Nabataean god Dushara was worshipped in the form of an obelisk or "an unhewn four-cornered blackstone."[303] Indeed, a modern example of such stone worship is the much venerated black stone kept in the Ka'aba shrine in Mecca, which is thought by geologists to be a meteorite recovered in antiquity.

British Egyptologist G. A. Wainwright has convincingly argued that iron in the Old Kingdom period was mostly obtained from iron meteorites.[304] It seems that man-made iron from terrestrial ores rarely contains nickel, whereas meteoritic iron contains a high proportion of this element—on average, 12 percent. Wainwright states that ornamental beads made of iron dating as far back as Predynastic times have been analyzed and shown to contain high levels of nickel, confirming their meteoritic origin.[305] Significantly, the word bja, meaning "iron" in ancient Egyptian, also meant the "material of which heaven was made."[306] It is therefore highly likely that meteoritic iron was also imagined to be the stuff from which were made the reborn kings who became star gods.[307] Certain passages in the Pyramid Texts are indeed very suggestive of such a concept:

> The king's bones are iron and the king's members are the imperishable stars . . . (pyr. 2051)

> I [the king] am pure, I take to myself my iron bones . . . my imperishable limbs are in the womb of Nut (pyr. 530)

> [M]y bones are iron and my limbs are the imperishable stars. (pyr. 1454)

It is also likely that chunks of iron meteorite—which generally have a lustred, black appearance—were associated or even confused with black hard stones like diorite, basalt, and dark-grey granite found in Upper Egypt. To a primitive mind unfamiliar with iron and its chemical properties, the resemblance can be uncanny. Not surprisingly, black basalt was called bja-kam, meaning "black iron,"[308] suggesting that basalt and similar stones were associated to meteoritic ironstone, and consequently to the "bones" of star gods.

Most capstones of monumental pyramids were probably made of granite.[309] The almost-black granite capstone of the pyramid of Amenemhet III in the Cairo museum is a fine example of this. It was discovered in 1902 by Maspero, who remarked that its surface had been "mirror" polished.[310] Such a description is typical for the appearance of a freshly fallen iron meteorite. Amenemhet III's capstone could well be the stylized man-made version of an oriented iron meteorite, symbolizing his materialized star soul.

The two lines of carved hieroglyphic inscriptions ornamenting the base of the capstone were first discussed by Maspero[311] and later by Breasted[312] and Piankoff.[313] In the inscriptions, several deities are evoked, among them supposedly the sun god (as The Lord of the Horizon) and

Orion-Osiris, the great star god of astral rebirth, depicted as a striding man holding a staff in one hand and cupping a large star in the other. On one side of the capstone are carved two large eyes surmounted by a disc with feathered wings. The inscription below states that "the face of Amenemhet is open, he sees the Lord of the Horizon as he sails in the sky." Incidentally, this curious winged face/head is also depicted in the Pyramid Texts in conjunction with iron:

> He has appeared upon the Stone (?), upon his throne, he has sharpened the iron by means of it . . . raise yourself, O king, gather your bones, take your head . . . O king, raise yourself as Min [the Phallic/fertility God], fly up to the sky and live with them, cause your wings to grow with your feathers on your head . . . (pyr. 1945–1948).

Another inscription on the Amenemhet III capstone states: ". . . the soul of King Amenemhet is higher than the heights of Orion."

Figure A7. The pyramidion/capstone of the pyramid of Amenemhet III.

Breasted's view that the inscriptions prove the solar symbolism of the capstone is surely incorrect, for it is fairly evident from such texts that we are to consider the capstone, not as the material representation of the sun god, but rather that of the king's star soul—a progeny of Ra, not Ra himself. It is in this capacity that the soul of the king, now established as a star object high above the base of the pyramid, does indeed participate in the eternal cycles of the sun god and the ancestral star gods as they sail across the sky each day.

The hieroglyphic sign for the word "pyramid" was sometimes depicted as a pyramid with a yellow apex, suggesting that the granite capstones of pyramids may have been gilded.[314] An inscription found by Jequier at the pyramid of a queen called Udjebten supports this hypothesis, for it speaks of a gilded capstone. A quasi-black granite capstone, the stylized representation of an oriented iron meteorite, finely polished and covered with a gold skin, would certainly bear potent symbolism associated to a primitive concept of a "living star"—i.e., a star soul shining in the sky, the bones of which were imagined to be made of iron, or bja-kam, and the "flesh" of which was gold. Evidence of this idea may be found in these passages:

> O King, raise yourself upon your iron bones and golden members, for this body of yours belongs to a god ... may your flesh be born to life and may your life be more than the life of the stars in their season of life ... (pyr. 2244)

> I [the king] row Ra when traversing the sky, even I a star of gold ... (pyr. 886–889)

As in many other cases of meteoritic worship by ancient peoples, it is likely that the benben stone once worshipped in the Mansion of the Phoenix was a meteorite. Its conical shape and its association with the pyramid's capstone—the latter a likely symbol of the star soul of the departed pharaoh made of "iron bones"—is very suggestive of an oriented iron meteorite, possibly a mass within the one- to fifteen-ton range. Such objects fallen from heaven were generally representative of "fallen stars," and likely provided the Egyptian clergy with a tangible sample of a star object, a "seed" of Ra-Atum.

It is recognized by many that the whole business of the rebirth rites performed for dead pharaohs was intensely, if not mainly, stellar. Krupp rightly noted that "the language of the stellar cycles appears to be interchangeable with the language of funeral rites."[315] It is also generally accepted that the essence of the royal funerary rites was the re-enactment of the resurrection of Osiris, the latter having been revived after death by magical rites of mummification performed by Isis, thus becoming the first royal mummy. But this resurrection of Osiris as a mummy is but an initial, partial stage of the magical rites; the second and final stage was his self-transfiguration into the star god Sahu-Orion, in whose form he becomes ruler of the Duat, a star world for the souls.[316] This second cosmic transfiguration is not often appreciated,[317] nor is its stellar implication properly understood. All the rituals, ceremonies, and litanies for the royal funeral, however, are implicit of such a two-step transfiguration of the dead king.

The fundamental point to be appreciated here is that both transfigurations—i.e., corpse to Osiris, and Osiris to star god—were deemed to be materially possible. First, the dead king was made into a dead Osiris;[318] then he was transfigured into a star soul. To achieve the first transfiguration, the corpse was actually dressed in the image of Osiris via a complex preparation that today is somewhat loosely termed mummification. Then the "Osirianized" corpse—i.e., the mummy—through its own latent power and aided by magical spells recited by the clergy, was expected to self-transfigure into a *Sahu*, or spiritualized body (pyr. 1716).[319] That no connection or word-play was intended between Sah (Orion, soul of Osiris) and Sahu (spiritual body of the dead Osiris-king) appears very unlikely.

In the Pyramid Age, this second stage of the self-transfiguration into a star was conveniently left in the charge of the pyramid itself, the latter proclaimed by the clergy as a monument endowed with the power to induce the metamorphosis of a dead Osiris into a living star.[320] This was probably imagined to happen by the upward transmittal of the soul of the entombed Osiris king into his star soul "seed"—i.e., the capstone/ star object crowning the pyramid. Thus the seed of Ra-Atum was thrust skyward into the custody of the cosmic mother, the sky goddess Nut, to be gestated and reborn at dawn as an established star in the firmament.

In the Pyramid Texts, we read:

Nut has laid her hands on you, O King, even she whose hair is long and whose breasts hang down; she carries you for herself to the sky, she will never cast the king down to earth. She bears you, O King, like Orion . . . (pyr. 2171–2172)

The King has come to you, O Mother of the king, he has come to Nut, that you may bring the sky to the king and hang up the stars for him, for his savior is the savior of your son who issued from you, the king's savior is that of Osiris your son who issued from you. (pyr. 1516)

If we link up these passages with passage 1657 ("this king is Osiris, this pyramid of the king is Osiris"), then much sense is made of, and modality given to, this esoteric litany.

THE GIZA DIAGONAL AND THE HORIZON OF KHUFU

ADAPTED FROM "THE GIZA DIAGONAL AND THE HORIZON OF KHUFU:
TRUE OR FALSE?" BY ROBERT G. BAUVAL

There are two persistent but erroneous theories regarding the layout of the Giza pyramids:

- The southeastern corners of the three main pyramids (G1, G2, and G3) form a diagonal deliberately intended to link up with the city of Heliopolis.

- The two larger pyramids of Khufu and Khafre on the Giza necropolis (referred to here as G1 and G2) were part of a unified plan initiated by Khufu in order to create a giant hieroglyphic sign representing the "sun disc between two mounds" (N27).

Figure A8. The hieroglyphic sign representing the sun—N27.

The two larger pyramids, G1 and G2, are of almost equal size and are placed in such a way as to have their northeast-southwest diagonals almost in alignment—i.e., not exactly 45° to their meridian, but 43° 27'. On maps and aerial photography, it does appear as if the southeastern corners of the three pyramids G1, G2, and G3 form a line about 45° to the meridian. All this implies, but not proves, that there was perhaps a deliberate intention for this relative positioning of the three pyramids. This has led various Egyptologists—including Hans Goedicke, Mark Lehner, and Kate Spence—as well as many archaeoastronomers—including Juan Belmonte and Giulio Magli—to perpetuate a claim that the ancient builders deliberately created a "Giza diagonal" to connect the pyramids to the city of Heliopolis symbolically.

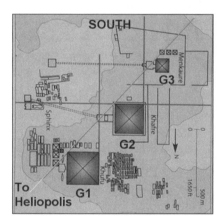

Figure A9. Schematic of the proposed Giza diagonal.

The idea of a symbolic link between the Giza pyramids and Heliopolis, however, is not new. In 1852, Hekekyan published a paper titled "Topographical Sketch of Heliopolis and Surrounding Lands," whose original is now in the manuscript archives of the British Library in London.[321] In it, he noted that the southwest-to-northeast diagonal passing through the apex of the Great Pyramid (G1), if extended toward the northeast, will also pass through the apex of the Sesotris I obelisk at Matareya-Heliopolis (a suburb of Cairo) some twenty-four kilometers away. According to Egyptologists, this monument probably marked the location of the Sun Temple of Re at Heliopolis.[322]

In 1970, George Goyon published an article on the astronomical orientation of the Great Pyramid that also pointed out that the line passing through the southwest-to-northeast diagonal of the Great Pyramid would extend all the way to the Sesostris I obelisk at Heliopolis.[323] Later, in 1983, Goedicke presented a variation to Hekekyan's original idea, claiming that a straight line could be drawn from the southeastern corners of the three Giza pyramids that was "deliberately aimed at Heliopolis and the sanctuary of the Benben Stone."[324] This line was dubbed the "Giza diagonal."

In 1984, Mark Lehner pointed out that this so-called Giza diagonal did not, in fact, link the southeast corners of the three pyramids, but that G2 (the middle pyramid) was "slightly stepped back."[325] Unfortunately the term "slightly stepped back" has misled many to assume that the Giza diagonal actually existed and was a deliberate alignment by the ancient builders, who had made only a slight error in setting it out. But closer scrutiny of the "slightly stepped back" position of G2 proved this to be a gross understatement when examined on the ground. Based on the accurate 1881 chain survey of Flinders Petrie, a line joining the southeastern corners of G1 and G2 would miss the southeastern corner of G3 by a massive twenty-three meters!

Even if another diagonal line were drawn between the southeastern corners of G1 and G3, it would still miss the southeast corner of G2 by twelve meters—the "slightly stepped back" distance noted by Lehner. In other words, the Giza diagonal simply does not exist. Yet the myth has persisted and is regularly used by Egyptologists to explain the layout of the three Giza pyramids,[326] with Giulio Magli being the latest victim of this erroneous theory. Yet Magli was well-aware of the twelve-meter discrepancy, because we informed him of it before he wrote his article. Indeed, Magli mentioned it in a footnote, but, like Lehner before him, chose words that are clearly intended to downplay the importance of the discrepancy:

It is known that the disposition of the Giza pyramids on the ground is characterized by what is customarily called the "Giza diagonal." It is an ideal line which connects the south-east corners of the three pyramids with good accuracy. It was observed already many years ago that this "Giza diagonal" might have had a symbolic meaning, since it points in the direction of the city of Heliopolis . . . the second pyramid "misses" the diagonal by 12 meters.

By any reckoning, missing a target by twelve meters can hardly be considered "good accuracy." The discrepancy is far too large to be regarded as an error, however inexperienced the ancient surveyor may have been. Indeed, judging from the extremely high level of surveying accuracy of other alignments at Giza—the square base of each pyramid is within fourteen arc minutes accuracy to the cardinal directions—the maximum error margin to be expected from the same ancient surveyor should not be more than 0.5 meters. To paraphrase Flinders Petrie when he showed that the so-called "Pyramid Inch" did not exist: The ugly little fact of a twelve-meter discrepancy has killed the beautiful theory of the Giza diagonal.[327]

Another "ugly little fact" that kills the second part of Magli's theory, namely that G1 and G2 were intended to create the hieroglyphic sign N27 ("sun disk between two mounds") is in the understanding of the hieroglyphic signs that form the name *Akhet Khufu*, often translated as "the horizon of Khufu." Magli finds particular significance in this, and concludes that, when the midsummer sun is seen setting between G1 and G2, it forms

> . . . a spectacular replica of the hieroglyphic sign "Akhet" which is the "sun disk between two mountains". . . . [T]he reason why I find striking similarities with what might have been the global Khufu project at Giza is firstly contained in the title of this paper, Akhet Khufu, "the horizon of Khufu". . . . Akhet Khufu is the name of the Giza 1 pyramid, according to inscriptions present in tombs dated some two hundred years later which report the names of all the three pyramids (Giza 2 at that time was "Khafra is great"). Thus, according to these sources the name of Giza 1 was a precise description of the main hierophany at the site, a hierophany which however could occur only if Giza 2 existed as well.

This "hierophany," as Magli calls it, was, in fact, first proposed by Lehner in 1985. According to Lehner:

> [A] dramatic effect is created at sunset during the summer solstice as viewed, again, from the eastern niche of the Sphinx Temple. At

Figure A10. The two pyramids seen as "the sun disk between two mountains."

this time, and from this vantage, the sun sets almost exactly midway between the Khufu and Khafre pyramids, thus construing the image of the Akhet, "horizon," hieroglyph on a scale of acres.[328]

Expanding on Lehner's theory, Magli added:

> The hieroglyphs were actually firstly used with the exact meaning of their images; for instance, the altar for offerings had precisely the same "arrow" form of the hieroglyph standing for "altar." Therefore, it is reasonable to think that the complex was called Akhet Khufu because it actually was it: the Akhet—the horizon—belonging to Khufu, the king who had "joined the sun-god" as the slightly later (but probably already existing) Pyramid Texts will say.

Magli thus concluded that G1 and G2 were deliberately positioned relative to each other to create the hieroglyphic sign N27, "Akhet"—i.e., "sun disk between two mountains"—and this is why Khufu called this project "Akhet Khufu."

At face value, this seems a reasonable conclusion. But there is a fatal flaw with this idea: The hieroglyphic sign of the "sun disk between two mountains" did not exist when Khufu built his pyramid! And even if it had, it was not used in the writing of the name "Akhet Khufu." In 1997, Lehner acknowledged this fact:

Khufu's pyramid was Akhet Khufu. Here, and in the Pyramid Texts, Akhet is written with the crested-ibis and elliptical land-sign, not with the hieroglyph of the sun disk between two mountains that was used later to write "horizon."[329]

Figure A11. Hieroglyphic signs for "Akhet" and "Khufu."

In fact, sign N27 is not found in the Pyramid Texts, where the word "Akhet" is written with the crested-ibis sign G25 and the elliptical-land sign N18. The same applies to the word "Akhet" in the name "Akhet Khufu," where "Akhet" is also written with the crested-ibis sign G25 and elliptical-land sign N16. If Khufu's intention was to associate his funerary area to N27 ("sun disk between two mounds"), let alone to build two giant pyramids to create this sign, then one would think that he would have used the N27 sign in the name of his funerary complex.

Amazingly, this mistake in interpretation of the name of the Great Pyramid is still found in recently published books. To be fair, Lehner did recognize that "Akhet"—although erroneously translated as "horizon" in many books—is written with the crested-ibis sign that also denotes the word *akh*, meaning a spirit who lives in the Duat (Afterworld), the latter

Figure A12. The name of Khufu's pyramid. From E. A. Wallis Budge's *An Egyptian Hieroglyphic Disctionary*, John Murray Publishers, London 1920

"often written with a star in a circle, a reference to Orion, the stellar expression of Osiris." Lehner thus offered another meaning for "Akhet Khufu": "The place where the deceased (king Khufu) becomes an Akh, a suggested translation is 'Spirit' or 'Light' Land."

So what does "Akhet" mean? Egyptologist James P. Allen, who is an expert on the Pyramid Texts, explains:

> The Axt (Akhet) is the place in which the king, like the sun and other celestial beings, undergoes the final transformation from the inertness of death and night to the form that allows him to live effectively—that is as an akh—in his new world. It is for this reason that the king and his celestial companions are said to "rise from the Axt (Akhet)," and not because the Axt (Akhet) is a place on the horizon or—as some have suggested—because it is a place of light.[330]

Akhet, therefore, must mean the "Place of Becoming Akh."

The theory of the Giza diagonal—that the southeast corners of the three pyramids form a diagonal leading to Heliopolis—as well as the theory that G1 and G2 were deliberately designed as one project to represent the sign N27 do not hold up to serious scrutiny. If we accept that the layout of the three pyramids was a deliberate act based on some plan or ideology, then some other explanation must be sought.

THE STEP PYRAMIDS AND STELLAR RITUALS

ROBERT G. BAUVAL 2002

After World War II, Egyptian archaeologist Zakaria Goneim returned to Cairo from Luxor, where he had been posted for the duration of the war. He joined Jean-Philippe Lauer at Saqqara.

Following the turmoil of the Free Officers Revolution of 1952 and the ousting of King Farouk I, Goneim created a media sensation when he announced the discovery of a "lost pyramid" a few hundred meters south of the Step Pyramid Complex of Netjerykhet/Djoser. The media frenzy was not over the discovery of the pyramid, which was in a pitiful state and hardly recognizable as a pyramid, but rather over the large alabaster sarcophagus that was intact and, more excitingly, appeared to be unopened. It had no lid, but rather a sealed portcullis, and "funerary wreaths" had been left on top of it—all indicating that the tomb had not been violated.

Figure A13. The burial chamber and alabaster sarcophagus of Sekhemkhet as found by Zakaria Goneim.

In spite of calls for caution by Lauer that the contents of the sarcophagus might, nevertheless, have been plundered in ancient times, Goneim was too excited and too hungry for fame to listen. He went ahead and invited important people, state officials, and the international media to the opening of the sarcophagus. Even Egypt's new president, Gamal Abdel Nasser, came to witness the historical event. As the lid was slowly lifted, spectators almost climbed over one another to get a glimpse of the

Figure A14. The alabaster sarcophagus of Sekhemkhet, with the portcullis opened.

contents. The expression of humiliation and embarrassment of Goneim's face, however, said it all: The sarcophagus was completely empty! Huge disappointment was expressed by the local and foreign media and Goneim never quite recovered from the experience, even though his discovery was of immense archaeological interest because inscriptions on potsherds proved that the pyramid belonged to Sekhemkhet, the son and successor of Netjerykhet/Djoser.

The Step Pyramid itself had never been finished. Today, only a few very dilapidated courses remain. Had this monument been finished, however, it would have been even larger that the Step Pyramid Complex of Netjerykhet/Djoser. Some of the boundary wall that survives is designed in the same way as that of Netjerykhet/Djoser, with bastions and panels. This led Lauer to conclude that Imhotep was still alive when Sekhemkhet's pyramid was begun, and thus the celebrated astronomer-priest-architect may well have been responsible for this project as well.

We have seen how careful Imhotep was to orient the Step Pyramid of Netjerykhet/Djoser northward toward the star Alkaid in the Big Dipper to mark the simultaneous rising of the birth star Sirius in the east. In order to achieve this, he aligned the Step Pyramid at azimuth 4° 35' (4° 35' east-of-north) and gave it an inclination of 16.5° to the horizontal. This alignment was almost certainly done in accordance with the Stretching of the Cord and rebirth rituals involving the circumpolar stars and the heliacal rising of Sirius. We would expect,

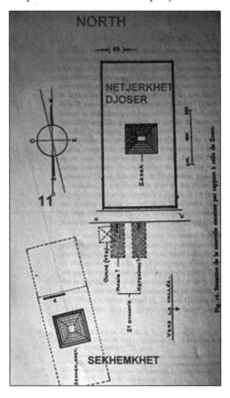

Figure A15. The orientation of the Sekhemkhet and Netjerykhet/Djoser complexes, based on the plan made by Lauer.

therefore, that the same alignment would have been done by Imhotep for Sekhemkhet's complex. Oddly, however, that was not the case. In fact, unlike all other pyramids in the region, the Step Pyramid of Sekhemkhet was a massive 11° *west*-of-north and its steps inclined some 15° to the horizontal. What could explain this odd orientation?

The topography of the ground was clearly not responsible. True, the Sekhemkhet complex had to be positioned farther south than the Netjerykhet/Djoser complex because of two massive rectangular mastabas (marked in dark) that already existed. Other than that, however, there were no practical reasons for the large 11° deviation west-of-north. Could there have been a ritualistic reason behind it?

The Pyramid Texts make it clear that the time of rebirth was at the heliacal (dawn) rising of Sirius (Sothis), identified to the Horus kings of Egypt. In the Old Kingdom, this event was witnessed in the eastern horizon near the time of the Summer Solstice at the start of the annual flooding of the Nile. On that day, Sirius would reappear (be "reborn") after having been invisible for seventy days. In Utterance 302 of the Pyramid Texts, it is said:

> The sky is clear, Spd (Sirius) lives, I am a living one (the reborn king as a 'star'), the son of Spdt (Canis Major), and the two Enneads have cleansed themselves for me in Mesekhtiu (Big Dipper), the Imperishable Stars. My house in the sky will not perish, my throne on earth will not be destroyed, for men hide, the gods fly away. Spdt (Canis Major) has caused me to fly up to the sky in the company of my Brethren.

Utterance 302 provides a visual interpretation of the heliacal rising of Sirius at dawn, although, paradoxically, it is inscribed not on the eastern wall toward the place that Sirius rises, but rather on the north wall, thus in the direction of the northern constellation of the Big Dipper. At the time of the rising of Sirius, the Big Dipper was in the lower northern sky.

In 1902, astronomer A. Romieu pointed out that, in the year 1800 BC in the location of Thebes in Upper Egypt, the rising of the star Sirius coincided with the lower culmination of the bright star AlKaid (Eta Ursa Major), which marks the handle of the Big Dipper. We have also shown how, in 3100 BC when observed at Saqqara, the bright star Alkaid was at azimuth 4° 35' (4° 35' east-of-north) and 16.5° above the horizon at the exact time of the rising of Sirius. This position is conspicuously close in orientation (4° 35' east-of-due north) and inclination (16° 30'), matching the orientation and inclination of Djoser's Step Pyramid and the serdab buttressed against it.

In 3100 BC, the heliacal rising of Sirius occurred on July 18 Julian, equivalent to June 21 Gregorian, thus the Summer Solstice. Seventy days earlier brings us to May 9 Julian (April 12 Gregorian), marking the beginning of the invisibility of Sirius. These seventy days of invisibility—seen as a sojourn in the cosmic underworld of the dead, the Duat—were deemed to be of supreme importance to the successful completion of the magical rites of astral rebirth for the Horus king, and may have been equated to the seventy days of the embalming/mummification period. In the Carlsburg Papyrus I, which draws much of its content from the astronomical ceiling of the tomb of Seti I and the Ramesside tombs (c. 1300–1150 BC), the "rising of the gods" (rebirth) took place in the east:

> [T]hese, Orion and Sirius, who are the first of the gods, that is to say they customarily spend 70 days in the Duat (and they rise) again . . . it is in the east that they celebrate their first feast. . . . Their burial takes place like those of men . . . that is to say, they are the likeness of the burial-days which are for men today . . . 70 days which they pass in the embalming-house . . . its duration in the Duat indeed takes place. It is the taking place of its duration in the Duat. . .every one of the stars, that is to say 70 days . . . this is what is done by dying. This one which sets is the one which does this.

In 3100 BC, the last day that Sirius was seen in the sky (death) was on May 9 Julian; seventy days later, on July 18 Julian, it would be reborn— i.e., rise in the east.

Where was Alkaid on May 9 at dawn? Setting StarryNight Pro for the latitude of Saqqara and the epoch 3100 BC, we can see that the star Alkaid was at 11° west-of-north and 18° above the horizon. From figures provided by astronomer Karine Gadre and the original plans of Lauer, the alignment of Sekhemkhet's complex is 11° west-of-north. Lauer gives an inclination for the Sekhemkhet pyramid of 15° to 22°, thus in the general direction of the stellar target.

Were the two step pyramids built by Imhotep part of a larger elaborate complex that, *inter alia*, serviced the astral rebirth/ascension rituals involving Sirius and the Big Dipper?

MEASURES
AND MYSTERIES
AT NABTA PLAYA

In 1973, the Combined Prehistoric Expedition (CPE) headed by Wendorf and Schild were about 100 kilometers west of Abu Simbel, taking a "comfort break" from their hot grueling cross-desert trek, when someone noticed numerous potsherds and fine stone tools—thus discovering what came to be known as Nabta Playa.

It soon became obvious that Nabta Playa was a very important site and the CPE focused its efforts on excavating there every winter when the heat became bearable. They uncovered, catalogued, and radiocarbon dated numerous layers of artifacts dating from c. 7000 BC to 3300 BC. They found tombs of cattle that had been ritually interred. Though no human remains were found at Nabta Playa, a cemetery from the same era was found about twenty kilometers away where they found remnants of jewelry that must have come through trade from as far away as the Mediterranean and the Red Sea.

The site was used extensively by peoples from around the region, and clearly involved important ritualistic activities. Wendorf and Schild began calling the site a Neolithic-era "regional ceremonial center" even before they noticed what Nabta Playa would become famous for—the megaliths. It seems strange they didn't notice the megaliths earlier, even to Wendorf himself, who wrote: "The megaliths of Nabta were not recognized or identified for a long time. We began to realize their significance only in 1992."[332]

> [I]t is not clear why we failed to recognize them previously, or rather why we failed to understand their significance. . . . It was not that we did not see them because we did, but they were either regarded as bedrock or, in some instances where it was clear they were not bedrock, regarded as insignificant.[333]

The megaliths and megalithic constructions at Nabta Playa clearly constitute the central aspect of the site and the rituals that were conducted there, and they required much effort and social organization to construct. There remain many mysteries about the megaliths, but one function that essentially everyone agrees on is that they served an astronomical purpose of some sort. Debate continues about which specific astronomy is involved, but clearly we can say that Nabta Playa was not only a regional ceremonial center; it was a Neolithic-era regional *astro-ceremonial center*.

A Neolithic Astro-Ceremonial Center

The visible portions of the megalith arrangements at Nabta Playa consist largely of six alignments of stones that radiate outward from one central point, like the spokes of a wheel. There are three alignments to the north-northeast and three alignments to the east-southeast. The most robust interpretation is that the north-northeast alignments refer to one or more circumpolar stars, especially in the Big Dipper constellation, which the ancient Egyptians called the Bull's Thigh. This same interpretation has the east-southeast alignments referring to the brightest star in the sky, Sirius, and the stars of Orion's belt. Given that Nabta Playa was used and constructed more than twenty-six centuries ago, it is likely the megalith alignments were used to represent celestial events at more than one epoch. Because stars "move" due to precession of the earth, however, any single alignment can refer to any given star at only one specific date. Thus the multiple megalith alignments may have been used to refer to certain sets of stars at certain ancient dates.

In 1997, the CPE finally invited the first astronomer to visit the site during the winter excavations—Kim Malville. In 1998, Malville and the CPE mentioned the megaliths in a report published in *Nature* magazine.[334] However, that paper focused mainly on the Calendar Circle—a separate device made of small stones, not megalithic large stones. They described the megaliths and their alignments, but did not associate them with astronomy, except to note that some alignments were close to northerly and to report that one megalith alignment was astonishingly precise to due east, with azimuths of 90.02°. But this alignment was never reported on again and apparently did not exist at all.

The first mention of astronomy concerning the megaliths was in a brief article by Wendorf and Malville within the massive book published by the CPE in 2001.[335] There, Malville proposed that the three northerly alignments of megaliths tracked the star Dubhe (in the Big Dipper) from 4742 BC to around 4200 BC. Of the three southeasterly alignments of megaliths, Malville claimed, one was aimed at Sirius about 4820 BC and the two others tracked the stars of Orion's belt at two other dates. That article also listed the exact GPS coordinates of each megalith.

When we attempted to reproduce these calculations, however, we found that some of the stars were not, in fact, at the locations given on the dates claimed. So we tried simply to calculate the megalith alignment azimuths from the CPE's raw GPS data and found that several of those calculations could not be reproduced either. The logical assumption was that the primary raw GPS data should be the most reliable, while the CPE calculations were in error. So, keen to decipher the astronomy of Nabta Playa, we took the raw GPS measures for the megaliths and attempted to solve the puzzle of the astronomy independently. We published the results in our book *The Origin Map*.

Our calculations showed that the megalith alignment the CPE had given to the rising of Sirius c. 4820 BC actually aligned with Sirius c. 6090 BC, a date that, as we have seen, was problematic for the CPE. As we show in this book, however, this date clarifies the symbology at the root of the very ancient system that the genius Imhotep tapped into when he designed the great Step Pyramid Complex at Saqqara.

We tasked the newly available Quickbird satellite to acquire image data (surely its first independent use for archaeoastronomy) and were elated to find that we could identify all of the megaliths described by Wendorf in his 2001 publication.[336] As we expected, the raw GPS data from the CPE seemed to be accurate. We confirmed these measurements on the ground in October 2003, then teamed up with our old colleague Paul Rosen (a leader in space-based-radar remote sensing) to help geo-rectify the satellite data and vet the scientific reasoning.

We presented the new results of our measures at Nabta Playa and our interpretations of the megalithic astronomy at a unique conference hosted by the University of the Aegean titled The Archaeology of World Megalithic Cultures. Following the conference, our paper was published in the *Journal of Mediterranean Archaeology and Archaeometry*, titled "Satellite Imagery Measures of the Astronomically Aligned Megaliths at Nabta Playa."[337] The substance of this paper is reproduced later in this appendix for those interested in further exploring the development of these ideas.

We reported that the date for the Sirius alignment given by Malville and Wendorf would have to be moved back in time to 6090 BC. Moreover, the three southeasterly megalith lines could also be interpreted as indicating the stars of Orion's belt, head, and shoulders all around the same epoch (c. 6200 BC), while the northerly megalith lines indicated the brightest star in the north at the same time, Vega. We also reported on our use of new space-based ground-penetrating imaging techniques to investigate the mystery of the "bedrock sculptures."[338]

The CPE responded in a paper by Malville et al. in 2007[339] that acknowledged our corrected data and calculations, and re-interpreted the megalith alignments. The authors now asserted that the megaliths they originally associated with Sirius c. 4820 BC (which we had shown must be corrected to 6090 BC) may have been off the playa; thus they now "decline[d] to interpret them." Instead, they suggested that the other southeasterly megalith lines may have indicated the rising of Sirius c. 4500 BC and 3500 BC. They also suggested an alignment to Orion's belt c. 4200 BC and possibly to Alpha Centauri at another date, and proposed a new target for the northerly megalith alignments—the star Arcturus. Moreover, they rejected any dates c. 6100 BC because that is "about 1,500 years earlier than our best estimates for the Terminal Neolithic."

The Stretching of the Cord at Nabta Playa

Meanwhile, we were making further progress researching the alignments. It became clear that the southeasterly megaliths very likely do indicate the rising of Sirius. Further, we remembered that early Old Kingdom Egyptian temples had been aligned simultaneously with the rising of Sirius and with the star Dubhe in the north. So we decided to test for such simultaneous alignments at Nabta. We were surprised to find very accurate simultaneous markings of the rising Sirius with Dubhe in the sky at both 4500 BC and 3500 BC. Moreover, these simultaneous alignments also formed very neat, precise right angles. These two sets of alignments thus associated with four of the six major lines of megaliths at Nabta Playa, as we wrote in *Black Genesis*:

> 1. There are at least nine megaliths that form the three lines—A1, A2, and A3—that point north. These track the star Dubhe in the Big Dipper over a considerable period of time.

> 2. There are at least six megaliths that form lines B1 and B2 pointing southeast. These track the bright star Sirius at two epochs.

> 3. Sirius also coordinated simultaneously with the star Dubhe in the Big Dipper so that their alignments formed an approximate 90-degree angle. (This curious connection also had been noted by Wendorf and Malville; they commented that the megalith builders of Nabta Playa had "a fascination with right angles.")

Note that these simultaneous Sirius-Dubhe alignments occur when Sirius is just rising above the horizon and Dubhe is at a low altitude in the sky—as signified both in the Egyptian temples and at Nabta Playa. At first, it may seem awkward for early astronomer-priests, using only the naked eye, to note a star (Sirius) breaking the horizon and at the same time to note its partner star (Dubhe) 90 degrees to the north and up in the sky. But recall that Nabta Playa was a seasonal lake that was filled with shallow water part of the year. The megaliths would have emerged out of still waters that may well have reflected starlight along the sight line to an observer. This would have made the alignments easily apparent to an observer situated at the central megalithic construction. In *Black Genesis*, we suggested that this ritual—the simultaneous sighting of the rising of Sirius together with a bright star in the circumpolar constellation (in this case, Dubhe in the constellation that we call the Big Dipper and the ancient Egyptians called the Bull's Thigh)—originated at Nabta Playa, and was later taken to the Nile Valley.

At Nabta Playa, the star sightings were both ritual and actual, involving the megalithic constructions and the giant natural reflecting pool that was the ancient seasonal lake. Later, in the pharaonic culture, the same ritual became more stylized and symbolic, embodied in the Stretching of the Cord ceremony that is depicted in temple art. As we describe in *Black Genesis*:

> The ancient Egyptian texts and temple reliefs explain that stretching the cord was carried out by a priestess, who represented a deity associated with the stars, and the pharaoh. Both the priestess and pharaoh held a rod and a mallet, and a rope or cord was looped between the rods. The priestess stood with her back to the northern sky and faced the pharaoh. This scene is depicted on many temples, and the texts alongside it tell us that the pharaoh observed the trajectory of the stars with his eye in order to establish the temple in the manner of ancient times. In the texts we are unequivocally told that the king looked at a star in the Big Dipper (called Mesekhtiu, the Bull's Thigh). Some of the texts, however, mention the star Sirius and imply that it also was somehow involved in the ritual. Exactly how was this stellar alignment ritual performed? . . . A further clue to the ritual is that the pharaoh observed carefully the motion of a star in real time. Inscriptions on the Temple of Horus at Edfu, accompanying portrayals of the ritual, quote the pharaoh: "I take the measuring cord in the company of Seshat. I consider the progressive movement of the stars. My eye is fixed on the Bull's Thigh constellation. I count off time, scrutinizing the clock . . ." This is also what might have happened at the ceremonial center of Nabta Playa thousands of years earlier.

Around 3300 BC, the Nabta Playa area became the uninhabitable extremely dry "hyper-arid" desert that it is today. Directly following that date is when the earliest temples of the ancient Egyptian civilization began popping up in the Nile Valley, especially the temple of the goddess Satis on Elephantine Island near Aswan. The temple was rebuilt several times over 3,000 years, its axis changing to align with the rising of Sirius as the star's declination changed through precession. The first known version of the temple was built c. 3200 BC.

Throughout ancient Egyptian civilization, the New Year was marked by the heliacal rising of Sirius, an astronomical event that also heralded the life-giving and civilization-supporting inundation of the Nile. In ancient Egypt, the brilliant Sirius would be "invisible" for a period of about two months every year, while it was too close to the sun in the sky. By the time of the New Kingdom, at least from what the great tourist Herodotus wrote, the Egyptians had forgotten that the source of the flooding of the Nile was the monsoon rains that engorged the river upstream. But they did remember that the floods would be heralded symbolically by the heliacal rising of Sirius.

Earlier, in the time of Nabta Playa, the megalith builders marked the rising of Sirius simultaneous with the Bull's Thigh constellation (Dubhe) for more than 1,000 years (certainly from 4500 to 3500 BC, and probably back to 6100 BC). And that was when the monsoon rains fell directly on the playa and inundated the seasonal lake that would, in turn, reflect the starlight along the megaliths they had constructed. There, the connection of the heliacal rising of Sirius with the coming of the annual life-supporting rains was direct, obvious, and visceral—the heavenly events coinciding with the annual renewal of the playa on earth. When the monsoon rains moved south and left their regional astro-ceremonial complex uninhabitably dry, the people of Nabta Playa moved to the Nile Valley and created the greatest temple-building civilization of history.

Clearly, we believe the megalithic tracking of Sirius and the circumpolar Bull's Thigh constellation is a very robust interpretation for the function of the megaliths at Nabta Playa. It is the astronomy associated with earlier dates that is more controversial and that also connects with the most mysterious aspects of the site.

The Calendar Circle Decoded

On the way to discussing these mysteries, however, we must mention the most reported feature of Nabta Playa—the Calendar Circle. The Calendar Circle is not megalithic; it is made of stones that come up to about one's knee, or smaller. As we describe in *Black Genesis,* the study, publication, and treatment of the Calendar Circle suffered a convoluted history. For some reason, the first publication of it did not appear until the CPE's famous 1998 *Nature* paper. However, the primary mapping and archaeological analysis of the circle was done in 1991 and 1992, and it was surely known about even back in 1974. Between then and 1998, the whole Nabta Playa site was left unguarded. Moreover, the megalithic excavation methods used there were generally destructive, not reconstructive. The remains of excavations of the megalithic "complex structures," for example, were left in a circle of detritus clearly visible in the satellite images.

As to the astronomy of the Calendar Circle, some is controversial, some not. The non-controversial part is that eight stones on the circumference of the circle form four "gates" that create two "sight-line windows," one of which indicates the north-south direction, while the other indicates the rising sun on Summer Solstice. Also, the location of the site itself at about 22.5° north latitude, near the tropic line, means the sun passed exactly overhead twice a year during the weeks around the Summer Solstice, at which time the standing stones would cast no shadow at noon. The solstice gates and the meridian (north-south) gates are "rough" alignments spread over a few degrees of arc and so cannot be used to date the circle from the small changes in earth's obliquity.

The controversial part of the interpretation of the Calendar Circle refers to the contents of the circle—six standing stones arranged in two sets of three. In *The Origin Map,* in professional conference proceedings, and again in our book *Black Genesis,* we suggest that the solstice and meridian gates of the circle give clues to its overall function.[340] The solstice gate tells a user what time of year is relevant—around the Summer Solstice. The meridian gate tells the user where to look in the sky—up along the north-south meridian (which is the same standard reference astronomers use today). Together, the gates also tell the user what time of day to look—just before sunrise while the sky is still dark. Then the contents of the circle form a simple "star map" that the user can visually "slide up into the sky" to identify the asterism indicated inside the circle. So, armed with the time of year, the time of night, and the area of sky to observe, the only other thing the user needs to know is which years to consider.

The radiocarbon dates from a nearby hearth supplied that clue—around 4800 BC. Calculating the appearance of the starry sky then, it was apparent that the three stars of Orion's belt would be a good candidate asterism for the lower set of three standing stones in the circle. Further investigation showed that the stars of Orion's belt best "fit" c. 4940 BC, and they generally "fit" during a time window from about 6400 to 4800 BC. Moreover, the fit occurred in multiple ways—just the right altitude was represented, and the best-fit date occurred at a special time in the long-term precession of those stars, exactly half-way between southern culmination and northern culmination. Thus, a more speculative interpretation for the other set of three stones inside the circle presented itself—that they match the top part of the Orion constellation (the shoulder and head stars) at the opposite part of the precession cycle (about 12,000 years earlier), again in multiple ways.

So it is likely that the Calendar Circle was constructed and used around 5000 BC (and certainly not 17,000 BC), and that it was a diagram to teach about the long-term motion of the starry sky. Just as the Summer Solstice sunrise "sight-line gate" on the outer part of the circle teaches about the annual motion of the sun through the sky over one year, the inner stones of the circle teach about the 26,000-year precession motion of the constellations. It is thus unified with the megalithic alignments at Nabta Playa, which also refer to Orion's belt, as well as to the rising of Sirius, tracked through precession.

The Mystery of the Bedrock Sculptures

The Calendar Circle gives us a hint about the more mysterious parts of Nabta Playa. The stellar-aligned megaliths are embedded in the playa sediments. According to paleoclimatologists and the radiocarbon dates of sediment layers, the last period of heavy sedimentation that laid down the final thick layer of sediment ended around 5000 BC. Therefore, megaliths embedded in that layer must have been placed then, or more recently. That is why controversy arose over the megalith alignment the CPE first ascribed to Sirius c. 4820 BC, which our measures and calculations proved actually aligned 1,270 years earlier, c. 6090 BC.

But the puzzle is complicated by what is found *underneath* the playa sediments, especially underneath the centerpiece called Complex Structure A. All the megalith alignments radiate out from Complex Structure A, which is composed of several parts: On top of the sediment are megaliths

Figure A16. Thomas Brophy with one of the megaliths that composed the surface of Complex Structure A (upper left); Artist's depiction of a complex structure surface arrangement of megaliths (upper right); Artist's depiction of Complex Structure A as it was before excavation, looking west, as if seeing through the sediments. The cow stone sculpture is suspended in the sediments between the surface of the ground and the bedrock sculpture (middle left); Complex Structure A viewed looking north (middle right); Excavators' line drawing of Complex Structure A, the cow stone sculpture, and the bedrock sculpture—on the left looking west; on the right looking north (bottom). Line drawings courtesy of the CPE.[341]

arranged in a large oval with a standing stone in the center; under that is some playa sediment and then a large sculpted megalith (called the cow stone); and underneath the cow stone sculpture is a sculpted lump of living bedrock about four meters under the surface of the playa sediment (see figure A16). Moreover, Complex Structure A sits in a field of about thirty other complex structures—all similar except that the others don't have the additional cow stone sculpture.

Nabta Playa is a bedrock basin covered by a few meters to several meters of sediments that were laid down over a period of about 8,000 years—from 15,000 to 7,000 years ago—especially in a series of "humid interphases" from around 9,500 to 7,000 years ago. When the CPE excavated the complex structures and found them to cover bedrock sculptures under three or four meters of sediment, they were at a loss to explain the creation of these structures. The conventional notion of Neolithic cultures is that such structures could not have been built by them. So the CPE theorized that the people of Nabta Playa, at some time more recent than 7,000 years ago, somehow located where the bedrock lumps of quartzitic sandstone (called "lenses") were located, and then dug through the sediment and sculpted the bedrock lumps. Then they filled the sediment back in and arranged the oval of megaliths on top of the sediment, leaving them thus for us to dig up today.

Obviously there are several problems with this scenario. For one, Complex Structure A is the centerpiece of all the megalith alignments, so it must predate them. The earliest of these is at least 6,500 years old (even by the most conservative accounts). Another problem with the scenario is that there was no possible way the Neolithic people could have figured out where the bedrock lumps were, under several meters of sediment, in order to carry out such a strange series of construction steps—not to mention *why* they would do such a thing in the first place.

We suggested that a more likely solution is that the bedrock sculptures are actually older.[342] By the time of their 2007 article, the CPE agreed that it is likely the bedrock sculptures pre-existed as part of an older "symbolic landscape" that was marked by humans with cairns or a sequence of constructions leading up to the complex structures we find today. The megalithic alignments placed on top of the sediment from 5000 BC to 3500 BC therefore incorporated—in fact, took as their centerpiece—the much older bedrock sculptures.

But when were they first constructed, and for what purpose? Why were they so important or sacred that people continued to maintain them and incorporate them into their ceremonial constructions for thousands of years? Does such continuity of construction through time imply a greater degree of cultural (or religious or technological) continuity than previously believed possible? If the later megalithic alignments were primarily astronomical (as well as religious), does that suggest that the much earlier bedrock sculptures were also astronomical?

The CPE completely excavated only two of these structures, partially excavated a third, and drilled test holes into two more. They concluded that all (approximately thirty) of the structures probably have a sculpted bedrock lump underneath. It is interesting that these bedrock sculptures date back to the same earlier epoch as has been proposed for the Great Sphinx at Giza, which itself is a giant bedrock sculpture. Geologist Robert Schoch and others have shown that the Sphinx and its bedrock enclosure are weathered by heavy rains that occurred before the standard dating of Dynastic Egypt. This is essentially the same rainy climate pattern that laid down the sediments on top of the bedrock sculptures at Nabta Playa.

When we first considered the astronomy of Nabta Playa, we approached the interpretation purely as an astronomical puzzle, unfettered by preconceived conventional notions of what the ancient people at the site "should" have been doing. Our interpretation of the Calendar Circle involves only "naked-eye" astronomy—observations easily visible to any user of the stone device with only the unaided eye. Similarly, the alignments of megaliths with stars rising over the eastern horizon involve only naked-eye observations. The puzzle solution, given in *The Origin Map* by Brophy, produced something amazing.

Working with the original archaeological drawings made by the excavators, and considering Complex Structure A as the centerpiece of all the alignments—and that perhaps it symbolically represented an astronomical center—it was clear that the disk-like mushroom shape of the bedrock sculpture roughly resembled the shape of our Milky Way galaxy. Moreover, the location of the centerpiece standing stone was positioned so as to be just about where earth is within the Milky Way. Further, the cow stone sculpture was found chocked in place on top of the bedrock sculpture. Its outer surface was sculpted/polished into what appeared to be a section of a sphere, and its sides were wedge-shaped such that its placement appeared to angle back to the "earth location" on the galaxy sculpture as a sort of symbolic viewing window to subtend the area of the sky that the center of the Milky Way transits.

One cannot help asking: Could that possibly be what those sculptures represented, if the people who built them only had naked-eye astronomy? The answer is probably not, but maybe. The Milky Way is a very prominent feature spread across the sky. It is possible (though generally believed not to be so) that some Neolithic sky-watchers realized that the Milky Way is a giant complex of which the earth and sun are only small parts. Some geometric thinking, without formal math, could yield the notion that the Milky Way is disk-shaped (as it is). Some more thinking could intuit from the anisotropy (variation) of the visual Milky Way that earth must be somewhere significantly off center in that disk (as it is). It has been suggested, for instance, that the gleaming white outer stones of the large megalithic disk-shaped mound at Newgrange, Ireland, could represent the Milky Way. So the concept of Neolithic people representing the Milky Way as a stone disk is not that far-fetched.

Could our hypothetical Neolithic geniuses at Nabta Playa have gotten the actual location of earth in the galactic disk so accurately? Probably not. The center of the galaxy is not visible to the naked eye. In an indirect way it is, however, because it is obscured by a dark patch of dust clouds, and that dark patch did have ritual significance in some ancient cultures. So, if the Nabta Playa sky-watchers guessed that that prominent dark patch was also the locus of the center of the galactic disk, and if they happened to guess correctly about how far from the center earth is, they could possibly have mapped it onto their bedrock sculpture. But it is not likely.

So, why go through this mental exercise? The concrete-thinking mind might say it is a useless exercise. We don't agree. For one thing, it sharpens our own thinking skills and stimulates learning astronomy. And there clearly is much we don't know about our vastly distant human ancestors. Completely unfettered thinking and problem-solving just may generate insight. So let's next consider the bedrock sculpture under Complex Structure B, the second biggest complex structure and companion to Complex Structure A.

Complex Structure B is an odd lumpy tilted oval bigger than the Complex Structure A bedrock sculpture—about six meters across, to Complex Structure A's four meters. If we suspend disbelief and consider that Complex Structure A may represent our Milky Way galaxy, the obvious guess is that Complex Structure B may represent the Milky Way's nearby much bigger companion, the Andromeda galaxy. Andromeda, as seen from earth, is a tilted oval or elliptical galaxy located a distance from us measured in galactic diameters that is similar to Complex Structure B's distance from Complex Structure A on the bedrock measured in sculpture diameters (2,500K light years to 220K light years versus forty-five meters to about six meters). Could our Neolithic sky-watchers have mapped the Andromeda galaxy from only naked-eye observation? No. Andromeda is visible to the naked eye, normally appearing similar to a star, although a Persian astronomer identified it as a small "cloud" as early as 964 AD. But there is no way for the naked eye to estimate the actual dimensions of the galaxy relative to the Milky Way.

In *The Origin Map*, we identified other astronomical coincidences that coincide with the megalithic features at Nabta Playa. Yet true mysteries about the site remain. So far, we have been limited to space-based remote-sensing attempts because we can "just do it" without the onerous barrier of getting permissions from the Supreme Council of Antiquities (which is often in turmoil). Ground-penetrating radar satellite technology isn't quite good enough yet to "see" the bedrock features at Nabt Playa. But some day, it will be. Suffice it to say here that Nabta Playa has provided a significant link in our knowledge chain that traces the ancestors of the pharaohs back in time and space to a black-African culture that thrived in the region before it was desert.

The Curious Case of the Artificial Human Tooth

In April 2008, we were four days, strenuous travel by 4-wheel-drive Jeep through totally desolate terrain into one of the driest deserts on earth—four days from any hint of modern civilization. As on an expedition to the moon or to the deepest oceans, we had to pack in all our supplies, even all our water. So, at our final destination we had only a precious few hours for free exploration beyond our specific expeditionary goals.

We were braving the blazing mid-day heat to explore the northwest faces of a small bluff on the north of an area called Jebel Uwainat, a massive table-topped mountain range straddling the uninhabited region of the Sahara where Egypt, Sudan, and Libya meet. It is so remote and inhospitable that, amazingly, the mere existence of this "Alps of the desert" was not even known to the modern world until the 1920s.

A member of our team scrambled twelve feet up the side of a cliff containing a faded prehistoric painting of a life-sized giraffe with a hunter or shaman-like figure. When he arrived at a small ledge of some natural flow-stone, he exclaimed: "Hey, there are engravings up here!" We joined him. And there, among the strange engraved markings, was a beautifully formed arrow that our compass confirmed pointed to the west-north-west—directly toward the Summer Solstice sunset! (see figure A17)

Figure A17. Elevated rock ledge at Jebel Uwainat, with engraved linear features and arrow pointing to the Summer Solstice sunset.

The rock art in this region generally dates from as far back as 12,000 years ago, up to the most recent about 6,000 years ago, when the region became the extreme desert it is today. The engraved rock art, like these markings, often tends to be even older than the painted rock art. Did the artist who engraved the arrow that points to the Summer Solstice sunset actually intend to indicate the astronomical event, or is the correlation only random chance? We may well be the first humans to see these engravings in thousands of years. Do they even represent some sort of early proto-writing? Who were the people who made them?

A clue to these questions can be gleaned from the astronomy at the Calendar Circle of Nabta Playa, some 500 kilometers due east, which also indicates the Summer Solstice. Could the two peoples who created the two artifacts be related? And could they be the people who later moved to the Nile and created pharaonic Egypt, precisely as the region suddenly transitioned from temperate savanna to the extreme desert that it still is today?

Some of the strongest physical evidence linking the peoples of Nabta Playa to the earliest Dynastic Egyptians comes from a study of their teeth. During 2001 to 2003, some twenty kilometers from Nabta Playa at a hill called Gebel Ramlah, the CPE discovered three Neolithic cemeteries that date to the middle of the 5th millennium BC. These cemeteries almost certainly contain people associated with the Nabta Playa regional ceremonial center of that time. Collaborating with the CPE, Joel D. Irish, a dental anthropologist from the University of Alaska, studied these teeth and compared them to the teeth of fifteen population groups—people from the Predynastic Hierokanpolis area, from the Early Dynastic Egyptians, from the Middle and New Kingdoms, and even from Roman-era Egypt. He published his study in 2006 in the *American Journal of Physical Anthropology*.[343] The teeth from Gebel Ramlah, the people of Nabta Playa, were the first (oldest) group of teeth in the study.

Irish conducted a comparative statistical analysis of twenty-two distinct dental traits across the fifteen groups, starting with the Gebel Ramlah/Nabta Playa teeth. His results show that the teeth of the people of Gebel Ramlah/Nabta Playa are "closest to predynastic and early dynastic samples from Abydos, Hierakonpolis, and Badari." Moreover, the Badari teeth are essentially the same as the Predynastic Naqada and Hierokonpolis teeth, and close to teeth of all fifteen sample groups. He concludes that the teeth of the Dynastic era Egyptian people "are an indigenous outgrowth from the Naqada culture." So essentially, the teeth tell us that ancient Dynastic Egyptians were indigenous Hierokonpolitans combined with an influx of peoples from the Gebel Ramlah/Nabta Playa culture—just as the megalithic astro-ceremonial evidence shows.

One specific tooth tells an even deeper tale. This is an artificial tooth crafted out of sea-water mollusk shell that probably came from the Red Sea. It was found on the desert surface near the Gebel Ramlah cemeteries among other fragments of human bone, probably excavated from a burial by 6,000 years of winds scouring the desert. Irish and a team of authors, including Romuald Schild, published a study of this curious artificial tooth.[344] The tooth (see figure A18) is very finely crafted and "anatomically accurate in size and appearance." Exactly what it was used for 6,500 years ago is unknown. Irish notes that it could have been an ornament or charm of some sort, but also concludes that "perhaps it was intended as a replacement for an actual human incisor." If so, it was either placed in a corpse in order to make the body whole for an afterlife journey, or it was a prosthetic implant for a living person.

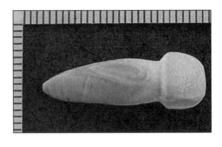

Figure A18. 6,500-year-old artificial human tooth found near the cemeteries of Gebel Ramlah.

The latter possibility would be astonishing, because clinical dental implantation was not thought to have been invented until 1918—6,400 years later. Even if the tooth was implanted postmortem, it was very advanced for its time. The next earliest known incidence of postmortem dental implantation of complete anatomically accurate artificial teeth was not until 600 AD by the Mayans—4,000 years later. In any case, this amazing prehistoric artificial tooth speaks to a refinement and advancement previously thought impossible for the people of Nabta Playa, about whom the more we learn the more mysteries remain.

Satellite Imagery
and the Megaliths at Nabta Playa

ADAPTED FROM "SATELLITE IMAGERY MEASURES OF THE ASTRONOMICALLY ALIGNED MEGALITHS AT NABTA PLAYA," BY THOMAS BROPHY AND PAUL ROSEN

The Nabta Playa megalithic complex consists of two types of features: large stones, many of them shaped, placed on or in the sediments of an ancient seasonal lake bed that is now hyper-arid; and large sculpted bedrock features underneath the sediments and associated with the surface megaliths.[345]

A group of three northerly lines were reported at azimuths of 24.3°, 25°, and 28°. A southeasterly line of slabs was reported with an azimuth of 126°. And a due east alignment of slabs was reported with a surprising accuracy of 90.02°. Coordinates of the megaliths were not reported.

Table 1. Comparative Coordinates of Nabta Playa Megaliths

Megalith	Wendorf and Malville 2001		Quickbird 2002		GPS 2003	
	lat (°)	long (°)	lat (°)	long (°)	lat (°)	long (°)
A	22.5080	30.7256	22.5079	30.7255	22.5080	30.7257
A-1	22.5159	30.7299	22.5158	30.7297	22.5158	30.7299
A-2	22.5158	30.7297	22.5157	30.7297	22.5157	30.7298
A-3	22.5155	30.7299	22.5155	30.7295	22.5155	30.7297
"A3"						
A-0	22.5165	30.7306	22.5164	30.7305	22.5164	30.7306
A-4	22.5150	30.7297	22.5149	30.7295	22.5149	30.7297
A-X	22.5137	30.7290	22.5136	30.7287	22.5136	30.7288
"A2"						
A-5	22.5134	30.7291	22.5135	30.7290	22.5135	30.7291
A-6	22.5132	30.7290	22.5131	30.7287	22.5131	30.7288
A-7	22.5130	30.7288	22.5129	30.7286	22.5131	30.7289
A-8	22.5128	30.7288	22.5127	30.7286	22.5127	30.7287
A-9	22.5120	30.7283	22.5120	30.7283	22.5121	30.7284
"A1"						
B-1	22.5059	30.7303	22.5058	30.7301	22.5058	30.7303
B-2	22.5059	30.7302	22.5059	30.7300	–	–
B-3	22.5061	30.7300	22.5059	30.7299	22.5059	30.7300
B-4	22.5061	30.7298	22.5060	30.7297	22.5060	30.7299
"B2"						
B-5	22.5061	30.7294	22.5061	30.7292	22.5061	30.7293
B-6	22.5064	30.7287	22.5063	30.7287	22.5063	30.7288
B-7	22.5066	30.7283	22.5065	30.7281	22.5065	30.7283
"B1"						
C-1	22.5021	30.7330	22.5018	30.7331	22.5018	30.7333
C-2	22.5022	30.7331	22.5018	30.7333	–	–
C-3	22.5028	30.7327	22.5024	30.7325	22.5024	30.7327
C-4	22.5025	30.7329	22.5025	30.7327	22.5025	30.7328
C-5	22.5029	30.7323	22.5027	30.7331	22.5027	30.7333
C-6	22.5032	30.7317	22.5029	30.7320	22.5029	30.7322
"C1"						

Table 2: Megalith Lines at Nabta Playa—Azimuth East-of-North (°)

line	Malville et al. *Nature* 1998	Wendorf and Malville 2001	From Wendorf and Malville 2001 data	This paper
A3	24.3	16.557	26.83	25.86
A2	25	18.524	28.60	27.68
A1	28	21.194	31.24	30.00
B2		113.771	115.81	117.49
B1		116.174	118.97	121.11
C1	126	125.373	129.71	130.10

Using satellite imagery, however, the placement of the astronomically aligned surface megalithic structures described in early field reports has been corrected.[346]

In 2001, GPS coordinates for twenty-four megaliths and Complex Structure A were reported,[347] based on simultaneous averaged measures from six to ten satellites with an elevated-antenna GPS. These values are given in Table 1, columns 2 and 3.

The CPE data contained a curious aspect, however.[348] The azimuths noted and used to derive stellar astronomy correlations are significantly different from the azimuths that can be calculated from latitude/longitude coordinates given in the reports. Table 2 compares the megalith alignment azimuths given in the 1998 *Nature* article[349] with the 2001 site report,[350] and with the azimuths that can be calculated from the 2001 site-report coordinates. These calculated values are a simple average of the azimuth for each megalith considered to be in each line. The alignment azimuths are the primary basis for calculating stellar correlations. An error of even one degree or less can significantly alter a stellar alignment date and the significance of an alignment. So it is relevant to determine which of the reported megalith locations may be in error.

On December 31, 2002, the Quickbird satellite acquired a high-quality 60-centimeter-resolution panchromatic geo-rectified image of Nabta Playa. Figure A19 on page 252 shows a reduced-resolution crop from the satellite image, showing the detritus rings from the excavations of Complex Structures A and B, and the megaliths labeled as lines B1 and B2 by Wendorf and Malville.[351] Figure A20 shows the individual named megaliths in line B1, as seen in the satellite image. Essentially all of the

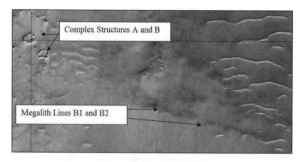

Figure A19. Reduced resolution crop from satellite image showing the detritus rings from the excavations of Complex Structures A and B, and the megaliths in lines B1 and B2.

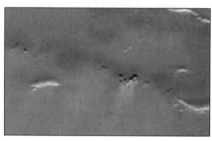

Figure A20. Individual named megaliths in line B1, as seen in the satellite image.

twenty-four megaliths and some of the complex structures identified by Wendorf and Malville were identified in the satellite image. Then the program ERMapper was used with the geo-rectified image coordinates delivered by the satellite to measure the latitude and longitude of the megaliths. These values are given in Table 1, columns 4 and 5.

To confirm the megalith location data, we used a handheld twelve-channel Garmin Etrex GPS to record the coordinates of the twenty-four megaliths and the center of Complex Structure A. These data are given in Table 1, columns 6 and 7. During the measurements, the real-time instrument-stated horizontal absolute accuracy was generally about five meters. The satellite imager was pointing five degrees off nadir east-west. Figures A21 and A22 show the differences, in meters, between the satellite-image-determined coordinates and the ground-GPS-determined coordinates.

There is a consistent east-west offset, ground versus satellite, of about twelve meters, and generally no north-south offset. This indicates there was a small inaccuracy of the pointing vector for the satellite image. Thus both the 2003 ground-GPS and the east-west-pointing corrected satellite-determined measures can be considered essentially the same and very accurate. The most variant north-south megalith (C-7) probably

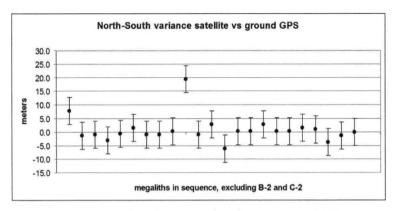

Figure A21. North-south variance of satellite versus ground GPS.

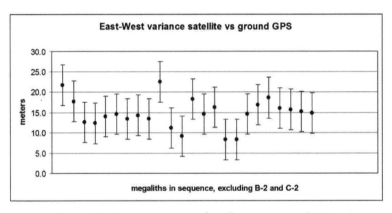

Figure A22. East-west variance of satellite versus ground GPS.

indicates visual identification on the ground of a different set of megalith fragments as the center for that megalith group.

Once clarified location coordinates for the megaliths were available, accurate azimuths from Complex Structure A could be determined. Table 2, column 4 gives the azimuths of the megalith lines from the 2003 ground–GPS measures and the pointing–corrected 2002 satellite image. Figure A23 on page 254 illustrates the megalith locations and orientation lines reported by the CPE team in 1998 and the lines reported by the team in 2001.

In the figure, the solid lines are the rising azimuths of stars ascribed to align with the megaliths reported in 2001.[352] The northerly three solid lines were reported to be the rising azimuths of Ursa Majoris on the dates 4742 BC, 4423 BC, and 4199 BC, with azimuths 21.2°, 18.5°, and 16.6° respectively. The southerly most line was reported to be the

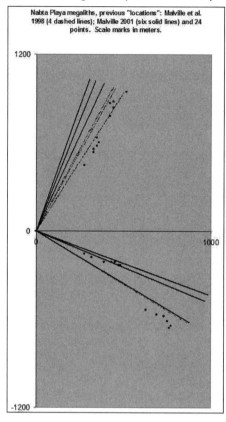

Nabta Playa megaliths, previous "locations": Malville et al. 1998 (4 dashed lines); Malville 2001 (six solid lines) and 24 points. Scale marks in meters.

rising azimuth of Sirius in 4820 BC at 125.4°. The other two southerly solid lines illustrate 116.2° and 113.8°, reported to be the rising azimuths of the stars of Orion's belt in 4176 BC and 3786 BC respectively. Thus Wendorf and Malville reported that the Nabta Playa megalith builders marked the bright star Sirius once in 4800 BC, and tracked the precessional movement of the star Ursa Majoris on three dates from 4742 BC to 4199 BC, and they tracked the precessional movement of the three stars of Orion's belt from 4176 BC to 3786 BC. However, our new data showed that the claimed alignments of those stars on those dates are significantly different from the locations of the megaliths.

Figure A23. Comparative Nabta Playa megalith locations and lines.

We considered if possibly the star-date reports fit correct alignments to the megaliths, while the star-azimuth numbers were in error.[353] An independent calculation of the actual rising azimuths (declinations) of those stars on the dates reported finds that the rising azimuths of Orion's belt stars were accurate,[354] while the rising azimuths of Sirius and Ursa Majoris were significantly in error—however not in a direction for which correction of the error moves the star risings closer to matching the megaliths. We estimate that in 4820 BC, Sirius had a declination of -30.165°, giving a rising azimuth of 122.95°. Figure A24 shows independently calculated rising azimuths, compared with the previous report.

So which prominent stars aligned with the megaliths, and when? The southerly most megalith alignment ("C" line) was reported by Wendorf and Malville to align with Sirius c. 4820 BC. Given these corrected data, we see that Sirius actually aligned with the C line c. 6000 BC. We estimate that in 6088 BC, Sirius had a declination of -36.51°, for a rising azimuth exactly on the C-line average given in Table 2. In Figure A25, plotted over the satellite image, one line is the rising of Sirius in 4820 BC and the other the rising of Sirius in 6000 BC.

The stellar correlations ascribed by Wendorf and Malville spanned more that 1,000 years and involved unrelated stars, with some of the stars purportedly being tracked through precession by the Neolithic megalith builders, and some stars not being tracked. If we consider the complex of megalith lines all on the same date c. 6270 BC, however, other possible stellar alignments become apparent. Figure A26 shows the rising azimuths of seven bright stars all on 6270 BC—Vega (the brightest star in the northern sky), the three stars of Orion's belt, and the three stars of Orion's head and shoulders (Betelgeuse, Bellatrix, and Meissa). All of them have near fits to megalithic alignments. Figure A26 also shows that the Calendar Circle, located just off the edge of the ancient playa, is nearly in line with the many northerly megalith lines, such that it may be warranted to consider whether the Calendar Circle is related to the complex of megalithic structures and alignments.

So let's now consider what may have been the meanings or alignments of the megaliths intended by the builders of the site. Although virtually all

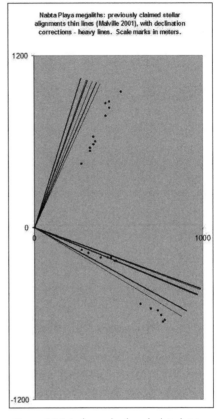

Figure A24. Independently calculated rising azimuths of Nabta Playa megaliths.

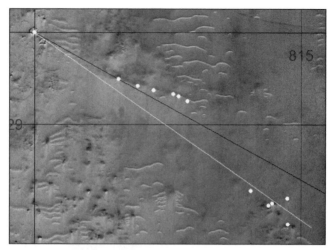

Figure A25. Nabta Playa megalith alignments plotted over the satellite image.

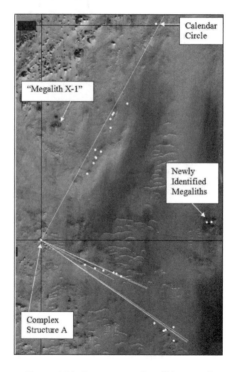

Figure A26. Rising azimuths of Vega and
Orion in 6270 BC.

prehistoric or otherwise undocumented stellar alignments in archaeology have been challenged as statistically unproveable,[355] the dates of activity at this site help constrain probable intended astronomy.

Figure A27 plots all of the radiocarbon dates younger than 10,000 years collected from Nabta Playa.[356] We see the most intense radiocarbon activity around 6000 BC, with steady activity continuing to the end of the last major humid interphase c. 5100 BC, and continuing less actively to the beginning of hyperaridity and year-round uninhabitability c. 3800 BC.

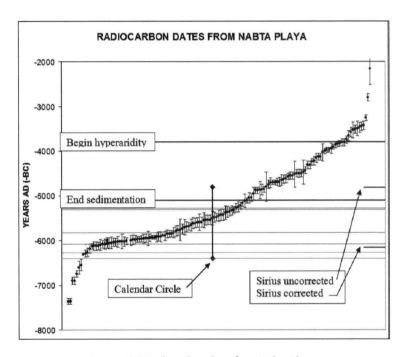

Figure A27. Radiocarbon dates from Nabta Playa.

The heavy horizontal lines in figure A27 mark the beginning of hyperaridity and the end of the last major humid interphase at Nabta, which is also the end of major playa sedimentation. The end of the last major humid interphase is relevant to the timing of the placement of the megaliths. Many of the megaliths lie on top of the playa sediments, and so are believed to have been constructed there more recently than 7,000 years ago.[357] The corrected star declinations and megalith coordinates given here show that Sirius aligned with the southerly major line of megaliths more than 1,000 years earlier, when the sediments were still accumulating.

This generates a number of questions about the megalith alignments. Is the primary, and earliest, alignment not intended for Sirius? Or is a constraint that the alignments postdate the end of the last major humid interphase unnecessary?

Related questions involve the construction of Complex Structure A, which consisted of a large oval of many megaliths—some finely worked, cut, or broken—on the surface of about three meters of sediment.[358] Underneath those surface megaliths, on the bedrock below and still attached to the bedrock, is the sculpted lump of bedrock said to be "shaped like a mushroom." On top of the bedrock sculpture was the cow stone—a finely sculpted megalith chocked in place by two other stones, all embedded in the sand underneath the oval of surface megaliths. All the megalith lines radiate out from this structure, indicating that Complex Structure A, or at least some part of it, is the earliest of the megalithic constructions.

Wendorf and Krolik theorize that Complex Structure A and thirty nearby similar complex structures were all constructed entirely after the sediments were laid down, and that the builders located the sub-surface bedrock lumps suitable for sculpting using some unknown method. It seems more reasonable, however, to think that possibly something was constructed there before or during the playa sedimentation, and only the final stage of construction occurred at or after the end of the last major humid interphase. Similarly, if the original placement of Complex Structure A predated the end of sedimentation, and if it is an element of all the megalith lines, that suggests that some of the megalith lines were also originally placed prior to the end of sedimentation. These megaliths, which now lie broken and cut on top of the sediment, may represent the final stages of construction—actually, destruction—with the earliest constructions originating earlier.

We suggest an alternative model—that the megaliths at Nabta Playa may represent a unified complex of related meanings, including the Calendar Circle. The southerly lines of megaliths correlated with the three stars of Orion's belt and with the shoulder and head stars of Orion all at the same epoch, c. 6270 BC. That was also the observationally relevant time of the Vernal Equinox heliacal rising for the center of Orion's belt. The "scatter" in the megalith lines may be such as to coordinate with the

Vernal Equinox heliacal rising of those same stars, spanning 6400 BC for the first star of Orion's belt to 5200 BC. (These dates are marked in figure A27 by the thin horizontal lines.) And the northerly lines of megaliths may have correlated with the motion of the brightest star in the north, Vega, starting with Vega rising over the Calendar Circle c. 6400 BC and then passing over the other north megalith lines during the same time window.

Interestingly, some of the southerly most megaliths may also have represented Sirius c. 6100 BC, for during that epoch the declinations of Sirius and Orion's belt differed by less than 2°. Elsewhere, we have shown that the standing stones within the Calendar Circle may have represented the appearance of the same stars on the meridian before Summer Solstice sunrise during the same time period (6400 BC to 4800 BC).

Thus, the corrected megalith locations at Nabta Playa simply do not support the notion that the earliest alignment was built in order to point to the rising of Sirius at some time subsequent to the end of playa sedimentation (7,200 years ago). If Sirius was the intended alignment, it had to have been built earlier, more than 8,000 years ago. A compelling model for the meaning of the various astronomical structures at Nabta Playa may thus involve a consistent complex of meanings, including alignments with the Vernal Equinox heliacal rising of Orion's belt and the appearance of Orion's belt on the meridian before Summer Solstice sunrise.

Bibliography

Allen, J. P. "Reading a Pyramid," in *Homages à Jean Leclant, IFAO* vol.1, 1994.

—————. *The Ancient Egyptian Pyramid Texts.* Leiden: Brill, 2005.

—————. *The Cosmology of the Pyramid Texts.* In Simpson, W. K. (ed.) Religion and Philosophy in Ancient Egypt. New Haven: Yale University Press, 1989.

Alliot, Maurice. "Les plus vieilles traditions du Temple D'Edfou," *Institut Francais d'Archeologie Orientale*, Melanges Mariette, T. xxxii, 1961.

Amer I. H., and B. Morardet. "Les dates de la construction du temple majeur d'Hathor à Dendara à l'époque Gréco-Romaine," *ASAE* 69, 1983.

Anthes, R. "Horus als Sorius in den Pyramidentexten," in *ZAS* (Zeitschrift für Ägyptische Sprache und Altertumskunde), 102 (1975).

Badawy, Alexander. "The Stellar Destiny of Pharaoh and the so-called Air-Shafts of Cheops Pyramid," *Mitteilungen der Instituts Fur Orient-forschung* (Akademie der Wissenschaften zu Berlin) Band 10, 1964.

—————. "The ideology of the superstructure of the Mastaba-tomb in Egypt," *JNES,* vol. XV, 1956.

Baines, J. "Bnbn: Mythological and Linguistic Notes," *Orientalia*, vol. 39, 1970.

Baines, J., and J. Malek. *Altlas of Ancient Egypt.* Oxford: Andromeda, 1996.

Baud, Michel. *Djeser et la IIIe Dynastie.* Paris: Pygmalion, 2007.

Bauval, Robert, and Graham Hancock. *Keeper of Genesis*. New York: Random House, 1997.

Bauval, Robert, and Adrian Gilbert. *The Orion Mystery*. New York: Crown, 1994.

Bauval, Robert, and Ahmed Osman. *Breaking the Mirror of Heaven*. Vermont: Inner Traditions Inc., 2012.

Bauval, Robert, and Thomas Brophy. *Black Genesis: The Prehistoric Origins of Ancient Egypt*. Rochester, VT: Bear & Company, 2011.

Bauval, Robert. "A Master-plan for the three Pyramids of Giza based on the Configuration of the three Stars of the Belt of Orion," *Discussions in Egyptology*, 13, Oxford, 1988–1989.

―――――――. *The Egypt Code*. New York: The Disinformation Company Ltd, 2008.

Beaux, Nathalie. "La Douat dans les Textes des Pyramides," *Bulletin de l'Institut Francais D'Archaeology Orientale* (BIFAO) vol. 94. 1994.

Belmonte, Juan. "Some open questions on the Egyptian Calendar: an astronomer's view," *TdE* 2, 2003.

Belmonte, Juan, and Mosalam Shaltout. "Keeping Maat: An astronomical approach to the orientation of the temples in Ancient Egypt," paper delivered to *WSEF* 2007.

―――――――. "On the Orientation of Ancient Egyptian Temples I: Upper Egypt and Lower Nubia," *ftp://ftp.ll.iac.es/pub/research/preprints/PP05003.pdf*.

―――――――. *In Search of cosmic Order: Astronomy, landscape and symbolism*. Cairo: American University in Cairo Press, 2010.

Bevan, E. R. *The House of Ptolemy*. London: Methuen Publishing, 1927.

Bolshakov, Andrey O. "Princess HMTR(W): The First Mention of Osiris?" *Chronique D'Egypte*, LXVII 1992.

Bomhard, Anne-Sophie. *The Egyptian Calendar: A Work for Eternity*. London: Periplus, 1998.

Boulter, Carmen. *The Pyramid Code*, episode 5, "A new Chronology," 2008.

Boussier, Gaston. *Tacitus and Other Roman Studies*. New York: Hutchison (Trans) Putnam, 1906.

Breasted, James H. *The Development of Religion and Thought in Ancient Egypt*. Philadelphia: University of Pennsylvania Press, 1972.

Brophy, Thomas. *The Origin Map: Discovery of a Prehistoric Megalithic Astrophysical Map of the Universe*. Bloomington, IN: iUniverse, 2002.

Brophy, Thomas, and Paul A. Rosen. "Satellite Imagery Measures of the Astronomically Aligned Megaliths at Nabta Playa," *Mediterranean Archaeology and Archaeometry* 5(1), 2005.

Brown, C. "A Theory on the Pyramids: Hopkins professor tells why they were put there," *Washington Post*, C8, 30.11.1983.

Brugsch, Heinrich. *Egypt under the Pharaohs*. London: Bracken Books (repr. 1996), 1891.

Buckwald, V. F. *Handbook on Iron Meteorites*. Berkeley, CA: UCLA Press, 1975.

Champdor, A. *The Book of the Dead*. New York: Garrett Publishing, 1966.

Church, Alfred John, and William Jackson Brodribb, trans. *Cornelius Tacitus: The Annals of Tacitus*. London: Macmillan, 1877.

Clagett, Marshall. *Ancient Egyptian Science,* Vol. I. Philadelphia: American Philosophical Society, 1995.

Clarke, Somers, and R. Englebach. *Ancient Egyptian Construction and Architecture*. London: Oxford University Press, 1930.

CPE Reports. Wendorf, Fred, and Romauld Schild, eds. *Holocene Settlement of the Egyptian Sahara. Vol. 1, The Archaeology of Nabta Playa*. New York: Kluwer Academic, 2001.

Cunnigham, Francis A. "The Sothic Cycle used by the Egyptians," *Journal of the American Oriental Society*, vol. 34, 1915.

Daremberg, Charles, and Edmond Saglio. *Dictionnaire Des Antiquites Grecques et Romaines*. Paris: Hachette, 1877–1919.

David, Rosalie. *Ancient Egyptian Religion, Beliefs and Practices.* London: Routledge & Kegan Paul, 1982.

de Maret, Pierre. "L'orycterope, un animale 'bon à penser' pour les Africains, est-il à l'origine du dieu Egyptien Seth?" *BIFAO* 105, 2005.

De Velde, H. *Seth, God of Confusion: A Study of his role in Egyptian Mythology and Religion.* Leiden: Brill, 1967.

Dodson, Aidan, and Dyan Hilton. *The Complete Royal Families of Ancient Egypt.* London: Thames & Hudson, 2004.

Dorner, Josef. *Die Absteckung und astronomische Orientierung agyptischer Pyramiden.* University of Innsbruck, 1981 (Thesis +C14169207).

Duguid, Euan. *The Sunday Post* [UK], 12-24-7.

Edwards, I. E. S. *The Pyramids of Egypt.* London: Penguin Books, 1993.

Egypt's Lost Cities, on BBC 1, 30 May 2011.

Fairall, A. "Precession and the Layout of the ancient Egyptian Pyramids," *The Journal of the Royal Astronomical Society,* June 1999.

Fairervis, W. A. "A Revised View of the Narmer Palette," *Journal of the American Research Centre in Egypt,* XXVIII, 1991.

Faulkner, R. O. *The Ancient Egyptian Pyramid Texts.* London: Oxford University Press, 1998.

Fiechter, Jean-Jacques. *Mykerinos, le Dieu Englouti.* Paris: Maisonneuve & Larose, 2001.

Flinders Petrie, William Matthew. *Researches in Sinai.* London: J. Murray, 1905.

—————. *Seventy Years in Archaeology.* New York: Grammond (repr. 1969), 1932.

Frankfort, Henry. *Kingship and the Gods.* Chicago: University of Chicago Press, 1978.

Friedman, Florence Dunn. "The Underground Relief Panels of King Djoser at the Step Pyramid Complex," *Journal of the American Research Center in Egypt*, Vol. 32, (1995).

—————. "Notions of Cosmos in the Step Pyramid Complex," in *Studies in Honor of William Kelly Simpson*, Vol. 1. Boston: Museum of Fine Arts, 1996.

Goedicke, Hans. "Zoser's Funerary Monument 1," *Esch996.*

Gordon, Gerard. "Etudes sur L'Epoque Archaique: Une mention de Sekhat-Hor dans la première dynastie," *BIFAO*, vol. 57, 1958.

Goyon, George. "Kerkasore et l'ancien observatoire d'Eudoxe," *Bulletin de l'Institut Francais d'Archeologie Orientale*, tome 74, 1974.

—————. "Nouvelles Observations relatives à L'Orientation de la Pyramide de Cheops," *Revue D'Egyptologie*, Tome 22, 1970.

—————. *Kheops: Le Secret des Batiseurs des Grandes Pyramides.* Paris: Pygmalion Press, 1990.

Graves-Brown, Carolyn. *Dancing for Hathor: Women in Ancient Egypt.* London: Continuum Publishers, London: Continuum, 2010.

Guksch, H., and D. Polz (eds). *Stationen: Beitrage zur Kulturgeschichte Agyptens.* Mainz: Rainer Stadelmann Gewimdet, 1998.

Gurshtein, A. "The Evolution of the Zodiac in the Context of Ancient Oriental History," *Vistas in Astronomy*, vol. 41, part 4, 1997.

Hart, George. *A Dictionary of Egyptian Gods and Goddesses.* London: Routledge & Keagan Paul, 1988.

Hassan, S. *Excavations at Giza.* Oxford: University Press, 1946.

Hawass, Zahi, and Mark Lehner. "The Sphinx: Who Built it and Why?" *Archaeology Magazine*, vol. 47, No.5, September, October 1994.

Hekekyan, Joseph. Brit. Lib. Add. MS 37458.21, 1852.

Herbich, Tomasz, and Aleksander Jagodzinski. "Geophysical Investigation on the Dry Moat of the Netjerykhet Complex at Saqqara," *Studies in Honour of Romuald Schild*. Warsaw: Polish Academy of Sciences, 2008.

Hitti, P. K. *History of Syria*. London: Macmillan, 1951.

Hoffman, Michael A. *Egypt before the Pharaohs*. London: Ark Paperback, 1984.

Hornug, I. *Ideas into Images*. Princeton, NJ: Princeton Press, 1992.

Ingham, M. F. "The Length of the Sothic Cycle," *Journal of Egyptian Archaeology* 55 (1969).

Irish, Joel D. "Who were the ancient Egyptians? Dental affinities among Neolithic through post-dynastic samples," *American Journal of Physical Anthropology*, 129:529–543.

Irish, Joel D., P. Bobrowski, M. Kobusiewicz, J. Kabaciski, and R. Schild. "An Artificial Human Tooth from the Neolithic Cemetery at Gebel Ramlah, Egypt," *Dental Anthropology*, Volume 17, No. 1, 2004.

Jacq, Christian. *Les Grands Sages de L'Egypte Ancienne*. Paris: Perrin, 2007.

—————. *Magic and Mystery in Ancient Egypt*. London: Souvenir Press, 1998.

Jeffreys, David G. "The topography of Heliopolis and Memphis: some cognitive aspects," in H. Guksch and D. Polz (eds), *Stationen: Beitrage zur Kulturgeschichte Agyptens*. Mainz: Rainer Stadelmann Gewimdet, 1998.

—————. "Regionality, Cultural and Cultic Landscapes," in *Egyptian Archaeology*, edited by Willeke Wendrich. Chichester, UK: Blackwell Publishing, 2007.

Kees, H. *Totenglauben und Jenseitsvorstellungen der Alten Agypter*. Leipzig: J. C. Hinrichs, 1926.

Kemp, Barry J. *Ancient Egypt: Anatomy of a Civilization*. London: Routledge, 1991.

Krupp, E. C. *Echoes of the Ancient Skies.* New York: Harper & Row, 1983.

—————. "Pyramid Marketing Schemes," *Sky & Telescope*, February 1997.

—————. *In Search of Ancient Astronomies.* Garden City, NY: Doubleday, 1978.

—————. *Skywatchers, Shamans, and Kings.* New York: Willey Popular Science, 1997.

Lacau, P., and J. P. Lauer. *La Pyramide à Degrés.* Cairo: Institut Francais d'Archeologie Orientale, 1959, 1961, 1965.

Lalouette, C. *BIFAO* 79.

Lauer, Jean-Philippe. *Saqqara, Une Vie.* Paris: Rivages, 1988.

—————. *Histoire Monumentale des Pyramides D'Egypte.* Cairo: Institut Francais d'Archeologie Orientale, 1962.

Lehner, Mark. "A Contextual Approach to the Giza Pyramid," *Archiv fur Orientforschung,* 32 (1985).

—————. *The Complete Pyramids.* London: Thames & Hudson, 1997.

Lichtheim, Miriam. *Ancient Egyptian Literature.* Berkeley, CA: University of California Press, 1975.

Lockyer, Norman. *The Dawn of Astronomy.* London: Cassell and Co, Ltd, 1894.

Lucas, A. *Ancient Egyptian Materials and Industries.* London: E. Arnold, 1934.

Magli, G. "Akhet Khufu: Archaeo-astronomical hints at a common project of the two main pyramids of Giza, Egypt," *NNJ-Architecture and Mathematics*, 11, 2009.

—————. "Topography, astronomy and dynastic history in the alignment of pyramids of the Old Kingdom," *http://arxiv.org/* .

Malek, J. "Orion and the Giza Pyramids," review of *The Orion Mystery, Discussions in Egyptology,* vol. 30. 1994.

Malville, J. M., et al. "Megaliths and Neolithic Astronomy in Southern Egypt," *Nature* 392 (April 1998).

Malville, J. M., R. Schild, F. Wendorf, and J. Brenmer. "Astronomy of Nabta Playa," *African Skies/Cieus Africains*, no. 11, July 2007.

Mariette, August. *Denderah*, Vol. I. Paris: A. Franck, 1870.

Mason, Brian. *Meteorites.* New York: Wiley, 1962.

Maspero, G. *Manual of Egyptian Archaeology.* New York: Putnam, 1926.

McCall, G. J. H. *Meteorites and Their Origins.* New York: Wiley, 1973.

Mercer, S. *The Pyramid Texts.* New York: Longmans, Green, 1952.

Mills, James O. "Astronomy at Hierakonpolis," paper presented at the 1990 Society for Africanist Archaeologists, March 22–25 1990, University of Florida, Gainesville.

Mond, Robert, and Oliver H. Myers. *Rock Drawings of Southern Upper Egypt: Sir Robert Mond Expedition, Preliminary Report 1937.*

Morley, Iain, and Colin Renfrew, eds. *The Archaeology of Measurements: Comprehending Heaven, Earth and Time in Ancient Societies.* New York: Cambridge University Press, 2010.

Morris, Ellen F. "On the Ownership of the Saqqara Mastabas and the Allotment of Political and Ideological Power at the Dawn of the State," *The Archaeology and Art of ancient Egypt: Essays in Honor of David B. O'Conner,* Annales du Service des Antiquités de L'Egypte, cahier No. 36, vol. II.

Malville, J. M., F. Wendorf, A. A. Mazar, and R. Schild. "Megaliths and Neolithic Astronomy in Southern Egypt," *Nature* 392, April 1998.

Mysliwjec, K. *Studien zum got Atum, Vol. 1.* Hildesheim: Gerstenberg, 1978.

Naville, Edouard. "Le nom du Sphinx dans le livre des morts," *Sphinx,* Vol. V, 188.

Neugebauer, O., and Richard Parker. *Egyptian Astronomical Texts,* Vol. 1. Providence: Brown University Press, 1964.

Nibbi, A. *JARCE* xiv, 1977.

O'Mara, Patrick. "Censorinus, the Sothic Cycle, and Calendar Year One in Ancient Egypt: The Epistemological Problem," *JNES*, vol. 62, 2003.

Parker, Richard. "Sothic Dates and Calendar Adjustments," *Revue D'Egyptologie*, vol. 9, 1952.

Peden, Alexander J. *The Graffiti of Pharaonic Egypt.* Leiden: Brill, 2001.

Piankoff, A. *The Pyramid of Unas.* Princeton, NJ: Princeton University Press, Bollingen Series XL.5, 1968.

Pogo, A. "Calendars on Coffin Lids from Asyut: Second Half of the Third Millennium," *ISIS*, vol. XVII, 1932.

Quaegebeur, J. "Cléopâtre VII et le temple de Dendara," *GM* 120, 1991.

Quirke, Stephen. *The Cult of Ra.* London: Thames & Hudson, 2001.

Radi, Abdel. (1936) [In book: Hans A. Winkler and Nicholas S. Hopkins. *Ghost Riders of Upper Egypt: A Study in Spirit Possession.* Cairo: American University in Cairo Press, 2009.].

Ramsey, Christopher, et al. "Radiocarbon-Based Chronology for Dynastic Egypt," *Science*, 18 June 2010: vol. 328 no. 5985.

Regulski, Illona. "Second Ink Inscriptions from Saqqara paralleled in the Abydos material from the Royal Museum of Art and history (RMAH) in Brussels," *https://lirias.kuleuven.be/bitstream/*.

Rice, Michael. *Egypt's Making.* London: Guild Publishing, 1990.

Romieu, A. "Calcul de l'heure chez les ancient Egyptiens," *Rec. Trav.* XXIV.

Rossi, C. *Architecture and Mathematics in Ancient Egypt.* New York: Cambridge University Press, 2004.

Roth, Ann Macy. "Fingers, stars, and the 'opening of the mouth': The nature and function of the ntrwj-blades," *JEA* 79, 1993.

Roux, G. *Delphes, son Oracle et ses Dieux.* Paris: Belles Lettres, 1976.

Rundle Clark, R. T. *Myth and Symbol in Ancient Egypt.* London: Thames & Hudson, 1959.

Saleh, Abdel Aziz. *Excavations at Heliopolis I & II.* Cairo: Cairo University, 1981.

Sarton, George. *Ancient Science through the Golden Age of Greece.* London: Dover Press, 1993.

Schaefer, B. E. "Atmospheric extinction effects on stellar alignments," Archaeoastronomy Supplement to *Journal for the History of Astronomy* 10:S32–S42, 1986.

Schild, Romuald, and Fred Wendorf. "Forty Years of the Combined Prehistoric Expedition," *Archaeologia Polona* 40 (2002).

Schnusenberg, Christine C. *The Mythological Traditions of Lithurgical Drama.* New Jersey: Paulist Press, 2010.

Shaw, Ian, and Paul Nicholson. *The Illustrated Dictionary of Ancient Egypt.* New York: The American University in Cairo Press, 2008.

——————. *The British Museum Dictionary of Ancient Egypt.* London: The British Museum Press, 2003.

Spence, Kate. "Are the Pyramids aligned with the Stars," in *The Seventy Great Mysteries of Ancient Egypt*, edited by Bill Manly. London: Thames & Hudson, 2003.

——————. "Ancient Egyptian Chronology and the astronomical Orientation of Pyramids," *Nature,* vol. 408, Nov. 2000.

Stadelmann, Rainer. *Der Aegyptischen Pyramiden.* Mainz am Rhein: Philipp von Zaber, 1985.

Stoley, R. W. "Primitive Methods of Measuring Time, with Special Reference to Egypt," *Journal of Egyptian Archaeology,* vol. 17, 1930.

Strawn, Brent A. *What is Stronger than a Lion? Leonine Image and Metaphor in the Hebrew Bible and the Near East.* Fribourg, Switzerland: Academy Press, 2005.

Swelim, Nabil. "The Dry Moat of the Netjerykhet Complex," *Pyramid Studies and Other Essays presented to I. E. S. Edwards.* London: Egypt Exploration Society, 1988.

The International Standard Bible Encyclopedia, Illustrated in Four Volumes, Revised Edition. Michigan: Wm. B. Eerdmans Publishing Co., 1986.

Tomkins, Peter, and Livio Catullo Stecchini. *Secrets of the Great Pyramid.* Edison, NJ: BBS Publishing, reprint March 1, 1997.

Trimble, V. "Astronomical Investigation concerning the so-called Air-Shafts of Cheop's Pyramid," *Mitteilungen der Instituts Fur Orientforschung* (Akademie der Wissenschaften zu Berlin) Band 10, 1964.

Van Sertima, Ivan. *Egypt: Child of Africa.* New Jersey: Transaction Publishers, 2002.

Verner, Mirolav. *Abusir: Realm of Osiris.* New York: The American University in Cairo Press, 2002.

Vyse, Richard W. Howard, and John S. Perring. *Operations Carried on at the Pyramids of Gizeh in 1837.* London: Fraser, 1840.

Wainwright, G. A. "Seshat and the Pharaoh," *JEA* 26, 1941.

—————. "Iron in Egypt," *JEA* 18, 1933.

Wallis Budge, E. A. *Egyptian Hieroglyphic Dictionary.* New York: Dover Publications, 1978.

—————. *The Book of the Dead; the hieroglyphic transcript of the Papyrus of Ani.* New Hyde Park, NY: University Books, 1960.

—————. *The Gods of the Egyptians.* New York: Dover Publications, 1969.

Warner, Marina Felipe, and Fernández-Armesto. *World of Myths.* Austin, TX: University of Texas Press, 2003.

Wells, Ron. "Sothis and the Satet Temple on Elephantine," *Studien Zur Altagyptischen Kultur* (ZAK) 12, 1985.

Wendorf, Fred, and Romuald Schild. *Holocene Settlement of the Egyptian Sahara: The Archeology of Nabta Playa*. New York: Kluwer Academic/Plenum, 2001.

—————. "The Megaliths of Nabta Playa," *Focus on Archaeology*, Academia No.1 (1) 2004.

Wendorf, F., A. E. Close, and R. Schild. "Megaliths in the Egyptian Sahara," *Sahara* 5, 7–16 (1992–1993).

Wilkinson, Richard. *The Complete Gods and Goddesses of Ancient Egypt*. New York: The American University in Cairo Press, 2003.

Wilkinson, Toby A. H. *Early Dynastic Egypt*. London: Routledge, 1999.

—————. *Royal Annals of Ancient Egypt: The Palermo Stone and Associated Fragments*. London: Keagan Paul International, 2000.

Williams, Bruce. "Forebears of Menes in Nubia, myth or reality?" *Journal of Near Eastern Studies* 46, No.1 Jan. 1987.

—————. "The Lost Pharaohs of Nubia," in *Archaeology* 33 No.5 1985

—————. *Excavations Between Abu Simbel and the Sudan Frontier, Part 1: The A-Group Royal Cemetery at Qustul, Cemetery L*. Chicago: Oriental Institute Nubian Expedition, 1986.

Winkler, Hans A. *Rock-Drawings of Southern Upper Egypt*. London: Bd. 2, 1939.

Winter, H. "A Reconsideration of the newly Discovered Building Inscription on the Temple of Denderah," *GM* 108, 1989.

Zaba, Zbynek. "L'Orientation Astronomique Dans L'Ancienne Egypte, et la Précession de l'Axe du Monde," Prague: Académie des sciences tchecoslovaque, 1953.

Ziegler, C. *Les Pyramides D'Egypte*. Paris: Hachette, 1999.

Endnotes

1   Ian Shaw and Paul Nicholson, *The Illustrated Dictionary of Ancient Egypt* (New York: The American University in Cairo Press, 2008).

2   Christian Jacq, *Magic and Mystery in Ancient Egypt* (London: Souvenir Press, 1998), p. 19.

3   I. E. S. Edwards, *The Pyramids of Egypt* (London: Penguin Books, 1993), p. 284.

4   Edwards, *Pyramids of Egypt,* p. 286.

5   The initial analysis of the Step Pyramid Complex astronomy is in Robert Bauval, *The Egypt Code* (New York: Disinformation Company Ltd, 2008), chapters 1 and 2.

6   Abdel-Aziz Saleh, *Excavations at Heliopolis* Vol. I. (Cairo: Cairo University, 1981), pp. 11, 23.

7   See *http://www.robertbauval.co.uk/articles/.* The *Orthodox Christianity Online Encyclopedia* contains this curious claim about a nearby street: "In one small street in the el-Matarya district of today's Cairo (Eid Street/Shek El-Te'eban Street), all kinds of bread and bakery cannot be leavened up to this day, since the Virgin Mary first visited that place with the Holy Family 2,000 years ago and they were refused bread and cast away. This is an ongoing miracle that anyone can witness till this very day. Bread leavens normally in all surrounding streets."

8   E. C. Krupp, *Skywatchers, Shamans, and Kings* (New York: Willey Popular Science, 1997), p. 223.

9   R.W. Stoley, "Primitive Methods of Measuring Time, with Special Reference to Egypt," *Journal of Egyptian Archaeology*, vol. 17, 1930, p. 167.

10   Richard Wilkinson, *The Complete Gods and Goddesses of Ancient Egypt* (New York: The American University in Cairo Press, 2003), p. 167.

11   Shaw and Nicholson, *Dictionary of Ancient Egypt*, p. 58.

12   For a full discussion on this issue, see Robert Bauval and Adrian Gilbert, *The Orion Mystery* (New York: Crown, 1994).

13   Patrick O'Mara, "Censorinus, the Sothic Cycle, and Calendar Year One in Ancient Egypt: The Epistemological Problem," *JNES* vol. 62, 2003, pp. 17–26; see also George Sarton, *Ancient Science through the Golden Age of Greece* (London: Dover Press, 1993), p. 29.

14   *Cornelius Tacitus: The Annals of Tacitus*, translated by Alfred John Church and William Jackson Brodribb (London: Macmillan, 1877).

15   See Gaston Boussier's *Tacitus and Other Roman Studies* (New York: Hutchison (Trans) Putnam), 1906.

16   R. T. Rundle Clark, *Myth and Symbol in Ancient Egypt* (London: Thames & Hudson, 1959), p. 246.

17   Quoted in William Matthew Flinders Petrie, *Researches in Sinai* (London: J. Murray, 1905), p. 164.

18   Clark, *Myth and Symbol in Ancient Egypt*, p. 263.

19   Bauval, *The Egypt Code*, pp. 64–65.

20   Bauval, *The Egypt Code*, pp. 64–65; see also Bauval and Hancock, *Keeper of Genesis: Message of the Sphinx* (London: Heinemann, 1996).

21   It was first presented by us in *The Orion Mystery* in 1993 (p. 193), then in *Keeper of Genesis* in 1996, and in *The Egypt Code* in 2006. We also discuss it and the important role of the subterranean passages in our last work, *Black Genesis: The Prehistoric Origins of Ancient Egypt* (Rochester, VT: Bear & Company, 2011).

22   E. C. Krupp, "Pyramid Marketing Schemes," *Sky & Telescope*, February 1997, pp. 65–75.

23   A. Fairall, "Precession and the Layout of the ancient Egyptian Pyramids," *The Journal of the Royal Astronomical Society*, June 1999.

24   For those wishing to know the full story of this bizarre episode, we refer them to these Internet publications: *http://www.grahamhancock. com* and *http://www.robertbauval.co.uk/articles/*.

25   From *http://www.pbs.org/wgbh/nova/pyramid*.

26   The two-volume thesis, *Excavations at Heliopolis I & II* (Cairo: Cairo University, 1981), by Abdel Aziz Salem, ex-Dean of Archaeology at Cairo University, shows the diversity of learned opinions on this topic.

27   See David Jeffreys, "Regionality, Cultural and Cultic Landscapes," *Egyptian Archaeology*, edited by Willeke Wendrich (Chichester, UK: Blackwell Publishing, 2007), p. 102.

28   J. Baines, "Bnbn: Mythological and Linguistic Notes," *Orientalia*, vol. 39, 1970, pp. 389–395.

29   Edwards, *Pyramids of Egypt*, p. 282; Henry Frankfort, *Kingship and the Gods* (Chicago: University of Chicago Press, 1978), pp. 153, 380 n. 26; J. H. Breasted, *The Development of Religion and Thought in Ancient Egypt* (Philadelphia: University of Pennsylvania Press, 1972), pp. 70–72.

30   Frankfort, *Kingship and the Gods,* p. 380 n. 26.

31   Bauval, *The Egypt Code*, p. 71.

32   Juan Belmonte and Mosalam Shaltout, *In Search of Cosmic Order: Astronomy, landscape and symbolism* (Cairo: Supreme Council of Antiquities Press, 2009), p. 260. Belmonte does not credit us for this discovery, although he surely was aware of it, since he lists *The Egypt Code* in his bibliography and also refers to it regarding another matter—the serdab of the Step Pyramid.

33   *http://www.aeraweb.org/projects/sphinx/*; see also Zahi Hawass and Mark Lehner "The Sphinx: Who Built It and Why?" *Archaeology Magazine*, vol. 47, no.5, September, October 1994, pp.30–41.

34   Edouard Naville,"Le nom du Sphinx dans le livre des morts," *Sphinx*, vol.V, 188, p. 193.

35   Rosalie David, *Ancient Egyptian Religion, Beliefs and Practices* (London: Routledge & Kegan Paul, 1982), p. 46.

36   K. Mysliwjec, *Studien zum got Atum, Vol. 1* (Hildesheim: Gerstenberg, 1978).

37   For a detailed study of the lion symbolism and iconography in Egypt, see Brent A. Strawn, *What is Stronger than a Lion? Leonine Image and Metaphor in the Hebrew Bible and the Near East* (Fribourg, Switzerland: Academy Press, 2005), pp. 174–178.

38   George Goyon, *Kheops: Le Secret des Batiseurs des Grandes Pyramides* (Paris: Pygmalion Press, 1990), p. 92.

39   Peter Tomkins and Livio Catullo Stecchini, *Secrets of the Great Pyramid* (Edison, NJ: BBS Publishing, reprint March 1, 1997).

40   David G. Jeffreys,"The topography of Heliopolis and Memphis: some cognitive aspects," in H. Guksch and D. Polz (eds), *Stationen: Beitrage zur Kulturgeschichte Agyptens* (Mainz: Rainer Stadelmann Gewimdet, 1998), pp. 63–71.

41   Joseph Hekekyan, Brit. Lib. Add. MS 37458.21, 1852. Hekekyan wrote:"Right Line identical with the South West and North Eastern Diagonal of the Soris (Cheops) Pyramid and the Obelisk."

42   George Goyon, "Nouvelles Observations relatives à L'Orientation de la Pyramide de Cheops," *Revue D'Egyptologie,* Tome 22, 1970, pp. 91–92.

43   C. Brown,"A Theory on the Pyramids: Hopkins professor tells why they were put there," *Washington Post*, C8, 30.11.1983.

44 *https://sites.google.com/site/okadct/home.*

45 From *The Seventy Great Mysteries of Ancient Egypt*, edited by Bill Manley (London: Thames & Hudson, 2003), p. 73.

46 Mark Lehner, "A Contextual Approach to the Giza Pyramid," *Archiv fur Orientforschung*, 32 (1985), pp. 136–158; G. Magli "Akhet Khufu: Archaeo-astronomical hints at a common project of the two main pyramids of Giza, Egypt," *NNJ-Architecture and Mathematics*, 11, 2009, 35–50, n.4; *http://arxiv.org/ftp/arxiv/papers.*

47 See, for example, Kate Spence, "Are the Pyramids aligned with the Stars?" in *The Seventy Great Mysteries of Ancient Egypt* (London: Thames & Hudson, 2003), p. 71. Also G. Magli, "Topography, astronomy and dynastic history."

48 Robert Bauval, "A Master plan for the three Pyramids of Giza based on the configuration of the three stars of the Belt of Orion," *Discussions in Egyptology,* vol.13, Oxford 1989, pp. 7–18.

49 J. Malek, "Orion and the Giza Pyramids," review of "The Orion Mystery," *Discussions in Egyptology*, vol. 30, 1994, pp. 101–114.

50 Mirolav Verner, *Abusir: Realm of Osiris* (New York: The American University in Cairo Press, 2002), p. 11.

51 Jeffreys, "The topography of Heliopolis and Memphis," p. 65.

52 Jeffreys did venture to offer "cultural and cultic" possible motives. See "Regionality, Cultural and Cultic Landscapes," p. 102.

53 Jeffreys, "The topography of Heliopolis and Memphis."

54 *http://www.robertschoch.net/Exploring%20the%20Great%20Pyramid%20*

55 Christian Jacq, *Les Grands Sages de L'Egypte Ancienne* (Paris: Perrin, 2007), pp. 18–22.

56 Edwards, *The Pyramids of Egypt*, p. 286.

57   *The Amazing Astronomers of Antiquity*, Houston Museum of Natural Science George Observatory, Scene 2.

58   Edwards, *The Pyramids of Egypt*, p. 34.

59   Lehner, "A Contextual Approach to the Giza Pyramid," p. 82.

60   Jacq, *Les Grands Sages de L'Egypte Ancienne*, p. 191.

61   Jacq, *Les Grands Sages de L'Egypte Ancienne*, p. 22.

62   Florence Dunn Friedman, "Notions of Cosmos in the Step Pyramid Complex," in *Studies in Honor of William Kelly Simpson*, Vol. 1 (Boston: Museum of Fine Arts, 1996), pp. 337–351; also "The Underground Relief Panels of King Djoser at the Step Pyramid Complex," *Journal of the American Research Center in Egypt*, Vol. 32, (1995), pp. 1–42.

63   *http://spaceupdate.com/shows/scripts/amazing_astronomers_of_antiquity-script.pdf.*

64   See Lehner, "A Contextual Approach to the Giza Pyramid," pp. 82–83.

65   Lehner, "A Contextual Approach to the Giza Pyramid," p. 7.

66   G. A. Wainwright, "Iron in Egypt," *JEA* 18, 1933, pp. 6–11.

67   Ann Macy Roth, "Fingers, stars, and the 'opening of the mouth': The nature and function of the ntrwj-blades," *JEA* 79, 1993, pp. 57–79.

68   George Goyon, "Nouvelles Observations Relatives à l'Orientation de la Pyramide de Kheops," p. 89. See Also Baines and Malek, *Altlas of Ancient Egypt*, (New York: Facts on File Publications, 1980), p. 15.

69   Roth, "Fingers, stars, and the 'opening of the mouth,'" p. 72.

70   George Goyon, "Kerkasore et l'ancien observatoire d'Eudoxe," *Bulletin de l'Institut Francais d'Archeologie Orientale*, tome 74, 1974, p. 135.

71   A. Lucas, *Ancient Egyptian Materials and Industries* (London: E. Arnold, 1962), 4th edition, pp. 52–53.

72   Somers Clarke and R. Englebach, *Ancient Egyptian Construction and Architecture* (London: Oxford University Press, 1930), p. 14.

73   Clarke and Englebach, *Ancient Egyptian Construction and Architecture,* p. 14.

74   Jean-Jacques Fiechter, *Mykerinos, le Dieu Englouti* (Paris: Maisonneuve & Larose, 2001), p. 228.

75   Richard W. Howard Vyse and John S. Perring, *Operations Carried on at the Pyramids of Gizeh in 1837* (London: Fraser, 1840), p. 37.

76   Vyse and Perring, *Operations Carried on at the Pyramids of Gizeh,* p. 41.

77   Vyse and Perring, *Operations Carried on at the Pyramids of Gizeh,* p. 43.

78   Vyse and Perring, *Operations Carried on at the Pyramids of Gizeh,* p. 46.

79   For a discussion on this, see Andrey O. Bolshakov, "Princess HMTR(W): The First Mention of Osiris?" *Chronique D'Egypte,* LXVII 1992, fasc. 133, p. 203.

80   R. O. Faulkner, *The Ancient Egyptian Pyramid Texts,* (Oxford: Clarendon Press, 1969), p. 120. Faulkner actually uses the Greek name "Sothis" for Sirius.

81   Nathalie Beaux, in *Hommages à Jean Leclant,* BdE 106/1, 1993, p. 64, n.14.

82   See O. Neugebauer and Richard Parker, *Egyptian Astronomical Texts,* Vol.1 (Providence: Brown, 1964), p. 25, n. 30–31.

83   For a full discussion on this issue, see Bauval, *The Egypt Code,* pp.45–47.

84   Stephen Quirke, *The Cult of Ra* (London: Thames & Hudson, 2001), pp. 116–117.

85   I. Hornug, *Ideas into Images* (Princeton, NJ: Princeton Press, 1992), p. 158.

86   Hornug, *Ideas into Images,* p. 121.

87   See R. Anthes, "Horus als Sorius in den Pyramidentexten," in *ZAS* (Zeitschrift für Ägyptische Sprache und Altertumskunde), 102 (1975), pp. 1–10.

88   Michel Baud, *Djeser et la IIIe Dynastie* (Paris: Pygmalion, 2007), p. 202.

89   Translation by Miriam Lichtheim, *Ancient Egyptian Literature*, Vol. 1 (Berkeley: University of California Press, 1975), p. 52.

90   Lichtheim, *Ancient Egyptian Literature,* p. 51.

91   Frankfort, *Kingship and the Gods*, p. 24.

92   Lichtheim, *Ancient Egyptian Literature*, pp. 52–53.

93   See Aidan Dodson and Dyan Hilton, *The Complete Royal Families of Ancient Egypt* (London: Thames & Hudson, 2004), p. 44.

94   Pierre de Maret, "L'orycterope, un animale 'bon à penser' pour les Africains, est-il à l'origine du dieu Egyptien Seth?" *BIFAO* 105, 2005.

95   E. A. Wallis Budge, *The Gods of the Egyptians* (New York: Dover Publications, 1969), pp. 249–250.

96   H. De Velde, *Seth, God of Confusion: A Study of his role in Egyptian Mythology and religion* (Leiden: Brill, 1967), p. 86.

97   Zbynek Zaba, "L'Orientation Astronomique Dans L'Ancienne Egypte, et la Précession de l'Axe du Monde," Prague 1953, p. 46.

98   Wallis Budge, *The Gods of the Egyptians*, p. 312. For a detailed study of Seth, the northern stars, the Opening of the Mouth adze, and the bull's foreleg/Mesekhtiu/Big Dipper, see De Velde, *Seth, God of Confusion*, pp. 83–89.

99   R. H. Wilkinson, *The Complete Gods and Goddess of Ancient Egypt* (New York: Thames & Hudson, 2003), p. 200.

100   See Christopher Ramsey, et al., "Radiocarbon-Based Chronology for Dynastic Egypt," *Science* 18 June 2010: vol. 328, no. 5985, pp. 1554–1557.

101 Mark Lehner, *The Complete Pyramids* (London: Thames & Hudson, 1997), p. 84.

102 Ian Shaw and Paul Nicholson, *The British Museum Dictionary of Ancient Egypt* (London: The British Museum Press, 2003), p. 87. Most of the graffiti dates from the time of Ramses II, c. 1250 BC, and some refer to "Djoser discoverer of stone working." See Alexander J. Peden, *The Graffiti of Pharaonic Egypt* (Leiden: Brill, 2001), p. 98.

103 Baud, *Djeser et la IIIe Dynastie*, p. 79. See also Berlin 7702; cf. Wildung, Die Rolle, 1969, 59–60).

104 E. R. Bevan, *The House of Ptolemy* (London: Methuen Publishing, 1927), pp. 79–80.

105 Baud, *Djeser et la IIIe Dynastie*, p. 17.

106 Baud, *Djeser et la IIIe Dynastie*, p. 18.

107 Robert Bauval and Ahmed Osman, *Breaking the Mirror of Heaven* (Vermont: Inner Traditions, 2012), chapter 4.

108 Jean-Philippe Lauer, *Saqqara, Une Vie*, (Paris : Rivages, 1988), pp. 44–45.

109 "[S]on orientation suggère qu'à travers les deux orifices il contemplait les étoiles 'imperissables' près du pole Nord..." C. Ziegler, *Les Pyramides D'Egypte* (Paris: Le Caire : Institut Francais d'Archeologie Orientale , 1999), p. 52.

110 Lehner, *The Complete Pyramids*, p. 28.

111 Lehner, *The Complete Pyramids*, p. 90.

112 A. Gurshtein, "The Evolution of the Zodiac in the Context of Ancient Oriental History," *Vistas in Astronomy,* vol. 41, part 4, 1997, p. 509.

113 Breasted, *Development of Religion and Thought in Ancient Egypt*, p. 101.

114 Rundle Clark, *Myth and Symbol in Ancient Egypt,* p. 58.

115 E. C. Krupp, *Echoes of the Ancient Skies* (New York: Oxford University Press, 1994), p. 212.

116 Lehner, *The Complete Pyramids*, p. 28.

117 G. A. Wainwright, "Seshat and the Pharaoh," *JEA* 26, 1941, pp. 30–40.

118 Krupp, *Echoes of the Ancient Skies*, p. 212.

119 Wainwright, "Seshat and the Pharaoh," pp. 30–40.

120 Anne-Sophie Bomhard, *The Egyptian Calendar: A Work for Eternity* (London: Periplus, 1998), p. 4.

121 Wallis Budge, *The Gods of the Egyptians* Vol. I, p. 425.

122 George Hart, *A Dictionary of Egyptian Gods and Goddesses* (London: Routledge & Keagan Paul, 1988), p. 193.

123 Edwards, *The Pyramids of Egypt*, p. 249.

124 Zaba, "L'Orientation Astronomique Dans L'Ancienne Egypte," pp. 58–59.

125 Lauer, *Saqqara, Une Vie*, p. 206.

126 Michael Rice, *Egypt's Making* (London: Guild Publishing, 1990), p. 175.

127 See Zaba, "L'Orientation Astronomique Dans L'Ancienne Egypte," p. 72. For the full story of how the bronze *pss-kf* was found in 1872, see also Bauval, *The Orion Mystery*, Epilogue, pp. 230–236.

128 See R. Stadelmann, *Der Aegyptischen Pyramiden* (Mainz am Rhein: Philipp von Zaber, 1985).

129 In a memoir, Lauer referred to Jéquier as being "a very cold man ... meticulous, cautious and, on the whole, very Swiss." Lauer, however, immediately warmed up to Cecil Firth who, "although British, was friendly and jovial."

130 Baud, *Djeser et la IIIe Dynastie*, p. 102.

131 Vyse, *Operations Carried on at the Pyramids of Gizeh in 1837*, Vol. III, p. 43.

132 Zaba, "L'Orientation Astronomique Dans L'Ancienne Egypte," p. 11.

133 Kate Spence, in Table 1 of the article "Ancient Egyptian Chronology and the astronomical Orientation of Pyramids," *Nature,* vol. 408, Nov. 2000, p. 320.

134 Lehner, *The Complete Pyramids*, p. 90.

135 Lauer, *Histoire Monumentale des Pyramides D'Egypte,* Tome 1, p. 169; see also p. 3.

136 Edwards, *The Pyramids of Egypt*, p. 41.

137 See *Manuel D'Archaeologie Egyptienne,* Tome I (Paris 1952), p. 936–937.

138 Josef Dorner, *Die Absteckung und astronomische Orientierung agyptischer Pyramiden*, University of Innsbruck, 1981 (Thesis +C14169207).

139 See Stadelmann, *Die ägyptischen Pyramiden,* p. 40.

140 Baud, *Djeser et la IIIe Dynastie*, p. 89–90.

141 Baud, *Djeser et la IIIe Dynastie,* p. 133.

142 Edwards, *The Pyramids of Egypt*, p. 295.

143 Quirke, *The Cult of Ra*, p. 117.

144 Maurice Alliot, "Les plus vieilles traditions du Temple D'Edfou," *Institut Francais d'Archeologie Orientale*, Melanges Mariette, T. xxxii, 1961, p. 14.

145 Bauval, *The Egypt Code*, p. 146.

146 Bauval, *The Egypt Code*, pp. 117–128.

147 Ron Wells, "Sothis and the Satet Temple on Elephantine," *Studien Zur Altagyptischen Kultur* (ZAK) 12, 1985, p. 258.

148 See Belmonte and Shaltout, "On the Orientation of Ancient Egyptian Temples I: Upper Egypt and Lower Nubia," *ftp://ftp.ll.iac.es/pub/research/preprints/PP05003.pdf*. See also Bauval, *The Egypt Code*, pp. 117–128.

149 Lichtheim, *Ancient Egyptian Literature*, pp. 94–100.

150 Lichtheim, *Ancient Egyptian Literature*, pp. 94–100.

151 Wells, "Sothis and the Satet Temple on Elephantine," p. 272.

152 A. Pogo, "Calendars on Coffin Lids from Asyut: Second Half of the Third Millemmium," *ISIS,* vol. XVII, 1932, pp. 11–12.

153 Jaun Belmonte and Mosalam Shaltout, "Keeping Maat: An astronomical approach to the orientation of the temples in Ancient Egypt," paper delivered to *WSEF* 2007, p. 17, fig. 8. See *http://www.uranos.fr/PDF/ETUDES_19_D02_TEN.pdf* .

154 We also discussed this matter in *The Orion Mystery* (1994) in Plate 15a.

155 I. H. Amer and B. Morardet, "Les dates de la construction du temple majeur d'Hathor à Dendara à l'époque Gréco-Romaine," *ASAE* 69, 1983, pp. 255–258; also H. Winter, "A Reconsideration of the newly Discovered Building Inscription on the Temple of Denderah," *GM* 108, 1989, pp. 75–85 and J. Quaegebeur, "Cléopâtre VII et le temple de Dendara," *GM* 120, 1991, pp. 53–55.

156 *http://www.culturediff.org/english/astroegypto5.htm.*

157 H. Brugsch, *Egypt*, quoted in Norman Lockyer, *The Dawn of Astronomy* (London: Cassell and Co, Ltd, 1894), pp. 204–205.

158 Lockyer, *The Dawn of Astronomy.*

159 A. Mariette, *Denderah,* vol. I (Paris: A. Franck, 1870), pp. 142, 263.

160 J. P. Allen, "Reading a Pyramid," in *Homages à Jean Leclant, IFAO* vol.1, 1994, pp. 5–28.

161 Allen, "Reading a Pyramid," pp. 26–28.

162 Bauval and Gilbert, *The Orion Mystery,* Appendix 4; for a fuller discussion on this issue, see also Nathalie Beaux, "La Douat dans les Textes des Pyramides," *Bulletin de l'Institut Francais D'Archaeology Orientale (BIFAO)* vol. 94, 1994, p. 6.

163 Dramatic Texts, Part II, VI, 43; see O. Neugebauer and R. Parker, *Egyptian Astronomical Texts*, vol. 1, 1964.

164 Beaux, "La Douat dans les Textes des Pyramides," p. 3.

165 Lockyer, *The Dawn of Astronomy*, p. 176.

166 Lockyer, *The Dawn of Astronomy*, p. 176–177.

167 Krupp, *Echoes of the Ancient Skies*, p. 26.

168 In a private communication, Egyptologist and philologist David Rohl has said: "The Arab astronomers seem to have been aware of the ancient Egyptian connections of the Opening of the Mouth ceremony and the prehistoric herald of the rain."

169 Belmonte and Shaltout, "On the Orientation of Ancient Egyptian Temple I," p. 8.

170 Zaba, "L'Orientation Astronomique Dans L'Ancienne Egypte," plate II Ca and Cb.

171 Lockyer, *The Dawn of Astronomy*, p. 179.

172 Alliot, "Les plus vieilles traditions du Temple D'Edfou," p. 14.

173 C. Rossi, *Architecture and Mathematics in Ancient Egypt* (New York: Cambridge University Press, 2004), p. 162–163.

174 Nadine Moeller, *Annual Report 2008, Annual Report 2010–11*, p. 119.

175 Baines and Malek, *Atlas of Ancient Egypt*, p. 76.

176 Lockyer, *The Dawn of Astronomy*, p. 204; the translation of this inscription was obtained by Lockyer from the German Egyptologist Heinrich Brugsch.

177 Heinrich Brugsch, *Egypt under the Pharaohs* (London: Bracken Books [repr. 1996], 1891), p. 189; also Lockyer, *The Dawn of Astronomy*, p. 205.

178 Brugsch, *Egypt under the Pharaohs*, p. 189.

179 Zaba, "L'Orientation Astronomique Dans L'Ancienne Egypte," p. 59: "A la manière d'autrefois." Zaba is quoting from the translations of Emile Brugsch, *Thesaurus VI*, p. 1272.

180 Lockyer, *The Dawn of Astronomy*, p. 177.

181 A. Romieu, "Calcul de l'heure chez les ancient Egyptiens," *Rec. Trav.* XXIV, pp. 135–142.

182 See Zaba, "L'Orientation Astronomique Dans L'Ancienne Egypte," p. 50.

183 Wilkinson, *The Complete Gods and Goddesses of Ancient Egypt*, p. 165.

184 Beaux, "La Douat dans les Textes des Pyramides," p. 3.

185 Pyramid Texts of Pepi I.

186 P. Lacau and J. P. Lauer, *La Pyramide à Degrés*, Tome IV, 1–2 ; Tome V (Cairo : Inst. Francais d'Archeologie Orientale, 1959, 1961; 1965).

187 Lauer, *Saqqara: Une vie*, p. 46.

188 Baud, *Djeser et la IIIe Dynastie,* p. 35.

189 Illona Regulski, "Second Ink Inscriptions from Saqqara paralleled in the Abydos material from the Royal Museum of Art and history (RMAH) in Brussels," *https://lirias.kuleuven.be/bitstream/*.

190 For a detailed, but controversial, analysis of the ownership of mastabas at Saqqara, see Ellen F. Morris, "On the Ownership of the Saqqara Mastabas and the Allotment of Political and Ideological Power at the Dawn of the State," *The Archaeology and Art of ancient Egypt: Essays in Honor of David B. O'Conner,* Annales du Service des Antiquités de L'Egypte, cahier No. 36, vol. II.

191 Badawy sourced H. Kees, *Totenglauben und Jenseitsvorstellungen der Alten Agypter* (Leipzig: J. C. Hinrichs, 1926), p. 131, where Kees discusses the stellar destiny of the king (see *Mitt. des Instituts fur Orientforschung* X, 1/3, Berlin 1964, p. 193).

192 *JNES,* vol. XV, Jan–Feb. 1956, pp. 180–184.

193 Alexander Badawy, "The Stellar Destiny of Pharaoh," Akademie der Wissenschaften zu Berlin) Band 10, 1964, p. 193.

194 *http://content.cdlib.org/view?docId=hb6z09p0jh&doc view=frames&chunk.id=div00003&toc.depth=1&toc.id=.*

195 A. Badawy, "The ideology of the superstructure of the Mastaba-tomb in Egypt," *JNES,* vol. XV, 1956, pp. 182–183.

196 G. Maspero, *Manual of Egyptian Archaeology* (New York: Putnam, 1952), p. 132.

197 Jacq, *Les Grands Sages de L'Egypte Ancienne*, p. 23.

198 For more recent information of explorations conducted by the Polish team, see Tomasz Herbich and Aleksander Jagodzinski, "Geophysical Investigation on the Dry Moat of the Netjerykhet Complex at Saqqara," *Studies in Honour of Romuald Schild* (Warsaw: Polish Academy of Science, 2008), p. 273.

199 Wainwright, "Seshat and the Pharaoh," pp. 30–40.

200 *The Archaeology of Measurements: Comprehending Heaven, Earth and Time in Ancient Societies*, edited by Iain Morley and Colin Renfrew (Cambridge: Cambridge University Press, 2010), p. 176; see also Toby Wilkinson, *Royal Annals of Ancient Egypt: The Palermo Stone and Associated Fragments* (London: Keagan Paul International, 2000).

201 Toby Wilkinson, *Early Dynastic Egypt: Stategies, Society and Security* (Oxon: Routledge, 1999), p. 294.

202 See Francis A. Cunnigham, "The Sothic Cycle used by the Egyptians," *Journal of the American Oriental Society*, vol. 34, 1915, p. 370.

203 Richard Parker, "Sothic Dates and Calendar Adjustments," *Revue D'Egyptologie*, vol. 9, 1952, p. 105.

204 M. F. Ingham, "The Length of the Sothic Cycle," *Journal of Egyptian Archaeology* 55 (1969): 36–40.

205 Baud, *Djeser et la IIIe Dynastie,* pp. 199–200; Edwards, *The Pyramids of Egypt,* p. 152.

206   Wilkinson, *The Gods and Goddesses of Ancient Egypt*, p. 206.

207   See Quirke, *The Cult of Ra*, p. 116; see also Hans Goedicke, "Zoser's Funerary Monument 1," *Esch996*, p. 51.

208   Lauer, *Histoire Monumentale des Pyramides De L'Egypte Ancienne*, p. 105.

209   Baud, *Djeser et la IIIe Dynastie*, p. 133.

210   Hans Goedick, *BACE 7*, p. 51.

211   Jacq, *Les Grands Sages de L'Egypte Ancienne*, p. 23.

212   Friedman, "Notion of cosmos in the Step Pyramid Complex," pp. 337–351.

213   Baud, *Djeser et la IIIe Dynastie*, p. 97.

214   Baud, *Djeser et la IIIe Dynastie*.

215   An interesting study on bja, meteoritic iron, and the belief that the sky was a slab made of bja was made by the (late) Alan Alford in his book *Midnight Sun: The death and rebirth of God in ancient Egypt* Eridu Books, 2004, chapter 10, p. 209.

216   Wallis Budge, *The Gods of the Egyptians*, p. 241.

217   Hart, *A Dictionary of Egyptian Gods and Goddesses*, p. 146.

218   Edwards, *The Pyramids of Egypt*, p. 147.

219   Ingham, "The Length of the Sothic Cycle," p. 39.

220   For a discussion on this issue, see by Juan Belmonte, "Some open questions on the Egyptian Calendar: an astronomer's view," *TdE 2*, 2003, p. 10.

221   Temple inscription at Dendera. See Zaba, "L'Orientation Astronomique Dans L'Ancienne Egypte," p. 59.

222   Fred Wendorf and Romuald Schild, "The Megaliths of Nabta Playa," *Focus on Archaeology*, Academia No.1 (1) 2004.

223 Michael A. Hoffman, *Egypt before the Pharaohs* (London: Ark Paperback, 1984), p. 227.

224 This notion was recently discussed by American Egyptologist Bruce Williams. See his articles "The lost Pharaohs of Nubia," *Archaeology* 33 no. 5 1985, and "Forebears of Menes in Nubia, myth or reality?" *Journal of Near Eastern Studies* 46, no.1, Jan. 1987, pp. 15–26.

225 W. A. Fairservis, "A Revised View of the Narmer Palette," *Journal of the American Research Centre in Egypt,* XXVIII, 1991, p. 20.

226 Wilkinson, *The Complete Temples of Ancient Egypt*, p. 16.

227 *Egypt's Lost Cities,* on BBC 1, 30 May 2011.

228 Douek, quoted from the TV documentary by Carmen Boulter, *The Pyramid Code*, episode 5, "A new Chronology," 2008; *http://www.youtube.com/*.

229 Thomas Brophy and Paul Rosen, "Satellite Imagery Measures of the Astronomically Aligned Megaliths at Nabta Playa," *Mediterranean Archaeology and Archaeometry* 5(1) (2005) 15–24.

230 Wendorf and Schild, *Holocene Settlement of the Egyptian Sahara: The Archeology of Nabta Playa* (New York: Kluwer Academic/Plenum, 2001), p. 498.

231 J. M. Malville, R. Schild, F. Wendorf, and J. Brenmer, "Astronomy of Nabta Playa," *African Skies/Cieus Africains*, no.11, July 2007.

232 Malville, et. al., "Astronomy of Nabta Playa."

233 Wendorf and Schild, *Holocene Settlement of the Egyptian Sahara*, p. 498.

234 Wendorf and Schild, *Holocene Settlement of the Egyptian Sahara,* pp. 500–501. See also Bauval and Brophy, *Black Genesis*, p. 92 and Wendorf and Schild, "The Megaliths of Nabta Playa," p. 12. *http://www.academia.pan.pl/*.

235 CPE Report 2001, pp. 500–502.

236 Wendorf and Schild, *Holocene Settlement of the Egyptian Sahara,* pp. 501–502.

237 Malville, et. al., "Astronomy of Nabta Playa," p. 5.

238 Brophy and Rosen, "Satellite Imagery Measures of the Astronomically Aligned Megaliths at Nabta Playa," pp. 15–24.

239 CPE 2001 Report, p. 471.

240 Msville, Wendorf, Mazar, et al., "Megaliths and Neolithic Astronomy in Southern Egypt," *Nature* 392, April 1998, p. 490.

241 *http://www.columbia.edu/~smt2141/MyWeb/regular_rain_seasons_in_the/*

242 Gerard Gordon, "Etudes sur L'Epoque Archaique: Une mention de Sekhat-Hor dans la première dynastie," *BIFAO,* vol. 57, 1958, pp. 143–155.

243 Carolyn Graves-Brown, *Dancing for Hathor: Women in Ancient Egypt* (London: Continuum Publishers, 2012), p.15–16.

244 Bauval and Brophy, *Black Genesis,* pp. 208–209.

245 Hoffman, *Egypt before the Pharaohs,* p. 354.

246 Euan Duguid, *The Sunday Post* [UK], 12-24-7.

247 *http://www.touregyptforums.com/index.php?showtopic=1804*

248 *http://www.glasgowlife.org.uk/museums/projects/saqqara/.*

249 In 1933, Hans Winkler met an Egyptian medium named Abdel Radi who claimed to be possessed by his uncle's ghost. Winkler wrote a book on this subject titled *Ghost Riders of Upper Egypt: A Study in Spirit Possession,* which was published in 1936 in German.

250 Hoffman, *Egypt before the Pharaohs,* p. 227.

251 Robert Mond and Oliver H. Myers, *Rock Drawings of Southern Upper Egypt: Sir Robert Mond Expedition, Preliminary Report 1937*; see also Hans A. Winkler, *Rock-Drawings of Southern Upper Egypt* (London: Bd. 2, 1939), Plate XXXIX and Plate XLV.

252 Rice, *Egypt's Making,* p. 175.

253 Lauer, *Saqqara, Une Vie,* p. 41.

254 Baud, *Djeser et la IIIe Dynastie,* p. 121.

255 Marina Warner and Felipe Fernández-Armesto, *World of Myths* (Austin, TX: University of Texas Press, 2003), p. 296.

256 Lichtheim, *Ancient Egyptian Literature,* p. 148.

257 Frankfort, *Kingship and the Gods,* pp. 93–94.

258 Baud, *Djeser et la IIIe Dynastie,* p. 122.

259 Hoffman, *Egypt before the Pharoahs,* p. xv. A colleague once told Hoffman: "Because you prehistorians deal with preliterate cultures is no excuse to write illiterate books!"

260 Bauval and Brophy, *Black Genesis.*

261 Barry J. Kemp, *Ancient Egypt: Anatomy of a Civilization* (London: Routledge, 1991), p. 48.

262 Bauval and Brophy, *Black Genesis,* pp. 48–49, 188–190.

263 Schild and Wendorf, "Forty Years of the Combined Prehistoric Expedition," *Archaeologia Polona,* 40 (2002), p. 18.

264 Frankfort, *Kingship and the Gods,* pp. 93–94.

265 Hoffman, *Egypt before the Pharaohs,* p. 127.

266 Kemp, *Ancient Egypt: Anatomy of a Civilization.*

267 *The International Standard Bible Encyclopedia,* Illustrated in Four Volumes, Revised Edition (Michigan: Wm. B. Eerdmans Publishing Co., 1986), volume 3, p. 437.

268 Wilkinson, *The Complete Gods and Goddesses of Ancient Egypt,* p. 197.

269 Rice, *Egypt's Making,* p. 142.

270 Christine C. Schnusenberg, *The Mythological Traditions of Lithurgical Drama* (New Jersey: Paulist Press, 2010), p. 45.

271 Toby A. H. Wilkinson, *Early Dynastic Egypt* (London: Routledge, 1999), p. 77.

272 Wilkinson, *Early Dynastic Egypt*, p. 78.

273 Baud, *Djeser et la IIIe Dynastie,* p. 60.

274 Bauval and Brophy, *Black Genesis,* p. 184.

275 James O. Mills, "Astronomy at Hierakonpolis," paper presented at the 1990 Society for Africanist Archaeologists, March 22–25, 1990, University of Florida, Gainesville. See also Marshall Clagett, *Ancient Egyptian Science* vol. I. (Philadelphia: American Philosophical Society, 1995), p. 497.

276 *http://oi.uchicago.edu/museum/special/nubia/*

277 Ivan Van Sertima, *Egypt: Child of Africa* (New Jersey: Transaction Publishers, 2002).

278 For more information, see Williams, *Excavations Between Abu Simbel and the Sudan Frontier.*

279 Published in *Discussions in Egyptology,* Volume 14, 1989.

280 pyr. 1652.

281 Baines, *Orientalia* 39, 1979, p. 391.

282 Baines, *Orientalia*, p. 391, fn. 2.

283 Edwards, *The Pyramids of Egypt*, p. 292; Badawy, "The Stellar Destiny of Pharaoh and the so-called Air-Shafts of Cheops Pyramid," *Mitteilungen der Instituts Fur Orientforschung* (Akademie der Wissenschaften zu Berlin) Band 10, 1964, p. 205.

284 Breasted, *Development of Thought and Religion in Ancient Egypt*, pp. 101–102.

285 Breasted, *Development of Thought and Religion in Ancient Egypt,* pp. 70–73.

286 Edwards, *The Pyramids of Egypt,* pp. 290–291.

287   Edwards, *The Pyramids of Egypt,* p. 287.

288   *JNES,* vol.xv 1956, p. 183.

289   Breasted, *Development of Thought and Religion in Ancient Egypt,* p. 72.

290   Rundle Clark, *Myth and Symbol in Ancient Egypt,* pp. 246–249.

291   Rundle Clark, *Myth and Symbol in Ancient Egypt,* p. 249.

292   Edwards, *The Pyramids of Egypt,* p. 24.

293   Frankfort, *Kingship and the Gods,* pp. 153, 380, and n. 26.

294   E. A. Wallis Budge, *Egyptian Hieroglyphic Dictionary* (New York: Dover Publications, 1978), p. 217.

295   Baines, *Orientalia,* p. 389–395.

296   Edwards, *The Pyramids of Egypt,* pp. 295–298; Badawy, *JEA* 63, p. 58.

297   V. F. Buckwald, *Handbook on Iron Meteorites* (Berkeley, CA: UCLA Press, 1975). See also Brian Mason, *Meteorites* (New York: Wiley, 1962), chap. 6.

298   G. Roux, *Delphes, son Oracle et ses Dieux* (Paris: Belles Lettres, 1976), p. 130.

299   G. A. Wainwright, Annal, Serv.xxviii, p. 185.

300   G. J. H. McCall, *Meteorites and Their Origins* (New York: Wiley, 1973), p. 17.

301   Charles Daremberg and Edmund Sangrio, *Dictionnaire Des Antiquites Grecques et Romaines* (Paris: Hatchette, 1877–1919, p. 529.

302   P. K. Hitti, *History of Syria* (London: Macmillan, 1951), p. 312.

303   Hitti, *History of Syria,* p. 385.

304   Wainwright, "Iron in Egypt," p. 3.

305   For a counter view, see Dunham, *JEA* 28, p. 57.

306 A few Egyptologists have recently questioned the bja = iron for the Old Kingdom epoch, suggesting copper instead; see A. Nibbi, *JARCE* xiv, 1977, p. 59; C. Lalouette, *BIFAO* 79, p. 67. Nonetheless, bja is widely accepted as being iron, and especially meteoritic iron in archaic times.

307 Wainwright, "Iron in Egypt," p. 11.

308 Wallis Budge, *Egyptian Hieroglyphic Dictionary,* p. 210.

309 Edwards, *The Pyramids of Egypt,* pp. 118, 151.

310 "poli a miroir . . . " Maspero, Annal.Serv. iii, p. 206.

311 Maspero, Annal.Serv. iii, p. 206.

312 Breasted, *Development of Thought and Religion in Ancient Egypt,* p. 73.

313 A. Piankoff, *The Pyramid of Unas* (Princeton, NJ: Princeton University Press, Bollingen Series XL.5), p. 5.

314 Edwards, *The Pyramids of Egypt,* p. 276.

315 E. C. Krupp, *In Search of Ancient Astronomies* (London: Chatto & Windus, p. 216.

316 S. Hassan, *Excavations At Giza,* Vol. vi, part i. 1946, p. 286; S. Mercer, *The Pyramid Texts* (New York: Longmans Green, 1952), p. 34.

317 Rundle Clark, *Myth and Symbol in Ancient Egypt,* p. 122.

318 A. Champdor, *The Book of the Dead* (New York: Garrett Publishing, 1966), p. 69.

319 E. A. Wallis Budge, *The Book of the Dead—Papyrus of Ani in the British Museum,* (London, 1895), lix; Hassan, p. 314.

320 R. G. Bauval, "A Master-plan for the three Pyramids of Giza based on the Configuration of the three Stars of the Belt of Orion," *Discussions in Egyptology,* 13, 1988. See also V. Trimble, "Astronomical Investigation concerning the so-called Air-Shafts of Cheop's Pyramid," *Mitteilungen der Instituts Fur Orientforschung* (Akademie der Wissenschaften zu Berlin) Band 10, 1964, pp. 183–187.

321 J. Hekekyan (Brit. Lib. Add. MS 37458.21), 1852. Hekekyan wrote: "'Right Line identical with the South West and North Eastern Diagonal of the Soris (Cheops) Pyramid and the Obelisk.'"

322 Jeffreys, "The topography of Heliopolis and Memphis, pp. 63–71.

323 Goyon, "Nouvelles Observations. . . ," pp. 91–92.

324 *Washington Post,* 30 November 1983.

325 Mark Lehner, "A contextual approach to the Giza pyramids," *Archiv. fur Orientforschung,* 1885, vol. 32, pp. 136–158.

326 Lehner, *The Complete Pyramids,* p. 107. Even more recently, in 2003, British Egyptologist Kate Spence reproduced the map with the so-called "Giza diagonal" and claims that "Mark Lehner suggests that the southeast corners of the pyramids may have been deliberately aligned" ("Are the Pyramids aligned with the Stars," pp. 71–73). Ironically, the reason Spence mentioned the Giza diagonal was to argue against the stellar-based Orion-Giza correlation plan that I proposed in my book *The Orion Mystery* (1994).

327 William Matthew Flinders Petrie, *Seventy Years in Archaeology* (New York: Grammond, 1932), p. 13. He was referring to his debunking of the so-called Pyramid Inch of John Taylor and the theory that Piazzi Smyth had built upon it.

328 Lehner, "A contextual approach to the Giza pyramids," p. 141.

329 Lehner, *The Complete Pyramids,* p. 29.

330 J. P. Allen, *The Cosmology of the Pyramid Texts,* in Simpson, W. K. (ed.), *Religion and Philosophy in Ancient Egypt* (New Haven: Yale University Press, 1989), pp. 19–20.

331 J. P. Allen, *The Ancient Egyptian Pyramid Texts* (Leiden: Brill, 2005), pp. 11, 425.

332 Wendorf and Schild, "The Megaliths of Nabta Playa," p. 11.

333 Wendorf and Schild, *Holocene Settlement of the Egyptian Sahara.*

334 J.M.Malville, et al.,"Megaliths and Neolithic Astronomy in Southern Egypt," *Nature* 392, (April 1998), pp. 488–491.

335 Wendorf and Schild, *Holocene Settlement of the Egyptian Sahara.*

336 Wendorf and Schild, *Holocene Settlement of the Egyptian Sahara.*

337 Brophy and Rosen, "Satellite Imagery Measures of the Astronomically Aligned Megaliths at Nabta Playa," pp. 17–31.

338 Brophy and Rosen, "Satellite Imagery Measures of the Astronomically Aligned Megaliths at Nabta Playa."

339 J. M. Malville, et. al., "Astronomy of Nabta Playa."

340 Our interpretation relied on the careful original mapping of the reconstructed circle by Applegate and Zedeno in 1991–1992. See Wendorf and Schild, *Holocene Settlement of the Egyptian Sahara.*

341 Adapted from "The Complex Structures or Shrines" by Fred Wendorf and Halina Krolik in Wendorf and Schild, *Holocene Settlement of the Egyptian Sahara,* p. 509. Image also appears in *Black Genesis.*

342 Brophy and Rosen, "Satellite Imagery Measures of the Astronomically Aligned Megaliths at Nabta Playa."

343 Joel D. Irish, "Who were the ancient Egyptians? Dental affinities among Neolithic through post-dynastic samples," *American Journal of Physical Anthropology.* 129:529–543.

344 Joel D. Irish, P. Bobrowski, M. Kobusiewicz, J. Kabaciski, and R. Schild, "An Artificial Human Tooth from the Neolithic Cemetery at Gebel Ramlah, Egypt," *Dental Anthropology,* Volume 17, No. 1, 2004, pp. 28–31.

345 Wendorf and Schild, *Holocene Settlement of the Egyptian Sahara.*

346 See Fred Wendorf and J. M. Malville, "The Megalith Alignments," in *Holocene Settlement of the Egyptian Sahara,* Vol. I, pp. 489–502 and J. M. Malville, F. Wendorf, A. A. Mazar, and R. Schild, "Megaliths and Neolithic Astronomy in Southern Egypt," *Nature,* V392, 488–91, April 2, 1998.

347 Wendorf and Malville, "The Megalith Alignments."

348 Wendorf and Malville, "The Megalith Alignments."

349 Malville, et al., "Megaliths and Neolithic Astronomy."

350 Wendorf and Malville, "The Megalith Alignments."

351 Wendorf and Malville, "The Megalith Alignments."

352 Wendorf and Malville, "The Megalith Alignments."

353 Wendorf and Malville, "The Megalith Alignments."

354 Wendorf and Malville, "The Megalith Alignments."

355 E.g., B. E. Schaefer, "Atmospheric extinction effects on stellar alignments," Archaeoastronomy Supplement to *Journal for History of Astronomy,* 10:S32–S42, 1986.

356 R. Schild and F. Wendorf, "Combined Prehistoric Expedition's Radiocarbon Dates Associated with Neolithic Occupations in the Southern Western Desert of Egypt," in *Holocene Settlement of the Egyptian Sahara,* Vol. I, pp. 51–56.

357 Wendorf and Malville, "The Megalith Alignments."

358 Fred Wendorf and H. Krolik, "The Complex Structures or Shrines in Holocene Settlement of the Egyptian Sahara," in *Holocene Settlements of the Egyptian Sahara,* Vol. I.

About the Authors

ROBERT BAUVAL was born in Alexandria, Egypt, in 1948. His father was Belgian and his mother Maltese-Italian. In 1967, he settled in England where he continued his studies. In 1973 he graduated from The University of the Southbank in London, with a Higher National Diploma in Building Management and Technology. He then worked as a construction engineer in Oman, Sudan, Iran, Guinea, Saudi Arabia, France, Australia, and England. In 1990, Bauval obtained a Postgraduate Diploma in European Marketing and Management.

Bauval published his first book on ancient Egypt, *The Orion Mystery*, which was a number one *Sunday Times* bestseller and has since been translated in more than 25 languages. Subsequently he has published a further seven books, including *The Message of the Sphinx*, and *The Egypt Code. Black Genesis,* published in 2011, is co-authored with Thomas Brophy. Another book, *The Master Game,* was co-authored with Graham Hancock. *Breaking the Mirror of Heaven* was co-authored with Ahmed Osman. His discoveries and theories have been the subject of dozens of TV documentaries on many channels, including BBC, ZDF, France A3, ABC, NBC, Fox-TV, History Channel, Discovery Channel and RAI-Italia.

Bauval speaks four languages (English, French, Italian, and Arabic) and is presently learning Spanish. He has two children who live in England, and he and his wife Michele live in Southern Spain.

THOMAS BROPHY has a Ph.D. in physics from the University of Colorado, was a staff research scientist at the Laboratory for Atmospheric and Space Physics, Boulder, with NASA interplanetary spacecraft projects, and was a National Science Foundation exchange scientist with the University of Tokyo and Japan Space Program. His work focused on planetary astrophysics problems. A member of one of the Voyager II spacecraft instrument teams, he developed theoretical understandings for data from the outer planets (Jupiter, Saturn, Uranus, Neptune), and was involved in defining science goals for space mission instrumentation. Those interests in fundamental theory, and teaching at the University level, led him to broader studies involving the non-calculable and immeasurable aspects of the universe, and to Integral philosophy. These Integral studies, together with practice of contemplative/yogic traditions, led to his book *The Mechanism Demands a Mysticism* and subsequent publications, and invited presentations on Integral theory and psychospiritual growth. He is former Dean of the California Institute for Human Science, a graduate school and research center dedicated to integrating the pyschospiritual and scientific worldviews. Recombining Integral philosophy with astrophysical dynamics led to his studies of the astro-archaeology of pre-history and proto-historic Egypt, and investigations into the origin of the Zodiac, and "Zodiac Ages" in early human cultures, and his book *The Origin Map*. His book *Black Genesis: The Prehistoric Origins of Ancient Egypt* about the origins of the pharaohs from a mysterious star-ceremonialist African peoples is co-authored with Robert Bauval. He has also worked in the IT/telecommunications industry and found application for fundamental dynamics calculation methods in gaming and investment theory. He has published peer reviewed scientific articles in premier journals including *Icarus, Mediterranean Journal of Archaeology and Archaeometry, IEEE Journal, Science,* and his work was reported on in *Nature* magazine. He has been a featured presenter at numerous scientific conferences and invited plenary speaker at Integral spirituality meetings in the United States, Europe, Japan, and New Zealand.